Affirmative Action for the Rich

Affirmative Action for the Rich

Legacy Preferences in College Admissions

Richard D. Kahlenberg, *editor*

A Century Foundation Book

The Century Foundation Press • New York

The Century Foundation sponsors and supervises timely analyses of economic policy, foreign affairs, and domestic political issues. Not-for-profit and nonpartisan, it was founded in 1919 and endowed by Edward A. Filene.

Library of Congress Cataloging-in-Publication Data

Affirmative action for the rich : legacy preferences in college admissions / Richard D. Kahlenberg, editor.

p. cm.

Includes bibliographical references and index.

ISBN 978-0-87078-519-1 (cloth)—ISBN 978-0-87078-518-4 (paper)

1. Universities and colleges--United States--Admission. 2. Rich people--Education (Higher)--United States. 3. Universities and colleges--United States--Endowments. 4. Discrimination in higher education--United States. I. Kahlenberg, Richard D. II. Title.

LB2351.2.A43 2010
378.1'61--dc22

2010024373

Manufactured in the United States of America
Cover design and art by Claude Goodwin, photo © iStockphoto.com/Terraxplorer

FOREWORD

American history does not reveal an unbroken pattern of increasing democratization and shared prosperity. Rather, progress has come in fits and starts. The long-term trend, however, generally has reflected forward movement, with growing expansion of political participation and economic well-being. Importantly, each generation has embraced the comforting and realistic belief that things would be even better for their children. Though buffeted by tumultuous periods of war, social change, and economic dislocation, the nation rightly was seen as a global model producing considerable advances in prosperity for the vast majority of its citizens.

In the post–World War II period, for example, income and wealth inequality narrowed, helped along by a progressive federal income tax rate on top earners, strong union leadership on economic issues, and rapidly growing wages and benefits for most workers. At the same time, the Civil Rights movement and the influx of women in the workplace clearly led to greater opportunities for more Americans. For twenty years after victory in World War II, the nation enjoyed a period of relentless advance toward fairness and shared prosperity. America reveled in this upward mobility, a country where hard work could overcome any obstacle and move one from the lowliest origins to the top of the society. College attendance, one of the keys to "getting ahead," vastly expanded from what once was a small slice of the population. The GI Bill alone sent 8 million veterans to post-secondary training. By the 1960s, the continued democratization of higher education seemed inevitable.

This golden age came to an abrupt halt in the 1970s. With the nation already increasingly split over involvement in the Vietnam War, and the ecumenical nature of the Civil Rights movement breaking down as sharp divisions emerged between mainstream rights organizations and the more radical elements, American society began to suffer further fractures along the lines of income and wealth. As the decade progressed, a much-heralded part of the American experience—continuing income growth—began to disappear for a majority of workers. There was a shift from rapidly growing incomes (not surprisingly, accompanied by fairly generous inclinations of the increasingly middle class majority) to wage stagnation for a vast segment of the American workforce. Over time, as workers struggled to maintain middle-class lives, that stagnation would lead to declining household savings as well as mounting levels of personal debt through the use of credits cards, second mortgages, sub-prime loans, and other devices that simply had not existed previously.

The patterns that surfaced in the 1970s have become a long-term trend, exacerbated by policy choices that have propelled us to the historically high level of wealth and income inequality that exist today. On a range of issues, there has been a backlash against the postwar pattern of social change and worker rights. Perhaps retrenchment was inevitable, given the scope and scale of the changes in society. There has been widespread resistance to affirmative action programs, including those intended to diversify college populations. For decades, these programs have come under relentless political and legal attack and seem very fragile. Taxes on the wealthy have been slashed several times, to a third of what they had been, and upward mobility now seems more of an empty slogan than a realistic possibility.

This virtual dismantling of the American Dream has had concrete results. The Pew Economic Mobility Project reports, for example, that the "best available evidence indicates that the United States stands out as having less, not more, relative mobility from one generation to the next." Furthermore, many industrialized nations now have more relative mobility than the United States—that is, children in other nations are more likely than American children to have their future economic success determined by merit, rather than by birth. Absent such economic mobility, Americans increasingly will have their futures determined by the economic class into which they were born.

At The Century Foundation, understanding the causes and cures of inequality is perhaps our central preoccupation and has been for nearly a century. Several of our recent publications outline an education reform agenda designed to reverse the trend toward inequality and to bring about greater opportunity for the vast majority of Americans. In higher education, the books include *Rewarding Strivers: Helping Low-Income Students Succeed in College* (2010), and *America's Untapped Resource: Low Income Students in Higher Education* (2004). Both volumes were edited by Century Foundation senior fellow Richard Kahlenberg.

In recent years, The Century Foundation also has published several books on elementary and secondary education, including Richard Rothstein's *The Way We Were? Myths and Realities of America's Student Achievement* (1998); Kahlenberg's *All Together Now: Creating Middle-Class Schools through Public School Choice* (2001); Joan Lombardi's *Time to Care: Redesigning Child Care to Promote Education, Support Families, and Build Communities* (2002); Jeffrey Henig's *Spin Cycle: How Research Is Used in Policy Debates—The Case of Charter Schools* (2008); and Gordon MacInnes's *In Plain Sight: Simple, Difficult Lessons from New Jersey's Expensive Efforts to Close the Achievement Gap* (2009). In addition, we have supported several volumes of essays on education edited by Kahlenberg, including *A Notion at Risk: Preserving Education as an Engine for Social Mobility* (2000); *Public School Choice vs. Private School Vouchers* (2003); and *Improving on No Child Left Behind: Getting Education Reform Back on Track* (2008). The Century Foundation also sponsored a task force, chaired by former Connecticut governor Lowell Weicker, Jr., that issued a report, *Divided We Fail: Coming Together through Public School Choice* (2002).

It is not surprising, in this context, that we would look at college admissions, particularly those at the elite institutions where entry and graduation is a ticket to higher incomes, greater wealth, and perhaps even longer life. Research shows that it not only matters whether you go to college, but where you go to college, and that if admission standards are loaded in your favor, you enjoy a substantial advantage over other applicants or aspirants. One aspect of this differential is the extent to which colleges take into consideration whether an applicant comes from a family that includes alumni of the institution. There is plenty of evidence that such a "legacy" attribute is a positive factor in college admissions. Legacy preferences turn out to be understudied causal factor in admissions, limiting opportunity for immigrant and minority groups and enhancing the life chances of those who come from families whose parents graduated from select institutions.

The contributions in this volume examine a range of issues related to this phenomenon and offer compelling arguments for why it should be addressed and reformed. Richard Kahlenberg again has assembled a group of researchers and writers who bring extraordinary credentials and insights to the questions of fairness and the implications for opportunity embodied in legacy preferences. The ten essays in this book offer a comprehensive picture of the way legacy preferences work in practice and of their impact on applicants. Taken together, the authors make a powerful case for change. This work and others like it deserve to become a call to action for those who seek to enhance fairness in college opportunities and the nation as a whole.

On behalf of the Trustees of The Century Foundation, I thank Richard Kahlenberg and his colleagues for this important contribution to our understanding of this important topic.

Richard C. Leone, President
The Century Foundation

Contents

Legal and Policy Options for Curtailing Legacy Preferences

1

Introduction

Richard D. Kahlenberg

The use of race-based affirmative action in higher education has given rise to hundreds of books and law review articles, numerous court decisions, and several state initiatives to ban the practice. By contrast, surprisingly little has been said or written or done to challenge a larger, longstanding "affirmative action" program that tends to benefit wealthy whites: legacy preferences for children of alumni.[1] Like racial preferences, preferences for legacies can be criticized for being based on ancestry rather than individual merit, yet they offer none of the countervailing benefits of affirmative action, such as remedying past discrimination or promoting educational diversity. (Nor, it turns out, do they boost college fundraising substantially.)[2] The evidence suggests, in fact, that in the early twentieth century, legacy preferences were born of anti-immigrant and anti-Jewish discriminatory impulses.[3]

Legacy preferences also are widespread. Among elite national institutions, almost three-quarters of research universities and virtually all liberal arts colleges grant legacy preferences.[4] While some colleges and universities try to downplay the impact of legacy preferences, calling them "tie breakers" in very close admission calls, the research suggests that their weight is significant. Princeton scholar Thomas Espenshade and colleagues find that, among applicants to elite colleges, legacy status is worth the equivalent of scoring 160 points higher on the SAT (on a 400–1600 point scale).[5]

To date, however, there have been no state ballot initiatives, only one lower court case, and not a single book-length treatment of the issue.[6] This volume of essays is an effort to begin to remedy the gap in the scholarly literature. Drawing upon a wide range of academics, journalists, and legal practitioners, this book sketches the origins of legacy preferences, examines the philosophical issues they raise, outlines the extent of their use today, studies their impact on university fund-raising, and reviews their implications for civil rights. In addition, the book outlines two new theories challenging the legality of legacy preferences, examines how a judge might review those claims, and assesses public policy options for curtailing alumni preferences.

Why Legacy Preferences Are Vulnerable and Why They Matter

One threshold question for a volume such as this is whether a policy that has been around for almost a hundred years—no matter how unfair—is ever going to change. The evidence in this book suggests that legacy preferences are in fact vulnerable. Over the past decade or so, sixteen leading institutions (including Texas A&M; the University of Arizona; the University of California, Berkeley; the University of California, Los Angeles; and the University of Georgia) have abandoned legacy preferences, joining institutions such as the California Institute of Technology (Caltech) and Cooper Union, which never employed them. Moreover, in the past year or so, plans have begun to challenge legacy preferences in federal court.[7] A serious legal challenge based on new claims has a very real possibility of succeeding on the merits, for the reasons outlined in Chapters 7, 8, and 9 of this book. At a minimum, litigation will produce, through the legal discovery process, greater understanding of the workings of legacy preferences, illuminating a practice that already is deeply unpopular with the American public. (One poll found Americans oppose legacy preferences by 75 percent to 23 percent).[8] Opposition to legacy preferences over the years has spanned the political spectrum, from

Senators Ted Kennedy and John Edwards and Representative George Miller on the left, to George W. Bush and Senators Charles Grassley and Bob Dole on the right.[9] A court case shining light on the issue could provide a political catalyst, particularly in a moment of profound populist anger in the country toward practices that unfairly advantage elites.

A parallel set of legal and political developments involving affirmative action further threatens the future of legacy preferences in university admissions. Race-based affirmative action policies are under attack from both popular initiatives and the courts. Justice Anthony Kennedy, who dissented in the Supreme Court's 2003 case, *Grutter* v. *Bollinger*, which affirmed the use of race in law school admissions at the University of Michigan, is the new swing vote on the Court. A new case challenging racial preferences at the University of Texas very well could provide the U.S. Supreme Court an opportunity to cut back on racial preferences significantly.[10] If this happens, legacy preferences will come under new pressure as well. Recent history suggests that preferences for the children of wealthy alumni are vulnerable in a post-affirmative action environment. After California banned racial preferences by voter referendum, for example, it soon moved to eliminate legacy preferences in the University of California system.[11] The same was true at other institutions. If change comes to affirmative action programs, legacy preferences may well be swept aside too.[12]

Another threshold question is whether legacy preferences matter. Preferences for the children of alumni are concentrated in selective institutions and may determine whether students are accepted at particular institutions, but not whether they will attend college at all. So how much does it matter if a given student goes to a more or less elite school?

The evidence suggests that going to a selective college or university does in fact provide considerable advantages. For one thing, wealthy selective colleges tend to spend a great deal more on students' education. Research finds that the least selective colleges spend about $12,000 per student, compared with $92,000 per student at the most selective schools.[13] In addition, wealthy selective institutions provide much greater subsidies for families. At the wealthiest 10 percent of institutions, students pay, on average, just 20 cents in fees for every dollar the school spends on them, while at the poorest 10 percent of institutions, students pay 78 cents for every dollar spent on them.[14] Furthermore, selective colleges are quite a bit better at retention. If a more-selective school and a less-selective school enroll two equally qualified students, the more-selective institution is much more likely to graduate its student.[15] Moreover, future earnings are, on average, 45 percent higher for students who graduated from more-selective institutions than for those from less-selective ones, and the difference in earnings is widest among low-income students. [16] And according to research by political scientist Thomas Dye, 54 percent of America's top corporate leaders and 42 percent of governmental leaders are graduates of just twelve institutions.[17] For all these reasons, legacy preferences matter.

The Shape of Legacy Preferences in the United States

This book begins with a philosophical discussion by Michael Lind of the New America Foundation outlining the ways in which legacy preferences are in direct conflict with bedrock principles of the nation's founding as a democratic republic. As Lind notes in Chapter 2, Thomas Jefferson sought to promote a "natural aristocracy" based on "virtue and talent," rather than an "artificial aristocracy" based on wealth.

In particular, Jefferson envisioned a society in which hereditary privileges of the Old World—in politics, the economy, and in education—were abolished in favor of structures that support merit and talent. In the political realm, he outlined plans to set up an elected Senate very different from the hereditary House of Lords. In the economic sphere, he advocated abolishing British practices of primogeniture and entails, which were designed to keep estates intact. And in education, Jefferson called for universal common schools and founded the publicly funded University of Virginia as an institution to draw upon the most talented students from all walks of life.

A system of legacy preferences, Lind writes, "is at odds with the fundamental design of a democratic republic such as the United

States of America."[18] In politics, legacy preferences artificially aid alumni children of lesser talents, undermining the "natural aristocracy" that Jefferson hoped would lead the nation. Given the importance of higher education in today's economy, legacy preferences undermine Jefferson's efforts in the agricultural economy of his day to prevent a "hereditary landed aristocracy." And in the realm of education, legacy preferences—including at Jefferson's beloved University of Virginia—directly undercut the meritocracy Jefferson sought to construct. "By reserving places on campus for members of the pseudo-aristocracy of 'wealth and birth,'" Lind writes, "legacy preferences introduce an aristocratic snake into the democratic republican Garden of Eden."[19] In a profound sense, by disrupting the ideal that "each generation starts life afresh," legacy preferences can truly be considered un-American.

This book then turns in Chapter 3 to a history of legacy preferences and privilege written by Peter Schmidt, a veteran reporter at the *Chronicle of Higher Education*. Schmidt, who is also the author of *Color and Money: How Rich White Kids Are Winning the War over College Affirmative Action*, cites the ugly origins of legacy preferences following World War I as a reaction to an influx of immigrant students, particularly Jews, into America's selective colleges. As Jews often out-competed traditional constituencies on standard meritocractic criteria at selective institutions, universities adopted Jewish quotas. When explicit quotas became hard to defend, universities began to use more indirect means to limit Jewish enrollment, including considerations of "character," geographic diversity, and legacy status.[20]

Legacy preferences took firmer root during the Great Depression, as universities believed that favoring alumni children might boost revenues.[21] Efforts to favor legacies came under attack in the 1960s and 1970s at places such as Yale University, which were seeking to democratize admissions, opening the doors to women, people of color, and financially needy students. But alumni ire from the likes of conservative writer William F. Buckley, Jr., effectively ended Yale's efforts to curtail legacy preferences.[22]

The advent of the influential *U.S. News & World Report* university rankings in the 1980s further solidified the place of alumni preferences, Schmidt contends, by considering the share of alumni who donate as a factor in the rankings.[23] Likewise, reductions in state financial support to public universities may have placed pressure on selective public institutions to adopt alumni preferences in the belief that doing so would raise further revenue.[24]

The biggest threats to legacy preferences, Schmidt argues, have come where affirmative action was banned. "Many minority lawmakers and civil-rights activists who had been willing to tolerate legacy preferences so long as colleges also used affirmative action would become staunchly opposed to legacy preferences where affirmative action was ended," he notes.[25] Legacy preferences were eliminated, Schmidt observes, following bans on affirmative action not only at the University of California, but also at the University of Georgia and Texas A&M.[26]

In Chapter 4, Daniel Golden, of Bloomberg News, provides an analytic survey of legacy preferences today. Golden won a Pulitzer Prize for his groundbreaking series of *Wall Street Journal* articles on legacy preferences and other advantages provided to privileged college applicants. He later elaborated on those articles in a 2006 book, *The Price of Admission*. Here, Golden extends that research and updates it.

If, as Lind argues, legacy preferences are in some sense un-American, Golden points out that they are also uniquely, and ironically, American. Universities in other nations, for the most part, do not provide legacy preferences in college admissions. Legacy preferences are "virtually unknown in the rest of the world"; they are "an almost exclusively American custom."[27]

In the United States, Golden finds, legacy preferences are pervasive—used by almost 90 percent of top universities.[28] And they make a real difference in admissions. William Bowen of the Mellon Foundation and colleagues found that, within a given SAT score range, being a legacy increased one's chances of admission to a selective institution by 19.7 percentage points.[29] That is to say, a given student whose academic record gave her a 40 percent chance of admission would have nearly a 60 percent chance if she were a legacy. Universities are quite open about the advantages provided to legacies. An admissions officer at the University of Miami told Golden, "Everybody gets the red carpet treatment when they come through admissions; for a legacy student, we'll vacuum the carpet, we'll get down and pick up the lint."[30]

The children of alumni generally make up 10 percent to 25 percent of the student body at selective institutions, Golden finds, and the proportion often varies little, suggesting, he says, "an informal quota system." (By contrast, at Caltech, which lacks legacy preferences, only 1.5 percent of students are children of alumni.)[31] As competition for university admission has increased, the power of legacy preferences has had to increase in order to maintain legacy representation. For example, in 1992, Princeton accepted legacy applicants at 2.8 times the rate of other candidates, but by 2009, 42 percent of legacies were admitted, more than 4.5 times the rate of non-legacies.[32]

Given the break in admissions provided to legacies, it is not surprising that, once on campus, they perform less well than students of similar demographic backgrounds who do not receive preference. Golden reports that a study by Princeton's Douglas Massey and Margarita Mooney of twenty-eight selective colleges and universities found under-performance by legacy admits was particularly pronounced when the gap between legacy SAT and the institution's SAT average was wide. The authors also found that "in schools with a stronger commitment to legacy admissions, the children of alumni were more likely to drop out."[33]

But are legacy preferences justified as a necessary evil to raise financial resources for colleges and universities? As a percentage of private donations, alumni giving is indeed substantial, totaling $8.7 billion in fiscal year 2008, accounting for 27.5 percent of private giving and coming in just behind foundation giving (of $9.1 billion).[34] (As a percentage of overall university budgets, by contrast, alumni donations account for just 5.1 percent of total expenditures at leading universities.)[35] While in theory legacy preferences go to all alumni equally, most people assume that giving counts in the weight provided such preferences.[36] One official at a highly selective institution told Golden that the university grants a larger preference to alumni donors. Because the cost of educating a student exceeds tuition, all students can be thought of as "trough drinkers." He said, "Just because you drank at a trough that others filled does not entitle your child to drink at the same trough. There are trough-fillers and there are just drinkers. Those two people are treated differently."[37]

Having said that, the research connecting legacy preferences and alumni giving is remarkably thin, and new research in this volume raises serious questions about the link. Golden begins by noting that several colleges and universities that do not employ legacy preferences nevertheless do well financially. Caltech, for example, raised $71 million in alumni donations in 2008, almost as much as the Massachusetts Institute of Technology (MIT, $77 million), even though MIT, which does provide legacy preference, is five times the size and has many more alumni to tap.[38] Berea College, in Kentucky, favors low-income students, not alumni, yet has a larger endowment than Middlebury, Oberlin, Vassar, and Bowdoin colleges. And Cooper Union in New York City does not provide legacy preference, but has an endowment larger than that of Bucknell, Haverford, or Davidson.[39] In terms of school quality, it is intriguing to note that, among the top ten universities in the world in 2008, according to the widely cited Shanghai rankings, are four (Caltech, the University of California at Berkeley, Oxford, and Cambridge) that do not employ legacy preferences.[40]

One interesting study by Jonathan Meer of Stanford and Harvey S. Rosen of Princeton finds that giving at one unnamed private non-profit university increased as children of alumni entered high school, but it also found that alumni giving "fell off a cliff" when a child was rejected.[41] The message sent—that even with a preference, your child was not good enough—may be particularly hard for alumni to take.[42] Indeed, they may be even more angered by rejection than would be the case had they not had their expectations raised by the existence of legacy preferences.[43] Significantly, as universities become increasingly selective, the proportion of alumni children rejected may increase, thereby angering donors. As a result, it is not clear that the net effect of legacy preferences on donations is positive, and Meer and Rosen make no claim that legacy preferences increase overall giving.[44]

To add to all this suggestive research, Chapter 5 includes a new rigorous study by Chad Coffman of Winnemac Consulting, LLC, and his coauthors Tara O'Neil and Brian Starr. They look at alumni giving from 1998 to 2007 at the top one hundred national universities as ranked by *U.S. News & World Report* to examine the relationship between giving and the existence of alumni preferences. Of those schools, roughly three-quarters provide legacy preferences.[45]

Coffman and his colleagues find that schools with preferences for children of alumni did have higher overall giving per alumni

($317 versus $201), but that this advantage resulted because the alumni in schools with alumni preferences tended to be wealthier. Controlling for the wealth of alumni, they find "no evidence that legacy preference policies themselves exert an influence on giving behavior."[46] After controls, alumni gave only $15.39 more on average in legacy-granting institutions, but even that slight advantage is from a statistical perspective uncertain.[47] They conclude: "after inclusion of appropriate controls, including wealth, there is no statistically significant evidence of a causal relationship between legacy preference policies and total alumni giving at top universities."[48]

Coffman and colleagues also examine what happened to giving at seven institutions that dropped legacy preferences during the time period of the study: Georgia Tech, Texas A&M, the University of Georgia, the University of Iowa, the University of Massachusetts at Amherst, the University of Nebraska, and Vanderbilt.[49] They find "no short-term measurable reduction in alumni giving as a result of abolishing legacy preferences."[50] After Texas A&M eliminated the use of legacy preferences in 2004, for example, donations took a small hit, but then increased substantially from 2005 to 2007.[51]

Of course, eliminating legacy preferences by itself would not guarantee that admission officials would discontinue favoritism of every other kind for the very wealthy. The top 1 percent of gift givers contribute 70 percent of alumni contributions, and the children of those individuals might continue to receive a nod based on wealth rather than legacy status.[52] But, eliminating legacy preferences and limiting favoritism to extremely large donors (whether or not they were alumni) would be an important step in the direction of fairness. Preferences based on raw wealth would be viewed by many as sordid, not something that universities would openly boast about as furthering a commitment to "tradition" and "family ties," values universities currently appeal to when defending legacy preferences. And the change would drastically decrease the number of casualties among qualified applicants who have the misfortunate of being born to non-alumni parents, compared to today's system in which between 10 percent and 25 percent of slots go to alumni children. (And, as we shall see below, under a more transparent system of donations in exchange for preferential treatment, the tax deductibility of such donations would come into serious question.)

In Chapter 6, John Brittain of the University of the District of Columbia Law School and former chief counsel at the Lawyers' Committee for Civil Rights and attorney Eric Bloom examine the impact of legacy preferences on students of color and the potential impact of curtailing preferences for alumni children on affirmative action policies.

Legacy preferences are an overt form of direct discrimination against "wrong ancestor" students whose parents did not attend the college to which students are applying. But preferring alumni children also has a disparate negative impact on students of color, essentially perpetuating discrimination and inequalities from the past.

As Brittain and Bloom point out, underrepresented minorities make up 12.5 percent of the applicant pool at selective colleges and universities, but only 6.7 percent of the legacy applicant pool.[53] At Texas A&M, 321 of the legacy admits in 2002 were white, while only 3 were black, and 25 Hispanic.[54] At Harvard, only 7.6 percent of legacy admits in 2002 were under-represented minorities, compared with 17.8 percent of all students. Likewise, at the University of Virginia, 91 percent of early decision legacy admits in 2002 were white, 1.6 percent black, and 0.5 percent Hispanic.[55]

After a generation of affirmative action, some civil rights advocates might argue that now is the wrong time to eliminate legacies—just as meaningful numbers of African-American and Latino families are beginning to benefit from the policies. But in fact, blacks and Hispanics continue to be grossly underrepresented at elite colleges, even with affirmative action policies in place. In 2008, African Americans and Latinos made up more than 30 percent of the traditional college-aged population, yet little more than 10 percent of the enrollees at the top fifty national universities in *U.S. News & World Report.*[56] The authors note that "affirmative action does not offset legacy preference: the use of legacy preference, in fact, requires college admissions [officers] to rely more heavily on affirmative action."[57]

Finally, Brittain and Bloom's chapter discusses the connection between legacy preferences and affirmative action. As we have seen, the elimination of affirmative action in places such as the University of California, the University of Georgia, and Texas A&M placed intense pressure on institutions to eliminate legacy preferences, given the "blatant inconsistency."[58] But would the reverse also be true?

Would the elimination of legacy preferences threaten the future of affirmative action?

That prospect is highly unlikely. As the authors point out, affirmative action policies to date have survived strict scrutiny because they enhance educational diversity. (For some members of the Supreme Court, though not a majority, affirmative action also has been justified as a remedy for centuries of brutal discrimination.) Legacy preferences, by contrast, have no such justification. Because they disproportionately benefit whites, they reduce, rather than enhance, racial and ethnic diversity in higher education. And rather than being a remedy for discrimination, legacy preferences were born of discrimination. Brittain and Bloom write: "If affirmative action is aimed at opening the doors to excluded minorities, legacy preferences were designed to slam those doors shut."[59] Affirmative action engenders enormous controversy because it pits two great principles against one another—the antidiscrimination principle, which says that we should not classify people by ancestry, against the anti-subordination principle, which says that we must make efforts to stamp out illegitimate hierarchies. In the case of legacy preferences, by contrast, the policy advances neither principle: it explicitly classifies individuals by bloodline and does so in a way that compounds existing hierarchy.[60]

Legal and Policy Options on Legacy Preferences

While the first portion of the book lays out the empirical evidence on legacy preferences, the second part examines legal and policy options for curtailing them. Remarkably, legacy preferences have been litigated only once in federal court, by an applicant to the University of North Carolina at Chapel Hill named Jane Cheryl Rosenstock. Rosenstock, a New York resident who was rejected, alleged that her constitutional rights were violated by a variety of preferences, including those for in-state applicants, minorities, low-income students, athletes, and legacies.

Rosenstock was not a particularly compelling candidate—her combined SAT score was about 850 on a 1600-point scale, substantially lower than most out-of-state applicants.[61] And if she was a weak applicant, she was also a weak litigant.[62] She never argued that, because legacy preferences are hereditary, they presented a "suspect" classification that should be judged by the "strict scrutiny" standard under the Equal Protection Clause. The district court judge in the case, *Rosenstock* v. *University of North Carolina*,[63] held that it was rational to believe that alumni preferences translate into additional revenue to universities, though absolutely no evidence was provided for this contention.[64] The decision was never appealed.

Given this sparse lower court history, legal scholars and practitioners believe the time is ripe for litigation of this question. This volume presents two distinct legal theories under which ancestry-based legacy preferences could be challenged.[65]

In Chapter 7, University of California at Davis School of Law professor Carlton Larson lays out the case that legacy preferences at public universities are not only unfair, but also "grossly unconstitutional."[66] In particular, he says, a state-sponsored preference based on hereditary status is a violation of a little-litigated constitutional provision—the Nobility Clause, which affects state governments. The clause provides that "No state shall . . . grant any Title of Nobility."[67]

Examining the early history of the country, Larson makes a compelling case that this prohibition should not be interpreted narrowly as simply prohibiting the naming of individuals as dukes or earls but more broadly to prohibit "government-sponsored hereditary privileges"—including legacy preferences at public universities.[68] In the Revolutionary era, Larson writes, hereditary privileges "were unthinkable." Indeed, "it is that British world of inherited privilege that the leaders of the American Revolution sought to overthrow forever."[69]

Larson focuses his chapter on a Revolutionary-era debate over the formation of the Society of the Cincinnati, a private, hereditary organization whose members were limited to officers of the Continental Army and their heirs. Even though the Society granted no formal "titles," was private in nature, and had no real power, its membership rules based on ancestry were denounced by all the leading figures of the time. Samuel Adams opposed the group's "odious hereditary distinctions." John Adams denounced the group as an "inroad upon our first principle, equality." Benjamin Franklin said the Society's members were acting "in direct opposition to the solemnly declared sense of their country." Thomas Jefferson labeled himself an "enemy of the institution." And George Washington said he would resign from the Society if it did not eliminate its hereditary succession.[70]

What would the Founders have thought of legacy preferences at state universities? "Selective college admissions were unknown in the eighteenth century," Larson notes, "but we do know what the Revolutionary generation thought about hereditary privilege." He argues: "Legacy preferences at exclusive public universities were precisely the type of hereditary privilege that the Revolutionary generation sought to destroy forever."[71] The Founders, Larson writes, would have resisted the idea of state-funded university admissions based even in part on ancestry "with every fiber of their being."[72]

Some might argue that legacy preferences are constitutional because they give just a boost, not guaranteed admission, to legacies. Larson asks, what if a state were to add points on a civil service exam to individuals who were the children of state employees? Such an arrangement would be considered bizarre and unconstitutional. He notes that "university admissions policies are perhaps the only area in modern public life where such practices persist."[73] Some might object that the Nobility Clause limits hereditary distinctions only in government positions, but that cannot be right, Larson says, or it would be constitutional to create hereditary exemptions from such obligations as paying income tax. Finally, he notes, the monetary justification—that legacy preferences help public universities raise money—cannot be a constitutional rationale, even if it were empirically valid. The Constitution often requires the government to do things that cost money: the Eighth Amendment prohibits housing convicts in dog cages, for example, even though it would be less expensive to do so.[74] Legacy preferences violate the Constitution's prohibition of state-sponsored hereditary privilege, Larson says, and none of the defenses suffices.

In Chapter 8, attorneys Steve Shadowen and Sozi Tulante outline another legal challenge to legacy preferences as a violation of both the Equal Protection Clause of the Constitution and the Civil Rights Act of 1866. Shadowen and Tulante concur with Larson's notion that the Founders were opposed to hereditary privilege and note that the essential purpose of the Fourteenth Amendment, adopted in 1868, was to codify within the Constitution the original promise of the Declaration of Independence that "all [white] men are created equal"—and extend it to black people.

Coming on the heels of the Civil War, passage of the Fourteenth Amendment, including its prohibition against state denial of "the equal protection of the laws," was fundamentally aimed at extending full citizenship to black Americans. But the wording and purpose of the Equal Protection Clause was also broader than that, as Shadowen and Tulante point out. The framers of the amendment, such as Charles Sumner and John Bingham, were seeking to prohibit all lineage discrimination, of which racial discrimination is a particularly noxious subset. As Justice Potter Stewart noted years later, the Equal Protection Clause applied to African Americans "a fundamental principle upon which this Nation had been founded—that the law would honor no preference based on lineage."[75]

Subsequent case law interpreting the Fourteenth Amendment bears out this reading, the authors contend. Courts have held that racial discrimination is forbidden in part because "it demeans the dignity and worth of a person to be judged by ancestry instead of by his or her own merit and essential qualities."[76] The prohibition of discrimination based on ancestry helps explain why the Court has interpreted the Fourteenth Amendment to go beyond race, and to apply heightened scrutiny to laws that punish children born out of wedlock, or whose parents came to this country illegally.[77]

If legacy preferences should be subject to strict scrutiny, as the authors suggest, can supporters of the policy show they have a compelling state interest, and that the policy is narrowly tailored to further that goal? Increasing donations is not a cognizable, much less a compelling, interest, Shadowen and Tulante argue. Suppose that, in *Brown* v. *Board of Education*, defenders of segregation could have proven that white taxpayers would be more likely to provide financial support to segregated public schools. Just because the beneficiaries of discrimination are willing to pay for it does not make the defense permissible.[78]

Nor are the means narrowly tailored, they say. Because the top 1 percent of alumni contributors provide 70 percent of the total donations, they argue, it would be far more efficient—and less discriminatory—to hold an open auction for a small number of university slots to go to the highest bidder than to discriminate against a broad swath of people who have the wrong set of ancestors.[79] Unlike affirmative action, the authors say, legacy preferences cannot survive strict scrutiny.

Shadowen and Tulante argue that legacy preferences at private universities are also illegal under the Civil Rights Act of 1866. Unlike Title VI of the 1964 Civil Rights Act, which outlaws discrimination only on the basis of "race, color or national origin," the 1866 Civil Rights Act prohibits discrimination on the basis of both "race" and "ancestry." The heavy use of legacy preferences at private universities, therefore, is also vulnerable to legal challenge.

How would a judge likely react to these new legal theories? In Chapter 9, the Honorable Boyce F. Martin, Jr., of the Sixth Circuit Court of Appeals in an article written with Donya Khalili, outlines the ways in which a judge will weigh the issues. Martin, who authored the Sixth Circuit's majority opinion supporting affirmative action at the University of Michigan Law School in *Grutter* v. *Bollinger*, writes that "legacy admissions are problematic legally."[80] He notes that the 1976 district court opinion upholding legacy preferences in *Rosenstock* addressed the issue "in a scant five sentences" and is "neither binding nor persuasive to future courts."[81]

Martin says he will "not hazard to guess" what level of scrutiny a court will apply to legacy preferences, but he does note that the argument for applying strict scrutiny, given that legacy preferences are based on "bloodline" is advanced "eloquently" by Shadowen and Tulante. He also notes that it is possible that a court will apply heightened scrutiny on the principle that "to penalize a child's ability to get into a school based on whether his parent was able to get in . . . would be unjust to the child because [he has] no control over this status." The third alternative is a "rational basis" test.[82]

If strict scrutiny were applied, Martin writes, defenders of legacy preferences could not point to the diversity justification used for affirmative action, given that legacy admits are "overwhelmingly white" and are likely to enjoy a "socioeconomic status that matches the historically dominant groups on campus."[83] Instead, legacy preferences are likely to be defended as a financial necessity, an argument, he says, that "evidence may not support." Even if evidence were produced,

Martin notes, a judge might find that a school "could increase donations by alumni by other means that do not require discrimination." An appeal to maintaining "a sense of tradition and community" appears to Martin to be "a fairly weak argument."[84]

The volume concludes with Chapter 10, a public policy analysis written by journalist Peter Sacks, author of *Tearing Down the Gates: Confronting the Class Divide in American Education*. Various sporadic attempts have been made over the years to curtail legacy preferences, without success. In the early 1990s, Senator Bob Dole asked the U.S. Department of Education's Office for Civil Rights to investigate the legality of legacy preferences, but the department never followed up on the request.[85] Likewise, in 2004, Senator Ted Kennedy proposed amending the Higher Education Act to require colleges to report the share of each entering class that were legacies, but he eventually backed down under pressure from higher education lobbyists.[86]

But the most powerful lever for attacking legacy preferences may lie elsewhere. Sacks asks the intriguing question: Suppose that supporters of legacy preferences are correct, and such policies are critical to fund-raising because donors would not give but for the expectation that doing so will help their offspring's chances of getting in? If that were true, then the donors are receiving something of real value—increased admission chances for their children—in return for their donations. Under IRS regulations, however, when donors receive a substantial benefit, the full measure of the donation is not tax deductible.

Sacks begins his chapter by noting the special tax provisions that apply to the nonprofit higher education sector, in contrast to for-profit higher education institutions. Because nonprofit colleges and universities serve the public interest, they are not required to pay taxes as corporations or individuals are.[87] As Senator Charles Grassley has noted, "John Doe pays taxes. John Deere pays taxes. But Johns Hopkins does not."[88] This tax exempt status costs the federal government some $18 billion annually, according to one analysis. Moreover, donations to nonprofit educational institutions are tax deductible to donors, a provision that cost the federal government $5.9 billion in 2007.[89] The philosophical rationale for making charitable donations tax deductible is that "unlike other uses of income, it does not enrich the disburser."[90]

So how do alumni donations aimed at increasing an offspring's chances of admissions fit into this framework? IRS publication 526 provides "If you receive or expect to receive a financial or economic benefit as a result of making a contribution to a qualified organization, you cannot deduct the part of the contribution that represents the value of the benefit you receive."[91]

As Sacks notes, the value of a legacy preference is quite substantial. Citing research, he estimates the lifetime benefit of attending a selective college compared to a less-selective college at $315,000. If legacy preferences increase one's chance of admission by 20 percentage points, the value is considerable.[92] If universities and colleges are conferring a monetary benefit in exchange for donations—as institutions themselves imply when they say legacy preferences are necessary for their financial health—then, says Sacks, "the arrangement shatters the first principle underlying the charitable deduction, that donations to nonprofit organizations not 'enrich the giver.'"[93] As Senator Grassley has argued, "We need to think whether these reserved spaces at our top colleges is a public policy that should be subsidized by the tax code—as is currently the case."[94] What is particularly outrageous is that under existing law, non-legacy taxpayers essentially are required to subsidize a practice that discriminates against their children.[95]

If Sacks's argument is right, universities and colleges are trapped in a logical box. Either donations are not linked to legacy preferences, in which case the fundamental rationale for ancestry discrimination is flawed; or giving is linked to legacy preferences, in which case donations should not be tax deductible, and the entire business model "may come crashing down."[96]

Conclusion

The chapters in this volume suggest that legacy preferences are an unfair and illegal anachronism. On one level, they are a uniquely American phenomenon, underlining the point that the rest of the world's universities somehow manage to survive without them. At the same time, they are fundamentally anti-American, at odds with the very founding of this nation. They were invented in a dark moment of early twentieth-century American history, even though they would have appalled the eighteenth-century founders of this nation.

For the most part, American higher education has sought to democratize, opening its doors to women, to people of color, and to the financially needy. Legacy preferences are an outlier in this trend, a relic that has no place in American society. In a fundamental sense, this nation's first two great wars—the Revolution and the Civil War—were fought to defeat different forms of aristocracy.[97] That this remnant of ancestry-based discrimination still survives—in American higher education of all places—is truly breathtaking.

Legacy Preferences in Action

2

Legacy Preferences in a Democratic Republic

Michael Lind

In 1940, shortly before U.S. entry into World War II, at a moment when democratic government survived in only a handful of countries encircled by totalitarian empires, one of the champions of expanded access to higher education, James Bryant Conant, delivered a Charter Day address at the University of California entitled "Education for a Classless Society: The Jeffersonian Tradition."

The questions that Conant raised are as relevant to the debate over the relationship of higher education to democracy in America today as they were on the eve of Pearl Harbor: "The possibility that each generation may start life afresh and that hard work and ability would find their just rewards was once an exciting new doctrine. Is it outworn? In short, has the second component of the Jeffersonian tradition in education still vitality? Can a relatively high degree of social mobility be realized in this modern world?"

Conant defended the Jeffersonian ideal of a democratic republic and argued for a close connection between education and social mobility:

> A high degree of social mobility is the essence of the American ideal of a classless society. If large numbers of young people can

> develop their own capacities irrespective of the economic status of their parents, then social mobility is high. If, on the other hand, the future of a young man or woman is determined almost entirely by inherited privilege or the lack of it, social mobility is nonexistent. You are all familiar with the old American adage, "Three generations from shirt sleeves to shirt sleeves." This implies a high degree of social mobility, both up and down. It implies that sons and daughters must and can seek their own level, obtain their own economic rewards, engage in any occupation irrespective of what their parents might have done.
>
> Contrast this adage with a statement of the aristocratic tradition—namely, that it takes three generations to educate a gentleman. . . . The distinction between a stratified class system and one with a high degree of social mobility is apparent only when at least two generations are passed in review. A class, as I am using the word, is perpetuated by virtue of inherited position.[1]

An "inherited position" is a perfect description of a legacy preference—that is, the policy of a college or university in giving preference in admissions to children or other relatives of alumni who would not otherwise be admitted. The number of students admitted to American schools on a hereditary basis by this mechanism is a closely guarded secret of university administrations, but according to some estimates, the beneficiaries of legacy preferences—disproportionately white, Protestant, and upper income—match or exceed the number of students admitted under race-based affirmative action programs, which have been much more visible and controversial.

Are legacy preferences in university admissions un-American? Critics of preferences in college admissions for the relatives of alumni argue that they are not only unfair, but also incompatible with America's democratic and meritocratic political traditions. Some argue that the spirit if not the letter of the ban on "titles of nobility" in the U.S. Constitution should discourage a quasi-heredity aristocracy of B.A.s, M.B.A.s, J.D.s, M.D.s and Ph.D.s. Others point out that legacy preferences are biased against non-whites and non-Protestants, inasmuch as they perpetuate a bias for descendants of white Protestant families who were admitted to colleges and universities that excluded or minimized the admission of blacks, Latinos, Asians, Jews, and Catholics before the Civil Rights movement.

By themselves, these would be compelling arguments for outlawing discriminatory legacy preferences in higher education. In addition, other powerful arguments against legacy preferences can be made, on the basis of the logic of America's democratic republican political creed. According to Thomas Jefferson, the most profound analyst of the American creed, a democratic republic is incompatible with political, economic, and educational aristocracy. Legacy preferences, however, promote aristocracy in all three areas.

Legacy preferences promote political aristocracy, because graduates of universities in general, and of elite universities in particular, are overrepresented both in the electorate and in the political elite. Legacy preferences promote economic aristocracy, because they promote privileged access by some families to the most precious income-generating assets in a post-agrarian economy of wage-earners—diplomas and professional credentials. Last but not least, legacy preferences promote educational aristocracy, because they ration access to higher education partly on the basis of birth rather than solely on the basis of individual ability.

Whether viewed from the perspective of political, economic, or educational opportunity, the system of legacy preferences is at odds with the fundamental design of a democratic republic such as the United States of America.

In the last letter he wrote, on June 24, 1826, Thomas Jefferson told Roger C. Weightman, mayor of Washington, D.C.: "All eyes are opened, or opening, to the rights of man. The general spread of the light of science has already laid open to every view the palpable truth, that the mass of mankind has not been born with saddles on their backs, nor a favored few booted and spurred, ready to ride them legitimately, by the grace of God."[2] Throughout his life, the author of the Declaration of Independence sought to make the United States a model of a democratic republic by purging it of institutions that were—if the wordplay may be forgiven—the *legacies* of aristocracy.

In an autobiographical note, Jefferson proposed "instead of an aristocracy of wealth, of more harm and danger, than benefit, to society, to make an opening for the aristocracy of virtue and talent, which nature has wisely provided for the direction of the interests of society, and scattered with equal hand through all its conditions."[3] In a letter to John Adams, Jefferson elaborated on the distinction he perceived between "natural" and "artificial" aristocracy:

> For I agree with you that there is a natural aristocracy among men. The grounds of this are virtue and talents. . . . There is also an artificial aristocracy founded on wealth and birth, without either virtue or talents; for with these it would belong to the first class. The natural aristocracy I consider as the most precious gift of nature for the instruction, the trusts, and government of society. . . . The artificial aristocracy is a mischievous ingredient in government, and provision should be made to prevent its ascendancy.[4]

In his letter to Adams, Jefferson goes on to discuss provisions he favored in order to prevent the ascendancy of an artificial aristocracy in the United States in the three interlocking realms of politics, the economy, and education.

With respect to politics, Jefferson rejects what he takes to be the view of Adams, that artificial aristocracies cannot be eliminated from politics and therefore should be co-opted by inclusion in a Senate designed to represent a propertied upper class. Jefferson writes,

> You think it best to put the Pseudo-aristoi into a separate chamber of legislation where they may be hindered from doing mischief by their coordinate branches, and where also they may be a protection to wealth against the Agrarian [redistributionist] and plundering enterprise of the Majority of the people. . . . I think the best remedy is exactly that provided by all our constitutions, to leave to the citizens the free election and separation of the aristoi from the pseudo-aristoi, of the wheat from the chaff. In general they will elect the real good and wise. In some instances, wealth may corrupt, and birth blind them; but not in sufficient degree to endanger the society.[5]

In the sphere of the economy, Jefferson sought to minimize the danger of an artificial aristocracy of "pseudo-aristoi" by using legislation to discourage the survival of landed family estates. "At the first session of our [Virginia] legislature after the Declaration of Independence, we passed a law abolishing entails. And this was followed by one abolishing the privilege of Primogeniture, and dividing the lands of intestates equally among all their children, or other representatives. These laws, drawn by myself, laid the axe to the root of Pseudo-aristocracy."[6]

Primogeniture and entail were the means by which the British aristocracy for centuries had sought to monopolize landed wealth among a small number of aristocratic families. Primogeniture preserved family dynasties by ensuring that the entire, intact estate was inherited by the eldest son, instead of being broken up into smaller estates among multiple children. The system of entail forced the heir to keep the estate intact.

Jefferson's claim that laws in Virginia and other states "laid the axe to the root of Pseudo-aristocracy" was not an idle boast. In *Democracy in America* (1831), Alexis de Tocqueville noted that laws of inheritance such as those written by Jefferson had nearly destroyed any trace of hereditary landed aristocracy in the United States:

> In the United States it has nearly completed its work of destruction, and there we can best study its results. The English laws concerning the transmission of property were abolished in almost all the states at the time of the Revolution. The law of entail was so modified as not materially to interrupt the free circulation of property. The first generation having passed away, estates began to be parceled out; and the change became more and more rapid with the progress of time. And now, after a lapse of a little more than sixty years, the aspect of society is totally altered; the families of the great landed proprietors are almost all commingled with the general mass. In the state of New York, which formerly contained many of these, there are but two who still keep their heads above the stream; and they must shortly disappear. The sons of these opulent citizens have become merchants, lawyers, or physicians. Most of them have lapsed into obscurity. The last trace of hereditary ranks and distinctions is destroyed; the law of partition has reduced all to one level.
>
> I do not mean that there is any lack of wealthy individuals in the United States; I know of no country, indeed, where the love of money has taken stronger hold on the affections of men and where a profounder contempt is expressed for the theory of the permanent equality of property. But wealth circulates with inconceivable rapidity, and experience shows that it is rare to find two succeeding generations in the full enjoyment of it.[7]

According to Jefferson in his letter to Adams, the third method of averting the formation of an artificial aristocracy in a democratic republic such as the United States is universal, publicly funded education. Jefferson regretted that the Virginia legislature had rejected his plan for democratic education:

> It was a Bill for the more general diffusion of learning. This proposed to divide every county into wards of 5 or 6 miles square, like your [Massachusetts] townships; to establish in each ward a free school for reading, writing and common arithmetic; to provide for the annual selection of the best subject from these schools who might receive at the public expence a higher degree of education at a district school; and from these district schools to select a certain number of the most promising subjects to be completed at an University, where all the useful sciences should be taught. Worth and genius would thus have been sought out from every condition of life, *and completely prepared by education for defeating the competition of wealth and birth for public trusts.* [emphasis added][8]

Note two aspects of Jefferson's scheme of education for a democratic republic. First, it is meritocratic. Jefferson wanted basic education to be universal. However, middle and higher education would be selective, intended to weed out everyone not naturally gifted with "worth and genius." Second, his educational system was intended not merely to recognize and promote the naturally talented, but also to turn them into a political force capable of doing battle in public with the "pseudo-aristoi." The meritocrats from all backgrounds would be "completely prepared by education for defeating the competition of wealth and birth for public trusts."

If Jefferson was right, then the citizens of a democratic republic needed to arrange their laws and institutions in order to discourage the formation of an "artificial aristocracy" of "wealth and birth" in the three realms of politics, the economy, and education. If we take Jefferson's philosophy to be the paradigmatic discussion of democracy versus aristocracy in America, then it is clear that legacy preferences in university admissions threaten democracy in politics, the economy, and education alike.

In politics, Jefferson's logic prevailed, and property restrictions on voting and office-holding, along with restrictions on gender and race, were abolished by the end of the twentieth century. Now and then, political dynasties have appeared at all levels of government, including the Harrisons, the Tafts, the Roosevelts, the Kennedys, the Bushes, and the Clintons. But these dynasties seldom last more than two generations. The influence of particular family fortunes on American politics, like that of particular political families, tends to be ephemeral. Jefferson's prophecy about the voters has been vindicated: in free elections, citizens generally have been able to sort "the aristoi from the pseudo-aristoi."

Even so, legacy preferences in higher education arguably are a threat, if only an indirect threat, to political democracy in America because of their influence on the composition of the electorate and the political class, including the vast numbers of political appointees and civil servants in modern America's enormously expanded government.

During the Progressive era of the early twentieth century, progressives and conservatives, frightened by immigrant voters and agrarian populists, enacted voter registration reforms at the state and local level intended to prevent working-class voters (and, in the South, black Americans) from voting and to increase the relative numbers of the college-educated and affluent in the electorate. While some of these devices, such as poll taxes and literacy tests, were struck down during the Civil Rights movement, others, such as Tuesday voting and complex registration procedures, still remain. U.S. voter participation has remained low since the early 1900s. Because the college-educated are overrepresented among voters, the allocation of access for some Americans to college on the basis of birth rather than talent makes an undemocratic gap between the population and the much smaller electorate even wider.

Jefferson would not have objected to the overrepresentation of college graduates among politicians, political appointees, and career civil servants. Indeed, the entire purpose of Jeffersonian education is to identify the "natural aristocracy" of "virtue and talents" that deserves to be entrusted by the less-educated voters with "the instruction, the trusts and government of society." But the idea of reserving a significant number of admissions to institutions of higher education for the children of alumni who could not have been admitted otherwise, thereby depriving more talented students of those places on campus, is obviously incompatible with the Jeffersonian ideal. Jefferson's university was supposed to help the meritocratic elite in its public purpose of "defeating the competition of wealth and birth for public trusts." By reserving places on campus for members of the pseudo-aristocracy of "wealth and birth," legacy preferences introduce an aristocratic snake into the democratic republican Garden of Eden.

Legacy preferences are particularly insidious in the branch of the federal government where a person's educational background tends to have the most weight: the judicial branch. Some observers have speculated that one reason why the Supreme Court has a tenuous majority in favor of another kind of ancestry preference—racial affirmative action—may be the fact that so many of its members have been able to benefit personally from this kind of affirmative action for the affluent white elite. Among the legacies on the recent Court have been Stephen Breyer, Anthony Kennedy, and Sandra Day O'Connor (Stanford University), and John Paul Stevens (University of Chicago and Northwestern Law School), while Ruth Bader Ginsburg is the mother of a legacy who followed her at Harvard Law School.[9]

Legacy preferences are even more of a threat to economic democracy than to political democracy. In order to understand why, it is necessary only to translate the function of a farm in agrarian America into the function of a diploma in urban, industrial America as an asset critical to an individual's struggle for economic opportunity and security.

Thinkers including Aristotle and Machiavelli have argued that a democratic republic could exist only where there was widespread ownership of small property. Most of America's Founders agreed. In the United States, where nine out of ten people lived on farms in 1800, that meant a focus on the widespread distribution of farms in the early years of the republic. As Senator Thomas Hart Benton of Missouri observed in 1826: "The freeholder . . . is the natural supporter of a free government, and it should be the policy of republics to multiply their freeholders, as it is the policy of monarchies to multiply tenants. We are a republic, and we wish to remain so; then multiply the class of freeholders."[10] In the nineteenth century, this sentiment was not limited to Jeffersonians and Jacksonian Democrats such as Benton. Henry Clay, one of the leaders of the anti-Jacksonian Whig Party, coined the phrase "self-made man" to describe the American ideal. In 1856, Abraham Lincoln told an audience in Kalamazoo, Michigan: "We stand at once the wonder and admiration of the whole world, and we must enquire what it is that has given us so much prosperity, and we shall understand that to give up that one thing, would be to give up all future prosperity. This cause is that every man can make himself."[11] From his hero Clay, Lincoln inherited the ideal of the self-made man or woman, as distinct from the daddy-made or mommy-made "legacy."

By the mid-twentieth century, the United States had completed its transition from an agrarian economy into an industrial society in which most Americans no longer owned the means of production, such as factories and offices, and had to compete for wages in a labor market. In today's wage-earner economy, the major economic asset for an individual is human capital, not agrarian capital, embodied in a diploma, alone or in combination with a professional degree. Americans with B.A.s tend to make more than those with only high school diplomas, and Americans with graduate and professional degrees, particularly those who belong to guilds such as the American Medical Association and American Bar Association and the professoriate, make even more, in part because educational and guild regulations artificially restrict the number of college graduates and licensed professionals.

To add insult to injury, there is the growing financial barrier to attendance at elite universities by middle-class and working-class Americans who are not poor enough to qualify for scholarships but who are unwilling to saddle themselves with massive and financially debilitating educational debt by taking out student loans. In 1979, children from families in the top 25 percent in terms of family income were only four times more likely to attend an elite university than those from the poorest 25 percent, most of whom are white; today, they are ten times more likely.[12] With the cost of tuition rising far more rapidly than wages and median family wealth, the broad American middle class is being priced out of elite schools. If legacy preferences favor some college applicants at the expense of others on the basis of birth, the high cost of a first-rate university education (which Jefferson hoped to be supplied entirely at public expense) creates an unfair advantage for the children of elite families on the basis of wealth.

A case can be made that the wage premium associated with higher education in the United States can and should be reduced. Sending more Americans to college might reduce wage inequality, but only by devaluing the worth of a diploma. There are more rational and direct ways to reduce education-based wage inequalities. One would be to raise the wages of non-college workers, by means of a higher federal minimum wage, greater unionization, or a tighter labor market created by reductions in unskilled immigration. The attempts to ensure that professions such as law, medicine, and the professoriate benefit from high barriers to entry also could be thwarted by legislative reforms that maintain standards while increasing the numbers of lawyers, doctors, and professors, leading to a decline in the fees and wages they can command from the rest of society.

Even if the economic assets of a degree and a professional license were more widely available, the case for purging nepotistic and aristocratic legacy preferences from higher education would remain. The fact that farm ownership in the United States following the American Revolution was extraordinarily widespread by European standards did not prevent Jefferson and other Americans from passing laws to kill off the threat of a hereditary landed aristocracy once and for all. Likewise, expanding educational opportunity, while it might dilute the advantage enjoyed by the relatives of university alumni, is no argument against "taking an axe to the root" of a quasi-hereditary, credentialed aristocracy based on campuses and the professions.

About the threat posed by legacy preferences to educational democracy, little need be said, so obvious is their incompatibility with a meritocratic educational system. Recognizing this, defenders of legacy preferences often contend that, while considered by itself the legacy preference system might be an evil, it is a necessary evil that contributes to the greater good of helping disadvantaged Americans attend universities. The argument given is that alumni are more likely to contribute money to private and state universities alike, if their undeserving children are admitted; and these contributions, which would not exist in the absence of legacy preferences, can be used to help pay for scholarships for those lacking alumni connections.

Let us ignore the obvious rejoinder—that it would be more efficient to raise money by selling diplomas directly to the undeserving children of alumni, rather than have them occupy classroom seats and dorm rooms that might otherwise be occupied by students who deserve to be in a selective university. The point I want to make about this argument for legacy preferences based on expedience—the argument that co-opting the nepotism of the rich on behalf of a generally democratic society—is that it resembles the argument that John Adams made for the alleged need, in the political sphere, to tame the rich by giving them their own branch of the legislature. Jefferson's reply to Adams's proposal applies with equal force to the argument that universities can help disadvantaged students by guaranteeing places on campus for the children of rich alumni: "I think that to give them power in order to prevent them from doing mischief, is arming them for it, and increasing instead of remedying that evil."[13]

When even the defenders of legacy preferences cannot invoke any principles to justify the policy and are forced to resort to arguments from expedience, it is impossible to speak of two equal sides in a debate. Legacy preferences are offensive to American ideals of political democracy, economic democracy, and educational democracy alike. If defenders of legacy preferences, having lost the argument, nevertheless prevail, it will be because they have wealth and birth, rather than talent and virtue, on their side.[14]

3

A History of Legacy Preferences and Privilege

Peter Schmidt

The history of admissions to America's selective higher education institutions generally has been one of increasing inclusion, as colleges, universities, and professional schools have opened their doors to women and students of color, used affirmative action to promote racial and ethnic diversity in their enrollments, and established financial-aid programs intended to provide greater access to the financially needy. This trend toward greater inclusion, however, has been slowed or halted at times by one common policy that serves a contrary purpose, enabling our society's elite to replicate itself by allotting a disproportionate share of seats at selective colleges to its children. That policy is known as the admissions preference for "legacies"—applicants somehow connected to alumni or enrolled students. It is used by nearly all of the nation's selective higher-education institutions.

In discussing the role that legacy preferences have played in American higher education, it is important to keep in mind that their emergence did not establish admission to selective colleges based on lineage: certain wealthy and powerful families had disproportionate access to the nation's selective colleges long before explicit legacy preferences were used. Legacy preferences, which first came into vogue among selective colleges in the 1920s, served mainly to formalize inherited access to seats in their entering classes in the face of unprecedented competition for admission from segments of American society that previously had not enrolled at such institutions in great numbers, such as the children of recent immigrants and, in particular, the children of upwardly mobile Jewish families from Europe.

It is also important to note that outright admission preferences are hardly the only advantages that colleges give to legacy applicants. In truth, such institutions have developed a host of other means of giving legacies an edge, including well-developed mechanisms for providing the children of alumni with coaching and "insider" information to improve their odds of acceptance; formal policies affording a second or even third chance to legacies who fail to make the cut; and scholarships and tuition discounts reserved specifically for legacy students.

This chapter seeks to provide a fuller picture of how legacy policies came into being and have evolved in American higher education, showing not only how they have survived past efforts to democratize selective college access, but also why they are likely to be difficult to eliminate, and could become an even bigger force in admissions down the road. The chapter begins by describing how selective colleges in the United States and Europe catered to the children of wealthy and powerful families long before legacy preferences came into being. It then offers an account of how legacy preferences developed and spread throughout selective higher education in decades following World War I. Then it describes how two trends under way in higher education in the 1940s—the promotion of meritocracy and of diversity—served to draw scrutiny to legacy preferences and, in some cases, to reduce the advantage enjoyed by legacy applicants. Next, it discusses how changes in the higher education market beginning in the early 1970s created incentives for colleges not to reduce legacy preferences any further. Finally, it discusses the legal and political challenges that have been mounted against legacy preferences in recent decades, and where they have succeeded or fallen short.

The Deep Roots of Inherited Privilege in Higher Education (1400–1900)

To frame the history of legacy admissions at U.S. colleges and universities in a broader context, it is worth noting that America's higher education institutions are hardly alone in having struggled to reconcile the ideal of broad educational access with a practical need to maintain the financial and political support of those with wealth and power. Universities in Europe were grappling with such tensions well before Columbus set foot in the New World.

The church-affiliated universities of the Middle Ages served both the rich and the poor, nobility and commoners, guided by a belief, rooted in Christianity, that education should be available to all. Moreover, their promotion of simple, frugal living on their campuses made it easier for students from poor backgrounds to fit in. They were hardly egalitarian, however. Mindful of family rank and the money associated with it, they reserved the choice seats within classrooms for the sons of the aristocracy and conferred additional privileges on those who came from high-status families or were able to pay additional fees. Although young people from noble backgrounds tended to be no more prevalent on university campuses than they were in society at large, their low enrollments were not a deliberate result of university admissions decisions, but instead reflected the reality that many had been taught the ways of the court by their families and tutors and regarded the knowledge of academic disciplines offered by a university education as unnecessary or irrelevant to their lives.[1]

The universities of the Holy Roman Empire, England, and Poland did not experience a significant increase in their enrollment of students of noble rank until the late 1400s, when Europe's nobility began to sense that it was losing some of its grip on power to the emerging bourgeoisie.[2] As nobles turned to universities to provide them with specialized training for future offices, and the children of the bourgeoisie turned to such institutions to prepare them for professions, the poor gradually were elbowed out, especially in the fields of law and medicine, and university life became much more aristocratic. Whereas few nobles had attended England's universities prior to 1500, by the early 1600s, there were six nobles for every five commoners enrolled at Oxford or Cambridge. In one history of admissions to European universities at that time, Maria Rosa di Simone writes that Spanish universities completely abandoned their efforts to reach out to the impoverished, and during the 1600s their "pupils tended for the most part to be sons of university lecturers, of loyal servants or of important and wealthy persons, and they in turn habitually went on to teach in the universities or hold high posts in the bureaucracies, the Inquisition or the church." As a result, "a genuine 'college-educated' caste was thereby created, which gathered into its own hands the key posts in university administration, the university chairs and the scholarships."[3]

With the dawning of the Enlightenment, Europe's universities became even less accessible to the poor, and more focused on perpetuating the ruling class. In eighteenth-century England and France, the recipients of university scholarships were virtually always "the sons and relatives of clerics, senior civil servants, university lecturers, and rich and influential persons."[4] Commoners, who made up 55 percent of the student body of Oxford and Cambridge as of 1600, accounted for just 1 percent of their enrollment as of 1810. Students from poor backgrounds were discouraged from even trying to come up with the funds to attend.[5] If the universities of old Europe did not widely use legacy preferences to ensure the admission of the children of the ruling class, it is because such children never needed them, for their admission was already assured.

A similar observation can be made of colleges in the United States, up until the early 1900s. Throughout the 1800s, most private colleges in the United States served fewer than one hundred students, drawn mainly from local communities, and relied so heavily on tuition revenue they had little incentive to turn anyone away.[6] As of 1870, many operated their own feeder schools and had arrangements with other private preparatory schools, allowing their graduates to be admitted based on their principal's recommendation.[7] Each private college had such distinct admissions criteria—generally spelling out how much applicants should have learned, and in which subjects—that young people tended to prepare themselves for entry into specific institutions. Many of those applicants who performed poorly on their entrance examinations nonetheless were admitted on a conditional basis, being allowed to stay so long as they remedied their deficiencies and kept their heads above water academically.[8]

The chief barriers precluding most working-class youth from attending private colleges were tuition costs and the scarcity of quality public schools offering subjects that the colleges required their students to have knowledge of, such as Latin and Greek. For the most part, those students whose families could not afford a private preparatory school or private tutoring were out of the running.[9] The public land-grant colleges that arose in the last half of the century were similarly disinclined to reject students who possessed minimal qualifications, as they sought to provide educational opportunity to segments of American society that had been denied it before. But they existed mainly to prepare people for careers in agriculture and engineering—not as training grounds for the elite—and, as a practical matter, also were out of the reach of the vast majority of Americans who never got as far as high school.[10]

Henry Adams, the great-grandson of John Adams and grandson of John Quincy Adams, captured the close ties between prominent families and private colleges through the 1800s in his own account of his plans to enroll in Harvard College, from which he graduated in 1858. After referring to attending Harvard as his "next regular step" in life, he wrote:

> For generation after generation, Adamses and Brookses and Boylstons and Gorhams had gone to Harvard College, and although none of them, as far as known, had ever done any good there, or thought himself the better for it, custom, social ties, convenience, and, above all, economy, kept each generation on track. Any other education would have required a serious effort, but no one took Harvard College seriously. All went there because their friends went there, and the college was their ideal of social self-respect.[11]

In an address given in 1869 upon his inauguration as Harvard's president, Charles W. Elliott appeared mindful of his institution's role in educating old-money families, declaring "the country suffers when the rich are ignorant and unrefined" and "inherited wealth is an unmitigated curse when it is divorced from culture."[12]

The extent to which the children of the upper class attended top colleges in their vicinity is evident from Richard Farnum's 1988 analysis of personal background data contained in past issues of the *Social Register* of various eastern cities. He found that Boston register entrants who earned their degrees during the 1880s did so at one of just six institutions, with 78 percent graduating from Harvard, 7 percent from the Massachusetts Institute of Technology, 5 percent from Yale, and 3 percent from Williams College. New York *Social Register* entrants who graduated from college during this period earned their degrees at just thirteen institutions, with 25 percent graduating from Columbia, 24 percent from Yale, 15 percent from Harvard, 14 percent from Princeton, and 3 percent from Williams.[13]

Such attendance patterns persisted through the early 1900s, as did top colleges' policy of basing admissions decisions on fairly undemanding entrance examinations and accepting—if not outright, at least conditionally—just about every product of their traditional feeder schools. American higher education had begun undergoing profound change to address major changes in society, by, for example, reaching out to the high schools that were sprouting up around the nation and establishing graduate programs to provide the specialized training that students would need to run large national companies.[14] But the growing demand for academic credentials did not translate immediately into growing academic demands on the students, who were encouraged to focus on traits such as "manliness" or "character," rather than their own intellects, and were allowed to devote much of their time to extracurricular activities and social organizations. Francis Landey Patton, who served as Princeton's president from 1888 to 1902, called his institution "the finest country club in America."[15] Although his successor, Woodrow Wilson, sought to raise Princeton's standards, as of fall 1907, it still allowed 230 of its 328 entering freshmen to gain admission on conditional basis.[16] The Big Three—Harvard, Yale, and Princeton—remained dominated by the children of high-status Episcopalian, Congregationalist, and Presbyterian families on the eastern seaboard.[17] Catholic families, being largely shut out from such institutions, flocked to colleges affiliated with their own church, with the more affluent enrolling at Holy Cross and Georgetown.[18]

Preserving Inherited Privilege through Legacy Preferences (1900–1940)

In a 2003 paper on legacy preferences at the University of Virginia, Sarah E. Turner, an economist at that institution, and Cameron

Howell, then a doctoral student in higher education, observed that selective colleges' routine admission of the minimally qualified children of alumni was a policy that "attracted no attention until it was threatened."[19]

What caused such a threat to emerge were two developments in the early 1900s. First, frustrated by the poor academic performance of their students and determined to serve a broader portion of society, elite colleges raised their admission standards while simultaneously abandoning those subject-based requirements, such as high-school credits in Latin, that had served as barriers to most students who did not attend elite preparatory schools. Second, the children of Jewish immigrant families, many of whom prized education and had come to the United States mainly to flee persecution, began knocking on college doors in large numbers and posting admission test scores well above those of many applicants from the families the elite colleges traditionally served.[20]

Harvard College's Jewish enrollment rose from 7 percent of the undergraduate population in 1900 to 21.5 percent in 1922. Jewish students accounted for 2 percent of Yale's 1903 graduating class and 9 percent of its class of 1921.[21] Anti-Semitism had flared up on Yale's campus as of 1911, when one of the secret societies, the Elihu, passed a motion saying, "Jews should be denied recognition."[22] At a May 1918 meeting of the Association of New England, representatives of Bowdoin, Brown, MIT, and Tufts all expressed alarm about their growing Jewish enrollments.[23] Ivy League institutions began to see limiting Jewish enrollments as a matter of survival; the University of Pennsylvania, which took no steps to keep Jews out, and Columbia University, which did not move quickly to hold down their numbers, lost a large share of their upper-crust enrollment and much of their cachet as Jewish enrollments surged.[24]

It was not just that elite colleges were enrolling more Jewish students—several also were beginning, for the first time in their histories, to turn significant numbers of minimally qualified applicants away. As the education historian David O. Levine has noted, by the end of World War I, "with the improvement in national transportation networks and the growth of the prosperous, mobile, and education-oriented upper middle class, the best American schools could engage realistically in a nationwide search for the most talented and socially desirable young men." A 1920 survey of the forty most prominent colleges of that time found that thirteen were rejecting applicants who had fulfilled their minimal entrance requirements. Among them, Dartmouth College, which was entering the heyday of its popularity, spurned 1,600 applicants; Princeton, 1,500; the University of Pennsylvania, 750; and Harvard, 229.[25] To be rejecting legacies while admitting Jews, Catholics, and other immigrants and people of modest means was risky behavior for the administrators of such institutions, which, as of the turn of the century, had been growing increasingly dependent on alumni contributions and had been giving alumni significantly more say in their affairs.[26]

Dartmouth College was one of the first to respond to the growing competition for its freshman class seats by adopting a comprehensive admissions process. And that process, adopted in 1919, included as one of its key elements what may have been the first officially stated legacy preference, a call for the admission of "all properly qualified sons of Dartmouth alumni and Dartmouth college officers." It also provided for alumni to take an active role in the recruitment and screening of applicants, especially in distant parts of the country that Dartmouth's own admissions officers had trouble reaching. Levine observed that involving alumni in admissions in such a manner served to give legacy applicants an added advantage, because such alumni "were less committed to a diverse, intellectually oriented student body than in ensuring the admission of their own children and those of others with whom they closely identified." Like many of the comprehensive admission policies subsequently adopted by other colleges, Dartmouth's process also took geographic diversity into account and called for applicants to undergo interviews, submit personal statements, and be rated on personal characteristics by people who knew them, including school officers.[27]

But, while other colleges later adopted such policies for the explicit purpose of limiting Jewish enrollments, Levine's account of the circumstances surrounding Dartmouth's decision suggests that it is a mistake to assume its new admission policies were motivated by anti-Semitism to any significant degree. There was little anti-Semitism reported at Dartmouth at the time, perhaps because its Jewish enrollment was so small—at about 2 percent—that the presence of such students was scarcely felt. Ernest M. Hopkins, who was Dartmouth's president, later insisted that limiting Jewish numbers had not even been a consideration when he devised the 1919 policy change. Hopkins did not make an overt effort to limit Jewish enrollments—by implementing a quota on their numbers—until the winter of 1931–32, after a decade in which Dartmouth's Jewish enrollments had risen fivefold, to about 10 percent of the entering freshman class. Even then, he approached the issue with much more subtlety than his peers elsewhere in the Ivy League, convincing many influential Jewish alumni that he actually was doing them a favor. He told one such alumnus that he had concluded over the past two years that Dartmouth was doing a disservice to its Jewish students and alumni "in allowing the percentage of Jews to increase rapidly, and in not being as exacting in regard to qualities of character and personality among Jewish boys as we were among others." He even managed to enlist Jewish alumni in his efforts to weed out Jewish applicants who were deemed undesirable because they were less prosperous and assimilated to the establishment culture than those who had passed through Dartmouth before.[28]

When other Ivy League institutions undertook similar admission policy overhauls, however, a desire to limit Jewish enrollments was clearly one of their central motives. Robert Corwin, the chairman of Princeton's Board of Admissions, would boast that its "Jewish problem" was largely solved through its 1922 adoption of a comprehensive admission system relying heavily on personal interviews to judge "character"—a trait that, one can assume from later admission statistics, admission officials there were disinclined to find in Jews but found abundantly in the children of alumni. Abbott Lawrence Lowell, who served as Harvard's president from 1909 to 1933, was a major figure in the Immigration Restriction League, which championed "further exclusion of elements undesirable to our citizenship and injurious to our national character." He allowed the segregation of Jewish students in Harvard's dorms, and had made an unsuccessful attempt to impose an outright quota on Harvard's Jewish enrollment in the early 1920s before turning to less obvious means to try to keep their numbers down. Internal memos from Yale show administrators there had a quota on Jewish enrollments in mind when they began tinkering with admission policies at about that time.[29]

Yale formalized its use of legacy preferences in 1925, when, as part of a broader effort to hold down Jewish numbers, its Board of Admissions adopted enrollment limits but stipulated that they "shall not operate to exclude any son of a Yale graduate who has satisfied all of the requirements for admission." During a 1927 endowment campaign, it would assure alumni of its commitment to admit all legacy applicants with reasonably good records, regardless of the number of other applications it received or the quality of outside candidates.[30] Over the course of the 1920s, the share of legacies in Yale's entering freshmen classes rose from 13 percent to 24 percent. By the latter part of the decade, legacies were being judged as qualified for Yale admission if they earned a score of at least 60 on its admission tests, whereas other applicants needed a score of at least 70 to stay in the running.[31]

Harvard adopted a subjective admissions process much like Princeton's in 1926. Among its provisions designed to limit enrollments of Jewish students and protect enrollments of the families it traditionally served was an explicit rejection of the idea that admissions decisions should be based on scholarship alone.[32] Harvard also used absolute enrollment limits and tuition increases to try to ensure it would continue serving its traditional constituency, the graduates of a few private preparatory schools and elite public high schools in Boston, New York, and Philadelphia.[33] Going forward, alumni connections would carry a great deal of weight in Harvard's subjective admission decisions, which, the legal scholar Alan Dershowitz later observed, assured not just homogeneity in its entering classes, but also "a degree of perpetuation of past discriminatory patterns."[34]

Other selective colleges similarly began trying to control the composition of their student bodies by sharply raising tuition, limiting enrollment, taking applicants' "character" into account, and, in some cases, asking applicants to submit photographs or their mother's maiden name. While many elite liberal arts colleges saw themselves as becoming "small but national" in an era when more Americans were traveling for college, there were limits to what parts of the nation they were willing to serve.[35] John Albert Cousens, the president of what was then Tufts College, urged people there to stop thinking of their institution as "a poor man's college and an asylum for the children of the foreign-born," and argued that its academic reputation depended on its enrollment of students from the "best families."[36] State-affiliated Rutgers University, which also was struggling with how to limit Jewish enrollments, established a program in which alumni clubs recommended students "of the right type" for scholarships.[37] Catholics, themselves largely shut out from many top colleges as a result of such policy changes, flocked to Catholic colleges,[38] which would come to favor legacy applicants with equal zeal. Jerome Karabel, a sociologist at the University of California at Berkeley who has extensively studied the histories of Harvard, Yale, and Princeton, would later observe that the admissions process that arose from that era had as its defining feature "the categorical rejection of the idea that admission should be based on academic criteria alone." Its cornerstones "were discretion and opacity—discretion so that the gatekeepers would be free to do what they wished and opacity so that how they used their discretion would not be subject to public scrutiny."[39]

The financial pressures placed on colleges by the Great Depression increased their financial dependence on alumni, and many institutions saw enrolling the children of alumni as a way to thank them for their contributions and keep classroom seats filled.[40] The education historian Marcia Graham Synnott later observed that alumni sons became "the backbone of Yale in times of financial adversity." Nearly 30 percent of the freshmen entering Yale in the fall of 1932 were legacies, up almost 3 percent over the previous year and almost 6 percent over the year before that.[41]

A 1945 survey of the nation's colleges found that 45 percent viewed "character" as an essential quality, 4 percent cited "home influence" as highly important, and preferences for legacies and applicants recommended by alumni and other insiders were widespread. Ohio Wesleyan listed coming from an alumni family as a factor that might get a subpar applicant admitted there, and Swarthmore reported making special provisions for legacies who did not meet its usual standard of being in the upper fourth of their high school class. "Agnes Scott College points out that unless they are daughter of alumnae or sisters of students 'in the family,' the college does not advise a borderline student to come to the campus," a report on the survey's findings said.[42]

Quests for Meritocracy and Diversity Threaten the Grip of Legacies (1940–1973)

By the late 1940s, American higher education was being transformed by two forces that would increase competition for admission slots greatly and would help give rise to long-term political opposition to the very existence of legacy preferences. One such force was a growing consensus that selective colleges had an obligation to seek out our society's most academically talented young people and admit them based on merit. The other was the long-term democratization of access to higher education brought about by government efforts to expand college enrollments and by the curtailment of discriminatory admission practices that had been barriers to women and to members of certain minority groups.

The idea that selective colleges had an obligation to foster meritocracy was largely the brainchild of one man, James Bryant Conant, who served as Harvard's president from 1933 to 1953. Assuming the reins of Harvard at a time when the Great Depression had shaken the nation's faith in its leadership, he made a personal crusade of promoting the idea that the nation needed to rid itself of leadership by a largely hereditary upper class and instead create an elite based on intellectual merit, drawn from all walks of life. In a series of widely read magazine articles, he framed his appeal in deeply patriotic terms, drawing from a letter that Thomas Jefferson had sent to John Adams in 1813.[43] In that letter, Jefferson had argued that the country should be led by "a natural aristocracy" based on "virtue and talents," rather than "an artificial aristocracy, founded on wealth and birth." [44] Conant persuaded the leaders of several other Ivy League colleges to join him in establishing a new scholarship program to recruit bright students from throughout the nation, and helped give rise to the widespread use by colleges of the SAT as a means of trying to objectively identify academic merit.[45]

Conant did not usher in a revolution in admissions at Harvard or, for that matter, stay true to his own ideals. Being profoundly elitist in his vision, it did not seem to bother him that, as of 1940, Harvard was drawing 60 percent of its students from the wealthiest 2.7 percent of the population and continuing to accept virtually anyone from the elite boarding schools that had supplied its student body in the past. Karabel writes that, despite Conant's meritocratic rhetoric, "Harvard did more than give preference to socially elite applicants from exclusive boarding schools; it actively solicited their interest and fretted over the ones who chose to go elsewhere." As of 1952, almost twenty years after Conant took office, Harvard was rejecting fewer than 13 percent of all legacy applicants who applied.[46]

But the popularization of the ideal of meritocracy, as well as the establishment of national tests intended to objectively identify academic talent throughout American society, greatly shifted the terms of the debate, so that it would no longer be assumed that elite colleges were reserved largely for the wealthy or that the only people qualified to attend them were the graduates of a fairly short list of prestigious high schools.

The democratization of higher-education access that occurred after World War II helped ensure that many more ambitious students would be knocking on selective colleges' doors. The federal government's efforts to expand college access were inspired largely by the work of the President's Commission on Higher Education, appointed in 1946 by Harry S. Truman and informally known as "the Zook Commission" after its head, George Zook, the president of the American Council on Education. Echoing Conant, Zook's commission denounced the liberal education offered by many colleges as having an "original aristocratic intent" and concluded that college enrollments had been suppressed artificially by nonacademic barriers—including financial constraints, discrimination, and regional variation in access to education—that must be lifted. Established at a time when only about half of Americans graduated from high school, the commission declared that about half of the American population was qualified intellectually to go on to college.[47] With college enrollments already swelling rapidly largely as a result of the G.I. Bill of Rights of 1944, the commission's report helped focus the government's attention on expanding college access in the long term.

In the short term, however, the federal government's push to expand access did not pose any real threat to the advantages that legacies enjoyed. As of 1946, Princeton systematically was rewarding alumni who gave it their time and money by admitting their children. It accepted 82 percent of the alumni sons who sought admission that year, as compared to 26 percent of other civilians and less than 38 percent of the 2,000 veteran applicants judged to have met its standards, just 5 percent of the 15,000 returning veterans who had inquired about enrolling.[48] Four years later, Yale's dean of freshmen publicly stated that "every break is given to a Yale son," with the institution holding such applicants to lower academic standards, allowing them to make a poor showing in the "personal attribute" department, making no demands that they help fulfill its goal of geographically diversifying its student body, and showing a willingness to take risks on those who nevertheless seemed questionable.[49]

But, although such institutions were able to continue smiling on legacy applicants, some of the mechanisms they had used to keep out nonlegacies were seriously under attack. Most significantly, a post-Holocaust backlash against anti-Semitism in the United States put the nation's colleges under tremendous pressure to stop discriminating against Jews. And the first stirrings of the civil rights movement, fanned by the demands for fair treatment coming from returning black troops, caused many colleges to grow uncomfortable with policies discriminating against black applicants.[50] Most institutions in the North dropped questions dealing with race, religion, or nationality from their application forms.[51] The onset of the cold war and the U.S.-Soviet space race, accompanied by a surge in federal spending on academic research, not only increased pressures on selective colleges to educate the best and brightest, but also pushed them to alter how they defined the best, to take in students who excelled in fields such as engineering or science and did not necessarily fit the "well-rounded" ideal used to rationalize the admission of generations of legacy dilettantes.[52]

A 1990 analysis of *Social Register* data determined that the richest American families lost some of their grip on prestigious local colleges in the decades following World War II. Harvard educated 61 Boston *Social Register* entrants in the 1940s, but just 38 in the 1960s, and similar declines in *Social Register* enrollments occurred at other Ivy League institutions.[53] But, in looking beyond the enrollment patterns of the exceptionally rich, and looking at the enrollment patterns of those who were just plain wealthy or upper-middle-class, it becomes clear that class stratification in higher education actually increased during the period after World War II, thanks in no small part to the high correlation between socioeconomic status and SAT scores. Even as the higher education system as a whole was expanding, its most selective institutions were raising their admission requirements and becoming even more exclusive than they had been before. Many colleges that had served students from middle- and lower-middle-class families in the 1930s were catering to the affluent as the 1960s rolled around.[54] As colleges became more differentiated from each other in terms of their prestige, they began to focus more on staying ahead in the prestige competition than on promoting access.[55] Rather than benefiting the children of poor or working-class families, the changes under way at selective colleges primarily served to cause the children of families with *financial* capital, such as the offspring of business executives, to lose many of their seats on campuses to children whose families had *cultural* capital, so that, for example, enrollments among children of the professoriate rose substantially.[56] In a century marked by profound change in how families transmitted wealth—so that most parents no longer bequeathed their children a family farm or family business upon death, but instead sought to give their children "human capital" by ensuring they acquire certain skills—having parents who could groom you for college became an increasingly important advantage.[57]

The same trends that intensified the competition for admission at colleges that had long favored legacies prompted other colleges that previously had felt no need for legacy preferences to adopt them, to avoid doing too much damage to their relations with alumni as they began spurning growing numbers of applicants. Although Vanderbilt had been rejecting highly qualified young women as far back as the 1920s—mainly because it had limited the number of women it accepted to one-third of each class—by 1960 it also was turning away highly qualified young men as rising numbers of students with strong SAT scores knocked on its doors. One history of Vanderbilt says, "Such changes created intense pressure from alumni parents, including those who loyally supported Vanderbilt fund drives." The institution responded by adopting a policy of having its admissions office read all legacy applications first and accepting all qualified children of alumni before moving on to other candidates. As of 1961, it admitted 97 of 117 applicants who were the sons of alumni and 31 of 63 applicants who were alumni daughters.[58] By the early 1970s, many of the more selective public universities had similarly gotten into the business of courting legacy students and doing their best to admit those who applied.[59]

At the same time colleges were facing increased competition for admission based on merit, they also found themselves under increasing pressure to make exceptions from their usual admission standards for athletes and minority students. As college athletic recruitment became more sophisticated—and college sports more commercialized—beginning in the 1950s, colleges came to see lowering the bar substantially for recruited jocks as a necessary evil to maintain the sort of winning teams that keep alumni happy.[60] Meanwhile, minority students gained the right to compete for admission at colleges that previously had barred them as a result of two 1950 Supreme Court decisions striking down racial segregation in public higher education and the Civil Rights Act of 1964, which empowered the federal government to withhold funds from any college that engaged in racial discrimination. Beginning at Yale in the 1965–66 academic year, selective colleges adopted policies calling for minority applicants to receive the same sort of extra consideration and preferential treatment that legacies had long been receiving, to increase minority enrollments well beyond the levels attained through mere color blindness.[61]

Two other Supreme Court rulings issued during this period would come to be interpreted as giving colleges broad latitude to set their own admissions without risk of government interference. In the Court's 1957 *Sweezy* v. *New Hampshire* decision, involving a University of New Hampshire lecturer accused of being a communist, Justice Felix Frankfurter borrowed from a statement previously issued by South African scholars to assert that every university has "four essential freedoms," those being "to determine for itself on academic grounds who may teach, what may be taught, how it shall be taught, and who may be admitted to study."[62] Although the South African authors of the statement intended it as a challenge to the segregation of higher education mandated by apartheid, U.S. courts would come to see the language asserted in Justice Frankfurter's concurring opinion (and embraced in subsequent Supreme Court majority decisions) as shielding colleges from judicial second-guessing of any admissions policy that was not challenged as violating federal civil rights laws. (That the Supreme Court generally gave concern for civil rights precedent over concern for academic freedom would be evidenced by its 1976 *Runyon* v. *McCrary* ruling, which held that private schools could not engage in racial discrimination in admissions; its 1978 *Regents of the University of California* v. *Bakke* ruling, which struck down the use of racial quotas by the medical school at the University of California at Davis; and its 2003 *Gratz* v. *Bollinger* ruling striking down a University of Michigan undergraduate admissions policy that mechanistically awarded a bonus to minority students in scoring student applications.) Ten years after the *Sweezy* decision, in *Keyishian* v. *Board of Regents*, also involving a McCarthy-era law meant to restrict subversive speech in college classrooms, the Supreme Court called academic freedom "a special concern of the First Amendment," thereby extending to it the same fundamental legal protections afforded freedoms enshrined in the Bill of Rights.[63]

Selective colleges used their power over their own admission policies to try to reassure alumni that their children would continue to receive special treatment, no matter how much competition there was for college seats. In 1958, Princeton issued a document declaring "the Princeton son does not have to compete against non-Princeton sons" in seeking admission. A pamphlet issued by Princeton that year, on the topic of frequently asked questions about the admission of legacy applicants, declared: "No matter how many other boys apply, the Princeton son is judged from an academic standpoint solely on the one question: Can he be expected to graduate? If so, he's admitted."[64] Legacies accounted for about 20 percent of all entering students, but about half of the bottom fourth of admitted applicants, during this time.

Eventually, however, pressures to admit applicants based on merit or diversity concerns would put pressure on legacy policies at even the most elite institutions.

In 1964, unable to ignore the relatively poor performance of legacy applicants, Princeton's admissions director, E. Alden Dunham, declared that the legacy policy was "becoming increasingly difficult to live with," and took steps to give applicants' legacy status less weight. He moved gradually, however, leaving intact policies calling for legacy applications to benefit from extra readings and reviews. The proportion of alumni sons annually admitted by Princeton dropped from 59 percent in 1964 to 55 percent in 1965. After plunging to 47 percent in 1966—probably due to miscalibration by the admissions office as much as anything else—it rebounded to 51 percent in 1967 and 56 percent in 1968, leaving Princeton admitting legacies at about two and a half times the rate of other applicants.[65] A 1973 poll of Princeton alumni offered a glimpse of just how much pressure Princeton was under to keep legacy preferences intact: 65 percent said an applicant's status as a son or daughter of an alumnus should be given "a great deal" or "a fair amount" of weight, compared to 63 percent who gave such responses in connection with athletes, and just 36 percent who did so in connection with applicants who might help Princeton become more racially balanced.[66] Princeton's alumni showed their appreciation by helping it take in new students; as of the mid-1960s, Princeton had about 140 school committees around the country, involving 1,400 alumni, which helped it both review students and interview applicants.[67] Given alumni support for legacy preferences, it is probably safe to assume that legacies fared well in school committees' assessments.

Harvard toyed with a radical change in its admissions policy—a model based strictly on academic merit—in 1971, but backed off the idea after a test run showed that high-scoring applicants from the Chicago, New York, and Philadelphia areas would supplant legacies, athletes, black students, and the graduates of New England's private schools.[68]

Yale treaded less lightly in reconsidering its admission policies, and ended up with an alumni revolt on its hands.

Yale's reconsideration of how it treated legacies began quietly in 1963—the same year a Phillips Andover senior named George W. Bush was applying. Faced with rapid growth in the number of applicants it was receiving, Yale administrators decided they no longer could treat all legacy applicants the same, and that they would take into account the prominence of a legacy's family and how much it had contributed to Yale.[69]

Historical accounts of what happened in the ensuing year differ greatly. In *The Big Test: The Secret History of American Meritocracy*, the journalist Nicholas Lemann contends that R. Inslee "Inky" Clark, who took over as Yale's admission dean in 1964, "turned Yale admissions upside down," replacing staff and otherwise taking aggressive steps to make the admissions process much more meritocratic.[70] Joseph A. Soares, a sociologist based at Wake Forest University, takes issue with Lemann's characterization of Clark as a crusader for meritocracy who sought to curtail legacy admissions, and blames a six-year dip in legacy enrollments that occurred at Yale beginning in 1967 on other admission trends such as increased competition for such applicants.[71] While crediting Clark with meritocratic impulses, Karabel likewise says special treatment for legacy applicants remained "built into the admissions process" during Clark's tenure.[72] Clouding the picture is disagreement among historical accounts—stemming largely from disagreements in institutional documents and among Yale administrators from that period—on the matter of just how much Yale's legacy enrollment dipped. Karabel says the share of freshman seats occupied by legacies fell from 18 percent in 1965 to a low of 10.6 percent in 1967; Soares maintains that it never went below 14 percent during this period.[73]

What is certain is that Clark's announced plans to have Yale recruit from more schools and diversify its student body left many alumni ill at ease and feeling convinced Clark had a hand in dropping legacy enrollments. Moreover, his efforts to assert more control over Yale's 260 alumni committees around the nation stirred tensions and exposed just how much disagreement there was between Yale's alumni office and the alumni it had been trusting to interview applicants. (Of those candidates the admissions office rated in the bottom 10 percent, 40 percent were rated as strong or exceptionally strong by alumni interviewers out in the field.)[74]

By 1966 Yale's alumni were in a state of rebellion, with the Yale Alumni Board establishing a special committee to look into the recent admission changes that fall. Alumni began withdrawing donations, and the admissions office witnessed a decline in the number of legacies applying and a rise in the share choosing to go elsewhere after being accepted. In a January 1967 letter to a fellow alumnus in the provost's office, a graduate of Yale's class of 1950 asked if Yale "can afford to ignore the natural desire of its alumni for their sons to be given the same opportunity they had" and why it was "digging around Berkeley or elsewhere for eccentrics with some special talent or a high SAT score."[75] That October, another member of the class of 1950, William F. Buckley, Jr., announced he would run for a seat on the Yale Corporation based partly on his opposition to its admission policies. In an interview published in the *New York Times*, Buckley complained that Yale was no longer "the kind of place where your family goes for generations," and had instead become a place where "the son of an alumnus, who goes to a private preparatory school, now has less chance of getting in than some boy from PS 109 somewhere." In an article he published in April 1968, Buckley betrayed his uneasiness with Yale's growing racial and socioeconomic diversity in even more stark terms, writing "a Mexican-American from El Paso High School with identical scores on the achievement tests, and identically ardent recommendations from their headmasters, had a better chance of being admitted to Yale than Jonathan Edwards the Sixteenth from St. Paul's School."[76] The number of people annually donating to Yale's Alumni Fund dropped by a thousand from fiscal 1967–68 to fiscal 1969–70. In just one year, from 1969 to 1970, the value of its endowment dropped from just over $520 million to less than $420 million, a decline of nearly 20 percent. Unhappiness with Yale's embrace of affirmative-action preferences and the poor performance of several of its athletic teams contributed to alumni anger. The decline in the value of Yale's endowment stemmed mainly from a souring of its investments. But there was no escaping the conclusion that Yale would have been financially better off if the legacy issue had not alienated much of its alumni base.[77]

Buckley's insurgent campaign for office failed, but his entry into the race served as a wake-up call that left Yale officials scrambling to tend to alumni complaints.[78] By 1970, Clark was out.

In selecting the entering freshman class of the fall of 1973, of those who applied, Yale admitted 24.2 percent of all applicants, 38.7 percent of the children of Yale College alumni, 37.9 percent of the children of Yale University alumni, and 76.2 percent of those alumni children rated as preferred by the development office. That October, with the stock market in bad shape, inflation running high, and Yale's endowment losing much of its value, Yale's president, Kingman Brewster, Jr., made plans to launch a $370-million fundraising campaign and announced that he had directed Clark's replacement "that every effort be made to attract, to admit, and to gain the acceptance of every qualified alumni son and daughter." In June 1974, an admissions office staff member, Steven E. Carlson, reported to Brewster that the office "is now bending over backwards to accept alumni children." That year, Yale admitted 49 percent of legacy applicants, the largest share in a decade.[79]

Today's college administrators may be overreacting in pointing to what happened at Yale in the late 1960s as reason not to attempt to tinker with legacy preferences. Few other institutions have alumni who are as prominent and powerful as Yale's and as hell-bent on seeing their own children follow their footsteps into the alma mater. Larger-than-life figures such as William F. Buckley are few and far between and unlikely to pop up to lead rebellions at just any selective college. In subsequent years, other universities, such as the University of Georgia and Texas A&M at College Station, managed to end legacy preferences without suffering financial losses comparable to Yale's. Nevertheless, Yale's experience clearly shows that alumni who feel the admission of their children is threatened can fight back fiercely and, in at least some cases, win.

The Market Provides New Legacy Preference Incentives (1973–2008)

While the gains in college access made by minority groups put pressure on colleges to reduce legacy enrollments, another key civil rights development in the postwar period—the transformation of many selective colleges from all-male to coed—would have the long-term effect of doubling the number of legacy applicants vying to get into such institutions.

As of 1960, women had accounted for just 22.5 percent of the enrollment in the Ivy League and less than 27 percent of the enrollment at prestigious colleges other than the all-female Seven Sisters.[80] But by that time they were emerging from high schools with academic profiles and SAT scores comparable to those of boys, and admission policies barring women were about the only thing keeping them out of many selective higher education institutions. As Karabel notes, "Female Yalies, Princetonians, and Harvardians were, after all, the daughters, sisters, and neighbors of the men who had historically attended the Big Three, and only their gender had prevented them from enrolling. . . . Once the doors were opened, they were deemed to possess no less 'merit' than their brothers."[81]

With the arrival of the 1970s, the economy, government financing of higher education, and the higher-education market all began changing in ways that gave colleges incentives to adopt or maintain legacy preferences, helping to counterbalance the societal forces that had been putting colleges under pressure to base admission decisions strictly on merit or on diversity concerns.

Faced with high inflation and meager growth in federal support, private colleges began raising tuition and fees rapidly. To keep such increases from triggering declines in enrollment, many tweaked their recruitment efforts to target affluent families that would be less sensitive to price. For many such families, the high tuitions of some prestigious colleges—and the exclusivity and cachet conveyed by it—actually was a selling point. Throughout higher education as a whole, professional marketing techniques caught on, with colleges using mass mailings to likely prospects around the nation to swell their application numbers.[82] Colleges came to rely even more heavily on distant alumni to aid their recruitment efforts—essentially enlisting alumni volunteers as their admission offices' auxiliary staffs—and such dependence created added pressure on such institutions to maintain legacy preferences, to reward those who gave their time.[83]

In a letter published in the *Princeton Alumni Weekly* in the fall of 1979, Dean of Admission James W. Wickenden, Jr., shed light on just how much legacy status was helping certain types of candidates. "In a process where very fine lines must be drawn, the advantage Princeton children receive can perhaps be best appreciated when one analyzes the admissions ratios of candidates with certain rankings," he wrote. He gave an explanation of how Princeton assigned candidates one score for "academic promise" and a second score for "character and personal promise," with a 1 being the highest possible score and a 5 being the lowest in each category. Among candidates with 3/2 rankings, he noted, Princeton accepted 100 percent of legacies, but just 21 percent of the broader applicant pool. Among applicants with a 3/3, Princeton accepted nearly 29 percent of legacies but less than 7 percent of the broader applicant pool.[84] An analysis of data about Harvard's applicants for the following year sheds light on how colleges had begun to draw distinctions between those legacies who were likely to contribute to their bottom lines and those who were not. Harvard admitted 42 percent of those legacies who were willing to pay their full fare, and just 35 percent of those legacies who had applied for financial aid.[85]

A 1979 survey of the nation's colleges found 23 percent of public four-year colleges and 32 percent of private four-year colleges reporting exceptions to their formal academic requirements for the children of alumni. Those numbers would decline over the next five years—reflecting a continuation of trends from the previous decades—but level off in the mid-1980s and then begin inching back up.[86]

One development that probably renewed colleges' interest in legacy policies was the emergence in the late 1980s of the *U.S. News & World Report* college rankings and, soon after, of other similar guides. While *U.S. News & World Report* did not take legacy preferences into account in assigning scores to colleges, many of the measures it developed for judging institutions had the indirect effect of encouraging them to favor legacy applicants. For example, the magazine based 10 percent of any given college's score on its financial resources and 5 percent on the share of its alumni who gave annually, putting pressure on colleges to inspire alumni generosity. Until 2003, it based 1.5 percent of any college's score on "yield," or the proportion of all applicants they admitted who actually showed up for class in the fall, giving such institutions added incentive to admit legacies whose family ties make them significantly more likely than others in the applicant pool to actually enroll.[87] Ironically, even the magazine's criteria that judged colleges based on selectivity—and thus, presumably, the academic merit of their admitted students—had the effect of boosting the case for colleges to continue legacy preferences. That is because one of the chief means colleges use to compete for talented students is offering various discounts on their tuition, and to be able to afford such discounts, colleges need to keep the alumni contributions coming in. The need to prop up the average SAT scores of their entering classes—and thus maintain their reputation for selectivity—prompted some colleges to limit how much preference they gave legacies, minority students, athletes, and other preferred categories of students. But many found they could have both high average SAT scores and extensively use preferences essentially by maintaining a two-tiered system in which students who did not fall into some preferred category generally were required to have exceptionally high scores, to counteract the downward drag on the average exerted by the connected.[88]

Public colleges came under additional pressure to favor legacy applicants as a result of the long-term decline in their state tax-dollar support that began after the 1960s, with each recession prompting a new round of meager state appropriations to colleges based on the assumption they could raise tuition to make up for inadequate state revenue. For the sake of building up the amount of private money they had at their disposal, flagship universities launched huge fundraising campaigns, in many cases eventually building up endowments that would surpass those of all but the wealthiest private universities in terms of their size.[89] "In light of very deep budget cuts from the state, our private support particularly from alumni is crucial to maintaining the quality of the institution," the University of Virginia's admissions dean, John Blackburn, would later explain. "The legacy preference helps ensure that support by recognizing their financial contributions and their service on university committees and task forces."[90]

Some newer public institutions wasted little time in establishing legacy preferences as a way to try to build their mystique and finance their expansions. A spokesman for the University of Central Florida (UCF), established in 1968, explained: "As a young university, it is important for UCF to build traditions, and that is one way to do so."[91] While public colleges were careful to downplay how much weight they gave legacy status, to avoid triggering a rebellion among the non-alumni lawmakers and taxpayers who also provide them support, the thumb they put on the scale for legacies was often a fairly heavy one. The formula for scoring undergraduate applications that the University of Michigan adopted in the late 1980s, for example, automatically gave legacy applicants 4 extra points on a 150-point scale and left the provost the discretion to arbitrarily lavish 20 extra points on any applicant, with the provost's bonuses often going to the children of favored alumni.[92] An analysis of 1999 admission data from the University of Virginia found that legacies were about 4.3 times as likely as applicants with comparable grades and admissions test scores to be accepted there.[93]

In a 1992 survey of the nation's colleges, 16 percent of four-year public institutions reported making exceptions from their formal academic requirements for the children of alumni, as compared to 14 percent that reported making such exceptions in a survey conducted in 1985. The share of four-year private colleges reported making such exceptions stood at 21 percent, compared to 20 percent in 1985. Caution should be exercised in deducing trends based on the survey results, because the colleges responding varied from one survey to the next. But another finding of the 1992 survey provided added evidence that colleges had recently become more interested in taking in legacies: both private and public colleges generally reported that they were more likely to target the children of alumni in their recruiting efforts than they had been five years earlier. Among the institutions responding to the 1992 survey, 34 percent of two-year privates, 49 percent of four-year privates, and 33 percent of four-year publics reported engaging in special recruitment activities targeting legacies. The willingness of top colleges to lower the bar for certain desired applicants was suggested by the survey's findings that the most selective four-year institutions—those accepting no more than 50 percent of applicants—were less likely to report having minimum standards for admission than those colleges that accepted 50 to 80 percent of those who applied.[94]

A separate analysis of data from the 1991–92 academic year found that, among the top seventy-five universities in the *U.S. News & World Report* rankings, just one, the California Institute of Technology, had no legacy preferences at all. The list of those that preferred legacy applicants included Cornell, Georgetown, Lehigh University, New York University, the University of Illinois at Urbana-Champaign, the University of Wisconsin at Madison, Rensselaer Polytechnic Institute, Ohio State, and the Colorado School of Mines. Legacy preferences also were used widely by the one hundred top-ranked liberal arts colleges, including Beloit, Bowdoin, Colorado, Dickinson, Grinnell, Middlebury, Pomona, Rhodes, and Vassar. The only liberal arts college in the top one hundred that explicitly said it did not have legacy preferences was Berea. Sixty others reported favoring legacies, and thirty-nine others did not provide information on the subject.[95]

In an interview given in the early 1990s to Bill Paul, the author of the college admissions guide *Getting In*, Princeton spokesman Robert Durkee described how institutions such as his had come to see legacy preferences as a necessity:

> Just look at the numbers. Look at the fact that eighty percent of college students in this country are not going to private colleges and universities. And some growing percentage of people in the Congress did not go to private colleges and universities. You've got to believe that the amount of public support for private colleges and universities is not going to increase and probably will decrease over a period of time. Well, one of the things that means is that the pressure on these institutions to cultivate support from private individuals is going to increase. One way you do that is to retain family ties to the institution. And one way you do that is to continue to enroll some significant fraction of alumni children.[96]

Princeton's dean of admissions, Fred Hargadon, acknowledged to Paul that admitting a high percentage of legacy applicants limited Princeton's freedom to make other admission choices it found compelling, such as accepting applicants from high schools that almost never sent their graduates Princeton's way. He also suggested that he was aware of the conflict between the public-interest-focused missions that earned colleges their tax-exempt status and the willingness of such institutions to show favoritism to legacies to reward those who helped their bottom lines. Hargadon recounted advising a trustee being hounded by the parents of rejected legacy applicants to tell them that showing too much preference for alumni could jeopardize Princeton's tax-exempt status, because the federal government might frown on the university using such a status to enrich itself.[97]

In recent decades, the use of legacy preferences has expanded well beyond the undergraduate level, also affecting admissions to graduate and professional schools. In 2002, Saul Levmore, dean of the University of Chicago Law School, estimated based on discussions with law school administrators elsewhere that up to 5 percent of law schools' entering classes got in partly through legacy status or some other personal connection. Recalling his own experience fielding communications from people lobbying him on behalf of applicants, he recalled "a surprising number in which the writer expects the letter or call to matter a great deal, even when the writer has no special knowledge of the applicant."[98]

Legacies also have become a fixture of many colleges that are not very selective—and, in some cases, even have trouble filling up their classes—as such small private institutions have come to see appealing to the children of alumni as crucial to their efforts to compete for students. Among them, Stephens College, a women's college in Columbia, Missouri, says its concerted efforts to reach out to alumni to send it their daughters, which included offering admitted legacy students $500 scholarships, played a significant role in its 50 percent increase in enrollment and financial rebound from 2003 to 2006. Legacies accounted for 107 of the 412 students who entered the University of the South (Sewanee) in 2006, and Calvin College, a religious institution in Grand Rapids, reported at that time that it was raising its graduation rate by admitting legacies, who are more likely than other students to stay in school and earn their degrees within six years.[99]

The advantages that colleges have come to offer legacies extend well beyond simple admission preferences. Many, for example, have developed mechanisms for coaching legacies through the admissions process and alerting them to the edge they can gain by applying early—in the fall as opposed to the winter—and committing to enroll if accepted. The University of Pennsylvania operates an alumni council that serves as a resource to alumni whose children or grandchildren are applying, provides legacies with special advising sessions, and has established a student-led buddy program through which current legacy students correspond with legacy applicants via e-mail. The edge offered legacies by such insider advice is suggested by Penn's statistics for the class that entered in the fall of 2008: it admitted 41.7 percent of legacies who applied during the "early decision" admission cycle and 33.9 percent of legacies who applied during the regular admission cycle, compared to 29.3 percent of all students who applied "early decision" and 16.4 percent of all who applied during the regular cycle.[100] Among other institutions, Duke University's alumni association hosts informational lunches and other events exclusively for the children of alumni.[101] Some public universities, including Oklahoma State and the University of South Dakota, offer scholarships or tuition discounts to the children of out-of-state alumni, in many cases enabling them to attend at roughly the in-state rate.

As of 2008, alumni accounted for 27.5 percent of all giving to higher education. Only foundations, which provided 28.8 percent, accounted for a bigger share of voluntary support to colleges.[102] Colleges clinging to legacy preferences argue that abandoning them would lead to a marked decline in alumni giving, even though the empirical evidence on this point is somewhat mixed. (See Chapter 5.) Selective higher education institutions and the associations that represent them have fiercely fought efforts to curtail admission preferences based on family connections, and appear unlikely to abandon them voluntarily any time soon.

Legal and Political Challenges (1975–2009)

The first significant challenge to the legality of legacy preferences was a lawsuit brought against the University of North Carolina system in federal court in November 1975. The plaintiff was Jane Cheryl Rosenstock, a nineteen-year-old resident of Ellenville, New York, who had been denied a seat in that fall's entering class at the University of North Carolina (UNC) at Chapel Hill. Rosenstock's lawsuit alleged that the university had violated several of her constitutional rights, including her rights to equal protection and due process, by holding her to more stringent standards than an array of different categories of applicants, including legacies from other states, in-state students, foreign students, athletes, and students from impoverished or minority backgrounds.

It may not have helped Rosenstock's cause that she had been a less-than-compelling candidate for admission. Her combined SAT score was about 850 on a 1600-point scale, well below what UNC-Chapel Hill generally expected of out-of-state applicants. Her high school grades were solid, but also lower than those of most other out-of-state applicants, and she had not taken a high school math course that the university required of its applicants. In December 1976, Judge Hiram H. Ward of the U.S. District Court in Durham came down solidly against her, issuing a summary judgment dismissing her lawsuit against the university system's board and several top Chapel Hill administrators.

Harkening back to the Supreme Court's previous decisions holding that colleges, as institutions, have certain limited freedoms rooted in the First Amendment, Ward said, "The questions raised here are, in large part, attacks on administrative decision-making, an area where the federal courts have not and should not heavily tread." Specifically addressing the lawsuit's challenge to the preferential treatment of those in the out-of-state applicant pool who were legacies, Ward said such a policy was neither constitutionally suspect nor a violation of Rosenstock's fundamental interests, and therefore the test for judging its legality was whether it had a rational basis. (Oddly, Rosenstock's lawyers did not allege that preference based on heredity and family lineage was a constitutionally "suspect" classification that should trigger strict judicial scrutiny.) Under the rational basis test, Ward ruled, legacy preferences were constitutional because the university had shown in its affidavits "that the alumni provide monetary support for the University and that out-of-state alumni contribute close to one-half of the total given." The judge did not cite any evidence suggesting that legacy preferences were a direct cause of any such alumni contributions.[103]

One commentator would later observe that Ward's reasoning could be interpreted as meaning "nothing could stop a college from admitting every legacy who applies, despite his or her qualification, in order to maximize alumni contributions." The ruling went unchallenged, however, and the question of whether legacy preferences are legal for the most part was ignored by the courts after that point.[104] Three years later, in a dissenting opinion in the U.S. Supreme Court's *Bakke* decision striking down the use of racial quotas by the medical school at the University of California at Davis, Justice Harry A. Blackmun wrote that he found it "somewhat ironic to have us so deeply disturbed over a program where race is an element of consciousness" given the preferences colleges give to legacies, athletes, and applicants connected to donors and to "celebrities, the famous, and the powerful."[105] But his opinion did not portend judicial scrutiny of those other preferences so much as a long-term intertwining of the debate over legacy preferences with the debate over college admission preferences based on race, ethnicity, or gender.

The next significant examination of the legality of legacy preferences would come in the late 1980s, and it would be mounted by the executive branch in response to complaints that elite colleges were biased against Asian Americans.

Suspicions that elite colleges were discriminating against Asian Americans had been in the air at least since 1983, when the East Coast

Asian Student Union—an intercollegiate advocacy organization—published an analysis of data from twenty-five universities showing that their Asian-American enrollments had stayed flat in a period of rapid growth in the Asian-American population, and that Asian-American applicants were being rejected in favor of other students with lesser credentials. Over the next few years, several prominent institutions—including Harvard, Princeton, Brown, Stanford, and the University of California at Berkeley—would be accused of anti-Asian bias. The Education Department's Office for Civil Rights (OCR) waded into the debate in 1988, by launching an investigation of admissions at Harvard and the University of California at Los Angeles. The impact of legacy preferences on Asian-American applicants was part of its review, as Harvard officials had responded to complaints of discrimination by blaming its rejection of a disproportionate share of Asian-American applicants partly on their relative scarcity in the pool of applicants who benefited from its consideration of legacy status. In seeking to justify its use of legacy preferences to the federal investigators, Harvard said alumni give it their time and money, including "the bulk of scholarship funds" that help make college affordable for other students. It said, "If their children are rejected by Harvard, their affection may decline; if their children are admitted, their involvement with the College is renewed." Harvard asserted such claims as if they were self-evident, without providing any empirical evidence to back them.[106]

The OCR issued the findings of its investigation of Harvard and UCLA in October 1990. It said it had determined that Harvard had admitted legacies at twice the rate of other applicants, that in several cases legacy status "was the critical or decisive favor" in its decision to let a student in, and that legacy preferences helped explain why it had admitted 17.4 percent of white applicants and just 13.2 percent of Asian-American applicants over the past ten years. Moreover, it found, legacies on average were rated lower than admits who were neither legacies nor athletes in every important area—except athletic ability—in which applicants were judged. But OCR nonetheless cleared both institutions. Its report cited the *Rosenstock* decision as "one court's willingness to recognize the legitimacy of a link" between a college's economic interests and its use of legacy preferences. Although the OCR's investigators had not examined the impact of legacy preferences on minority groups other than Asian Americans, the office's report concluded that legacy preferences were not a pretense for discrimination. The office accepted Harvard's assertion that there were no alternatives to legacy preferences that could accomplish the same legitimate institutional goals effectively. Seconding the report's conclusion, Secretary of Education Lauro F. Cavazos declared that he did not see any conflict between legacy preferences and our nation's "principles of justice and equity."[107]

Soon after the report was released, the U.S. Department of Education's assistant secretary for civil rights, Michael Williams, provoked outrage among colleges and civil rights groups by expressing his view that another common college policy—the offering of scholarships specifically for minority students—generally violated the Civil Rights Act of 1964. As the debate over such scholarships raged, Senator Bob Dole of Kansas, the Republican leader in the Senate, urged the Education Department to have OCR look into whether legacy preferences violated the Civil Rights Act by broadly discriminating against minority students. "At a time when the Republican Party is promoting the ideal of a 'merit society,' we ought to be applying this principle across-the-board, and not selectively," Dole said in a letter to President George H.W. Bush's nominee as education secretary, Lamar Alexander. Legacy preferences, he said, have "the effect of benefiting those at the upper end of the income scale to the detriment of the economically less advantaged." Nothing came of his request.[108]

Dole's letter presaged an extended period in which legacy preferences would be invoked often in the debate over affirmative action at colleges, and would come under serious attack—in essence becoming collateral damage—in some situations where challenges to affirmative action prevailed. Some prominent critics of affirmative action—including Ward Connerly, the organizer of several successful campaigns for state ballot measures to ban affirmative-action preferences—would criticize legacy preferences, especially at public colleges, as inconsistent with their belief that colleges' admission decisions should be based on merit. And many minority lawmakers and civil rights activists who had been willing to tolerate legacy preferences so long as colleges also used affirmative action would become staunchly opposed to legacy preferences where affirmative action was ended.[109]

When the University of California's Board of Regents voted to ban the use of affirmative action preferences throughout that system in 1995, they included in their resolutions provisions ending a policy that had allowed each campus to waive its usual admission requirements for up to 6 percent of its students. A year later, in the wake of the state's 1996 adoption of a constitutional amendment prohibiting most uses of affirmative action preferences by public colleges and other state agencies, the regents specifically prohibited the system's campuses from giving preferences to legacies. Campus chancellors continued for a few years to quietly hold the children of alumni living out of state to the same standards as in-state applicants, but the regents banned that practice in 2000.[110]

Texas lawmakers considered, but did not pass, legislation prohibiting public colleges from giving admission preferences to legacies or applicants connected to major donors in response to a 1996 federal appeals court striking down race-conscious admission policies there. After the University of Georgia's use of affirmative action preferences was struck down by a federal appeals court in 2001, its president, Michael F. Adams, eliminated legacy preferences on his own, at the advice of a faculty committee assigned to revise admission policies to comply with the court ruling. "Certainly the notion of fairness was very much at issue," Delmer D. Dunn, who was the university's vice president for instruction at the time, recalled in a later interview. "If you could not provide weight for one group, on what basis could you justify giving it to another group?" Contrary to what many there feared, the university's abandonment of legacy preferences did not lead to a drop in alumni giving, Dunn said.[111]

As it became clear that the Supreme Court was going to have to weigh in on affirmative action in college admissions, there was talk among lawyers from minority advocacy groups of responding to any unfavorable court ruling by mounting discrimination lawsuits challenging legacy preferences and other admission policies that disproportionately benefit white students. "We will have to turn up the scrutiny," said Ted Shaw, the NAACP Legal Defense and Educational Fund's top lawyer at the time. "We are not going to sit around and allow double standards to apply in terms of who gets access to higher education." Legal briefs filed on behalf of minority students who intervened as defendants in two lawsuits challenging the University of Michigan's use of affirmative action argued that race-conscious admission policies were necessary to offset legacy preferences and other admission criteria that favored white applicants.[112]

Some key Democrats on Capitol Hill honed in on legacy preferences as well. Driving the effort was Michael Dannenberg, a lawyer working in the office of Senator Ted Kennedy, then chairman of the Senate education committee. Dannenberg's interest in having Democrats take up the cause stemmed from a combination of ideology and political calculation. He regarded legacy preferences as profoundly unfair and harmful to both the quality and the diversity of colleges' student bodies. At the same time, he also saw attacking legacy preferences as a way to justify support for race-conscious admissions (as a counterbalance) and as a way to appeal to middle- and working-class voters. Looking ahead to the 2004 elections, he also believed a public campaign against legacy preferences would help the Democrats score points against George W. Bush, who had been a mediocre student and used family connections to get into Yale. He persuaded one top Democratic contender for the presidency, Democratic U.S. senator John Edwards of North Carolina, to take up the issue. Edwards railed against legacy preferences as "a birthright out of eighteenth-century British aristocracy, not twenty-first century American democracy" in a November 2002 speech, and continued to oppose legacies throughout the remainder of his campaign. Meanwhile, Dannenberg and other members of Kennedy's staff contemplated trying to insert some sort of provision barring or discouraging legacy preferences in a key federal law appropriating funds to colleges and student aid programs.[113]

College officials, annoyed that legacies had even become an issue, put pressure on Kennedy's staff to abandon their antilegacy efforts. They argued that legacy preferences help build a sense of tradition on their campuses and are vital to their fundraising efforts. In an essay published by the *Chronicle of Higher Education*, two public relations officials at Rice University argued that legacy preferences are defensible because, in college admissions, "objective merit and fairness are attractive concepts with no basis in reality."[114] Public sentiment, however, was on the side of legacy opponents and would remain so in the ensuing years, with one national poll, conducted by the *Chronicle of Higher Education* in early 2004, finding that about three-fourths of Americans believed colleges should do away with legacy admissions.[115]

The Supreme Court upheld the use of race-conscious admission policies in its June 2003 *Grutter* v. *Bollinger* decision, involving the University of Michigan's law school. With its own members having deep ties to their elite alma maters, and several being either former legacy students or the parents of legacies, the Court majority showed no eagerness to ask the broader question of whether colleges were using race-conscious admission policies to solve a problem of their own making, one stemming from their legacy preferences and other admission practices that tend to give an edge to white students from economically privileged backgrounds.[116] The only significant criticism of legacy preferences offered by any member of the Court came in a stinging dissent written by Justice Clarence Thomas, the only member of the Court to grow up poor. He suggested that affirmative action preferences were being defended partly to keep alive an admissions process that had been "poisoned" by legacy preferences and other exceptions to merit. "Were this Court to have the courage to forbid the use of racial discrimination in admissions, legacy preferences (and similar practices) might quickly become less popular—a possibility not lost, I am certain, on the elites (both individual and institutional) supporting the Law School in this case," he wrote. Nevertheless, Thomas said he would not "twist the Constitution to invalidate legacy preferences or otherwise impose my vision of higher education admissions on the nation." He did not cite any case law supporting his conclusion that legacy preferences were in fact constitutional.[117]

The *Grutter* decision had the effect of reversing decisions striking down affirmative-action preferences issued by the U.S. Court of Appeals for the Eleventh Circuit, which covers Alabama, Georgia, and Florida, and the U.S. Court of Appeals for the Fifth Circuit, which covers Louisiana, Mississippi, and Texas. But the University of Georgia, which had been the focus of the Eleventh Circuit's decision, chose to continue operating without either legacy or affirmative action preferences. And when Texas A&M at College Station, which had continued to use legacy preferences after the Fifth Circuit's ruling, chose in December 2003 to continue using race-blind admission policies on the stated grounds that all applicants should be evaluated based on academic merit, its legacy preferences came under harsh attack from lawmakers and minority activists.

Fueling the criticism of Texas A&M's legacy policy, which awarded 4 points on a 100-point scale to the children, grandchildren, or siblings of is graduates, was a recognition that it had the effect of perpetuating the discrimination minority applicants to that institution had faced in the past. In 2003, for example, Texas A&M enrolled 312 white students—and just 27 Hispanic and 6 black students—who would not have been admitted if not for their family ties, according to a *Houston Chronicle* analysis of the university's data.[118] An analysis of University of Virginia data issued that year pinned down just how much legacy preferences worked to the detriment of minorities, concluding that, as a result of the lingering effects of Jim Crow, it would be about 2020 before the black share of its pool of legacy applicants matched black students' share of its overall student body.[119] The Democratic chairman of the Texas Legislative Black Caucus, State Representative Garnet F. Coleman, protested that university officials were being hypocrites in calling for an objective admissions process while "awarding admissions points to a student just because of bloodline." Among others who opposed the legacy policy were representatives of the League of United Latin American Citizens, the Mexican American Legal Defense and Educational Fund, the Texas Civil Rights Project, and the Urban League. In January 2004, the university's president, Robert M. Gates, heeded such criticism and ended legacy preferences there, calling the decision "difficult" but "one that had to be made to maintain consistency in an admissions policy based on individual merit and the whole person."[120]

Leading congressional Democrats kept pressing on the legacy issue through the summer of 2004, when Senator Kennedy proposed an amendment to the Higher Education Act calling for colleges to report annually what shares of their entering classes were legacies or had benefited from early decision programs. College officials and the lobbyists for several of their major associations remained staunchly opposed to the measure. The president of the American Council on Education, higher education's umbrella organization, protested in a letter to Kennedy that the measure would likely lead to more federal intrusion into colleges' affairs and would set "a very desirable precedent" for opponents of affirmative action in college admissions, who presumably could push for a similar measure requiring colleges to report how many admitted students had benefited from similar consideration of their ethnicity or race. One insight into just how much college leaders remained wedded to legacies was offered by William Bowen, the former president of Princeton University and a leading researcher on admission policies, in an April 2004 speech delivered at the University of Virginia. Bemoaning how under-represented low-income students are at selective colleges, Bowen suggested the solution was giving such students the same degree of preference as legacies. Abolishing legacy preferences to promote socioeconomic diversity did not seem to register as an option for him.[121]

Kennedy eventually backed off his anti-legacy amendment for the sake of keeping higher education interests on his side as he pushed other legislative priorities. George W. Bush, for his part, thwarted Democratic efforts to make legacy admissions an issue in the 2004 presidential election by declaring that he, too, opposed such preferences. The debate over legacies soon died down.[122]

During Washington State's 2009 legislative session, three Democratic state senators—Rodney Tom, Fred Jarrett, and Adam Kline—introduced a resolution urging President Barack Obama, Congress, and the secretary of education to withhold federal money from colleges and universities that grant admission preferences to legacies. The measure declared that legacy preferences "are benefits given to alumni children based not on merit, but on the identity, status, or accomplishments of their parents"; that the granting of inherited preferences for publicly available goods is "appropriate only in status-based feudal societies"; and that "legacy preferences in college admission offend the American egalitarian tradition and should be neither tolerated nor enabled." The measure was still in committee when the legislature adjourned its session, but the lawmakers involved planned to bring it up again when the legislature reconvened the following year.[123]

It is difficult, at this point, to say how such attempts to curtail legacy preferences in selective higher education will fare down the road. Selective colleges generally have succeeded in keeping legacy preferences in place so far, and financial pressures stemming from economic downturns and declines in government support are likely to increase their desire to use any policy they (rightly or wrongly) believe improves their bottom line. But the legal status of a separate group of admission preferences—those based on race or ethnicity—remains precarious, and should the courts put pressure on colleges to eliminate affirmative-action preferences, then other exceptions to admission based on merit are likely to face renewed opposition. It also is entirely possible that the new legal arguments against legacy preferences offered by contributors to this volume could sway the courts. The admission policies of select colleges have undergone such profound change over the past one hundred years that there is no reason to believe those policies in place today will be used tomorrow.

4

An Analytic Survey of Legacy Preference

Daniel Golden

Virtually unknown in the rest of the world, legacy preference is almost universal among America's premier universities and liberal arts colleges, casting doubt on their commitment to meritocracy and equal opportunity. These institutions cling fiercely to the preference for alumni children, largely for the monetary windfall they believe it bestows, even though it conflicts with their professed embrace of low-income and minority students. Ignoring the apparent contradiction, they seek economic diversity in their student bodies—through such means as increasing financial aid and eliminating requirements for applicants to take standardized tests on which scores correlate with wealth—while giving admissions preference to the largely white, affluent, and privileged group of alumni children.

Although polls show that the American people strongly oppose legacy preference, its beneficiaries hold key positions in Congress and the judiciary, protecting it from political and legal challenge. Yet legacy preference faces increasing pressure. As they seek greater selectivity in admissions, many American colleges are forced to make harder choices among applicants, including legacies. Some distinguish more than they used to between offspring of major alumni donors, who continue to receive a massive admissions boost, and legacies from less wealthy or philanthropic families, who may get squeezed out. Other schools, reacting to alumni complaints about the impact of rising standards on their children, have designed separate programs or staff positions to guide legacies through the admissions process.

A growing body of evidence, meanwhile, undercuts the financial justification for legacy preference. This research suggests that, even though one reason that alumni contribute money is to enhance their children's chances for admission, universities can raise ample sums without compromising the integrity of their admissions process through lowering standards for alumni children. A few private institutions, such as the California Institute of Technology, have accumulated healthy endowments without giving an edge to legacies. Several public universities that discarded legacy preference in recent years have seen no adverse impact on fundraising—and in fact have enjoyed higher levels of contributions. Successful fundraising tactics include appealing to alumni pride in the college's aspirations for higher academic status and in the mission of fostering upward mobility for talented low-income students. Institutional courage also is required; one state university that had eliminated legacy preference hurriedly recanted for fear of jeopardizing a multibillion-dollar fundraising campaign.

Simply discarding legacy preference, however, may not ensure that colleges evaluate candidates without regard to parental wealth and philanthropy. Many colleges also give what is known as "development preference" to applicants recommended by the development, or fundraising, office—children of major donors, trustees, politicians, celebrities, and others. It is possible that some universities have been able to drop legacy preference without hurting fundraising because they still are lowering standards for children of key alumni under the development mantle. As endowment values tumble in the current recession, colleges have an increasing incentive to bend admission standards for alumni donors. Thus, more sweeping reforms than the ostensible elimination of legacy preference may be needed to purge advantages for affluent alumni children from college admissions.

The Scope of Legacy Preference

Schools differ in how broadly they extend legacy preference. At Harvard, for instance, only children of undergraduate alumni formally receive preference in freshman admissions. At Stanford and Vanderbilt, children of alumni of undergraduate or graduate programs enjoy an edge. Many schools also give a boost, formal or informal, to siblings, grandchildren, nephews, and nieces.

However they are defined, legacies enjoy an edge at nearly all selective private universities and liberal arts colleges and most flagship public universities. More than 90 percent of schools generally ranked in the top tier say that they consider legacy status in admission decisions, with several calling it "important" and a few "very important."[1] At public universities, legacy preference sometimes has taken the form of evaluating children of out-of-state alumni according to the lower admission standards for in-state applicants.

Most colleges flag legacy applicants early in the admissions process. College officials often learn in advance, through alumni or fundraising channels, that the son or daughter of a notable or generous graduate plans to apply. Otherwise, they identify legacy candidates through the application form; the "Common Application" used by many U.S. schools asks candidates where their parents attended college and graduate school and the highest degree they attained.

Ivy League and other top schools typically admit legacies at two to five times their overall rate. As overall admission rates have declined, the power of legacy preference at some elite institutions has increased substantially. For instance, Princeton admitted 41.7 percent of legacy applicants in 2009—more than 4.5 times the 9.2 percent rate of non-legacies.[2] That is a far greater disparity than in 1992, when legacy applicants were accepted at 2.8 times the rate of other candidates.[3]

Elsewhere among the Ivies, Brown University admitted 33.5 percent of alumni children in 2006, compared to a 13.8 percent overall rate. The year before, Brown accepted 36 percent of legacies, compared to 15.1 percent of all applicants. The University of Pennsylvania admitted 33.9 percent of legacy applicants in 2008, about double its overall admission rate of 16.4 percent. The University of Pennsylvania alumni office, according to its website, "is very sensitive to the fact that nearly two-thirds of legacy applicants are not admitted to Penn each year." Dartmouth accepted 29.7 percent of alumni-child applicants in 2008, compared to an overall rate of 13.5 percent. Alumni children make up 10–11 percent of Dartmouth's student body.[4]

In 2003, Harvard admitted 40 percent of legacy applicants, compared to an overall 11 percent acceptance rate.[5] (The university declined to provide more recent legacy admission data.) In 1990, an investigation of Harvard admissions by the U.S. Office for Civil Rights underscored the importance of legacy status. Assessing applications from alumni children, Harvard reviewers had written such comments as: "Dad's connections signify lineage of more than usual weight," "Two legacy legs to stand on," "Without lineage, there would be little case. With it, we will keep looking," and "Not a great profile, but just strong enough numbers and grades to get the tip from lineage."[6]

It seems likely that, if these same legacy applicants to the Ivy League were to be evaluated without any preference, their acceptance rate—instead of being two to four times higher than the overall rate—would be the same or lower, for two reasons. First, preferences for other groups, such as recruited athletes and underrepresented minorities, inflate the overall rate. Second, alumni children as a group may have weaker credentials than applicants who do not receive any preference. Knowing that they qualify for preference, some alumni children with marginal records may take a fling at applying to a top school that otherwise would be out of their range.

Although significant, the boost given to alumni children in admissions is not quite as sizable as the boosts for racial minorities and athletes. A 2004 study of 124,000 applicants to elite colleges and universities found that legacy status was worth 160 points on the then-1600 point SAT scale, compared to 230 points for African Americans, 200 points for recruited athletes, and 185 for Hispanics. Athletes and legacies were twice as likely to be accepted as applicants who did not receive those preferences.[7] A 2005 analysis of 180,000 student records obtained from nineteen selective colleges and universities found that, within a given range of SAT scores, being a legacy raised one's chances for admission by 19.7 percentage points.[8]

Alumni children often magnify their edge by applying under early-decision programs. Colleges typically lower standards somewhat for early applicants in return for a commitment to enroll if admitted. Early decision programs suit alumni children who have long since made up their minds to go to the same college as their parents. The chief disadvantage of the commitment to enroll—that accepted students cannot shop around at other colleges for a better financial aid offer—does not hurt most legacies, since they are too affluent to qualify for need-based aid. The University of Pennsylvania promises "maximum consideration" to legacies who commit themselves to attend by applying under its early-decision plan.[9] One southern university admits 75 percent of its early-decision applicants—mostly legacies or siblings of current students—but only 21 percent of applicants during the regular cycle.[10]

At many universities, legacy applicants enjoy not just a higher likelihood of admission but also special treatment throughout the process, from alumni-only recruiting events to help, in the event of rejection, with placement at another college. Both Brown and the University of Pennsylvania have programs to advise legacy applicants, while the University of Miami offers legacy admission counseling. Legacies with indifferent academic records are often encouraged to enroll at a lesser school for one or two years to prove themselves and then reapply as transfer students. Since rankings by *U.S. News & World Report* and other media take into account only the SAT scores and high school grades of entering freshmen, a college can accept low-achieving legacies as transfer students without hurting its standing in the public eye.

Harvard caters to children of well-connected alumni and big donors with what is known as the Z-list. Although Z-listers are often assured in advance that they will get in, they officially are waitlisted until they graduate from high school. Then they are admitted, not for the following September but the year after. How they spend the intervening year is largely immaterial; they are not required to take courses or improve their academic records.

The special treatment often continues after enrollment. For instance, legacies often have a leg up in making varsity rosters. The last player on the bench on men's college basketball teams tends to be the son of a prominent alumnus.[11]

Alumni children generally make up 10 percent to 25 percent of the student body at elite universities. At Stanford, 22 percent of freshmen who enrolled in 2008 were legacies; at Cornell, it was 14 percent; at Princeton, 13.7 percent; at Yale, 13.3 percent. At Vanderbilt, 19.4 percent of entering freshmen in 2008 were alumni children, but the admission rate for legacies—29.8 percent—was only slightly higher than the 25.3 percent rate for all applicants. "If somebody is a legacy or has a current sibling here, that would bode in a positive favor for them, but it doesn't mean you get in," says Vanderbilt admissions dean Douglas Christiansen. "Our children of our alumni are highly prepared students. In a large, whole host of cases, they would have been admitted anyway."[12] At many elite universities, the number of alumni children in the freshman class hardly varies year after year, implying an informal quota system.

Legacy enrollment is often highest at faith-based schools. Alumni children make up almost 40 percent of Calvin College in Grand Rapids, Michigan, run by the Christian Reformed Church.[13] Similarly, at the University of Notre Dame in South Bend, Indiana, nearly one-fourth of students are alumni children. Notre Dame accepts half of its legacy applicants, double its overall admission rate.[14] These schools defend their use of legacy preference on the grounds that it helps to perpetuate their religious traditions. Yet this policy in effect discriminates against members of the sponsoring religion whose parents did not attend the school. For instance, in 2004 Notre Dame rejected one applicant who was a parochial-school valedictorian and devout Catholic, while admitting a high school classmate with a lesser record, whose father was a Notre Dame alumnus and donor.[15] A fairer and more direct approach might be simply to set aside a certain percentage of admission slots for a particular religious group. Legacy enrollment is relatively low at many second- and third-tier private colleges, despite the admissions preference, because successful alumni parents often aspire for their children to attend schools ranked higher than their own alma mater.

Once enrolled in college, alumni children tend to be average academically. They typically under-perform classmates from similar demographic backgrounds who did not receive preference, and they may be at higher risk of dropping out. A study of 3,900 students who entered 28 selective colleges in 1999 concluded that "the greater the gap between a legacy student's SAT and the institutional average SAT, the lower the grades he or she earned." Indeed, "in schools with a stronger commitment to legacy admissions, the children of alumni were more likely to drop out."[16]

Demographically, a large legacy population on campus limits racial and economic diversity. Duke University's 1,700 freshmen in 2007 included a school-record 230 alumni children, or 16 percent of the class.[17] According to a 2008 study, Duke's legacies are more likely to be white, Protestant, U.S. citizens, and private school graduates than the overall student body. They also are considerably richer, with a family income of $250,000 a year.[18] Of 567 alumni children attending Princeton in 2000–01, ten were Hispanic and four were black.[19] In general, "preferences for athletes and legacies are likely to boost the proportion of whites among admitted students."[20] Similarly, a 2005 study reported that half of legacy applicants to selective colleges boasted family incomes in the top quartile of American society, as against 29 percent of non-legacy applicants. It concluded that "legacy preferences serve to reproduce the high-income/high-education/white profile that is characteristic of this school."[21]

Despite their privileged backgrounds, alumni children frequently enjoy special tuition discounts. Growing numbers of public and private institutions—including the University of California at Santa Barbara, Colorado State University, the University of Virginia, and the Rochester Institute of Technology—provide legacy scholarships, typically through their alumni associations. Calvin College, for instance, annually awards thirty-six scholarships of $500 each to incoming freshmen whose parents are both Calvin alumni; candidates gain a leg up if they also have alumni grandparents, great-grandparents, and great-great-grandparents.[22]

The University of Arkansas' scholarship program for legacies from out-of-state started in 1995 and has steadily expanded from 90 beneficiaries in 1998 to 185 in 2008. "Its fundamental purpose is to recruit and retain legacy students from outside of the state of Arkansas and defray their cost of attendance," says Tysen Kendig, the university's associate vice chancellor for university relations.[23] The scholarships reduce the legacy student's tuition from the out-of-state to in-state rate, a difference of about $9,000. That translated in 2008–09 into a loss of $1.7 million in university revenue that could have funded scholarships for low-income students.

Legacy preference also is prevalent in admission to private high schools—and is even starting to surface at public elementary and secondary schools. Beverly Hills and Santa Monica/Malibu recently became the first public school districts in the country to adopt legacy policies. Hoping to elicit parental donations, Beverly Hills makes room for children of out-of-district graduates ahead of nonresidents without alumni connections. "What's wrong with being elitist?" asked one district trustee. "We're Beverly Hills."[24]

The Reasons for Legacy Preference

College officials offer a number of justifications for legacy preference. For instance, they point out that legacies, if accepted, are more likely than other students to matriculate, reducing the uncertainty of enrollment planning and boosting the "yield rate" often used to evaluate colleges in media rankings. Of legacy applicants accepted by Princeton in 2009, 72.2 percent enrolled, well above the 57.5 percent yield rate for other students whom the university admitted.[25] Almost 75 percent of alumni children accepted by the University of Notre Dame matriculate there, exceeding the school's overall 57 percent yield rate.[26] College officials also argue that alumni deserve a reward for volunteer service to the institution, and that legacies are a good fit on campus because they know a university better than other applicants and are devoted to its traditions.

While these motivations play a role, the primary reason for legacy preference today is financial. Alumni donated $8.7 billion in fiscal 2008, amounting to 27.5 percent of all private giving to colleges and universities in the United States, just behind foundations ($9.1 billion, or 28.8 percent), according to the Council for Aid to Education.[27] Reflecting the impact of the recession, alumni giving slumped to $7.1 billion in 2009. College administrators often defend legacy preference by pointing out that alumni donations underwrite financial aid for needy students, faculty salaries, and other worthy expenditures. Asked by the *Wall Street Journal* in 2006 why Princeton gives an edge to legacies, university president Shirley Tilghman said, "We are deeply dependent on the generosity of our alumni each and every year. . . . They are extremely important to the financial well-being of this university." "And wouldn't they continue to be even if you didn't give their children the preference?" the reporter pressed. "We've never done the experiment," Tilghman responded.[28]

The University of Notre Dame, which has an unusually high legacy enrollment, has sought to capitalize on these multigenerational ties in its fundraising campaigns. Alumni donations have helped Notre Dame amass a $4.8 billion endowment, the fourteenth largest in the United States.[29] Nearly three-fourths of alumni contributed to Notre Dame's 1994–2000 "Generations" campaign, the first by a Catholic university to raise $1 billion.[30] Its "Spirit of Notre Dame" campaign, launched in 2007, surpassed its $1.5 billion target in 2009. Nineteen of the twenty-six campaign leaders are alumni.

On the campaign's website, several alumni donors express hope that their children will attend Notre Dame. "I support Notre Dame because I believe in the mission of this University," wrote one alumnus, "and because I hope that members of my family and future generations will have the opportunity to be a part of that mission too." Added an alumna: "My father, a Notre Dame alum, taught me the Fight Song when I was just two. My son Michael is two now. He sings the Fight Song . . . and we're working on the alma mater."[31]

Alumni themselves recognize the monetary basis for legacy preference—and behave accordingly, timing their donations to boost their children's admission chances. A study of alumni donations to an anonymous research university between 1983 and 2006 found that alumni with a child are 13 percent more likely to give than those without children. Parental giving rises when the child is in high school if he or she ends up applying to the university, but drops if not. Favorable admission decisions mean more donations. "Interestingly, having a child rejected lowers the probability of giving to the level of alumni who have no children," the authors observe. Their conclusion: nearly half of giving by alumni whose children apply to the university "is due to self-interest. . . . Alumni giving varies systematically with the age and admissions status of the alumni's children."[32]

Just as a premier quarterback may enjoy a bigger admissions boost than a third-string tight end, so the extent of legacy preference varies in individual cases depending on the alumni parent's wealth and importance. A 1991 study of Harvard admissions found that, when a legacy seeks financial aid, the admissions boost disappears almost entirely.[33] At the other extreme, the boost swells for children of alumni who are especially important to the university—major donors, politicians in a position to provide earmarked funding, celebrities whose presence on campus would create desirable buzz.

One senior official at a highly selective university, who requested anonymity, defends legacy preference. "Those who went here are a part of the family," he says. But he adds that the university gives a bigger edge to children of alumni donors than non-donors. Because the cost of educating a student is one-and-a-half times tuition, he said, alumni who are not involved with their institution should not expect special treatment. "Just because you drank at a trough that others filled does not entitle your child to drink at the same trough. There are trough-fillers and there are just drinkers. Those two people are treated differently. For alumni who support, it's easier to make a case for the university going out on a limb to make an admission possible that wouldn't otherwise be possible."

This administrator tracks about seven hundred applicants a year, most of them legacies, whose parents are "trough-fillers." He and his staff stay in touch with their parents from beginning to end of the admissions process, managing their expectations and providing vital information—for instance, about the university's acceptance rate, and the advantage of applying early. Before each acceptance round, he meets with the admissions office to discuss a dozen applications, "where a child is right on the bubble and a parent has been faithful over the years. That doesn't mean just giving money. It means regularly being responsible not to this university but for it." On these dozen candidates, he says, "we can have some influence."

When it has to turn down children of alumni donors, the university sometimes encourages them to improve their academic credentials elsewhere and reapply in a year or two as transfer students. "We try to make the parents see that the child's record was too far from the norm to make an admission possible," he says. "Maybe that child is just beginning to bloom. Go somewhere else, lay down a more substantial record, and transfer in here." Inevitably, he says, some alumni reduce their level of giving after a rejection, perhaps shifting their charitable dollars to another university where their child does go. "To paraphrase the Scripture, where your child is, there will your heart be also."[34]

Legacy Preference and Increased Selectivity

In the past quarter-century, applications to private colleges and universities in the United States have soared. Yet few of these schools have significantly expanded their student bodies. As a result, colleges that were already selective in admissions are now even more so, while those that used to accept the bulk of their applicants increasingly have turned competitive.

With this shift, legacy preference has become more important to colleges than ever—but also more awkward and problematic. When a college rejects only a small proportion of candidates, legacy preference hardly matters, since most alumni children would get in regardless. As a school becomes more choosey in admissions, it needs to exercise legacy preference more often if it wants to satisfy alumni.

Yet there is an inherent tension between raising selectivity and sustaining legacy preference. In essence, admission officials are asked to fulfill two very different and conflicting goals: to enhance the college's academic prestige by raising standards for entry, and simultaneously to boost fundraising by making exceptions for alumni children who do not measure up to the new criteria.

As admission officials balance these two imperatives, what often happens is that acceptance rates for legacies in particular and for applicants overall both decline—thus preserving the gap between the two rates. This compromise does not please everyone. Rejected non-legacy applicants bemoan what they consider the unfairness of favoring alumni children, while alumni parents whose sons or daughters were spurned recall being admitted themselves with lesser credentials, wax nostalgic about the old days, and complain that the institution is disloyal to those who built it. Under such pressures, some colleges—particularly during fundraising drives—have been obliged to step up outreach efforts to alumni, assuring them of continued special attention in admissions.

The University of Miami in Coral Gables, Florida, illustrates this pattern. The number of applications to Miami nearly tripled in fifteen years, from 7,219 in 1993 to 21,774 to 2008. But the size of the freshman class did not keep pace, rising only 21.6 percent, from 1,653 to 2,010 over the same period. With more applicants per slot, Miami's admission rate dropped from 75 percent in 1993 to 44 percent in 2003 to 39 percent in 2008, and the average SAT score of entering freshman rose 138 points, on the 400–1600 scale.[35]

Although Miami still gave a break to legacy applicants, standards rose for them as well. Jim Sullivan, who joined Miami's admissions staff in 1999, recalls that in the midst of the boom in applications, the president and provost "would be getting calls from alumni that were livid because their son or daughter had been denied. Didn't we realize that they went here or their wife went here? Wasn't that taken into consideration? It was. But we're not the same university. Our alumni were not keeping up to date on what it takes to get admitted."[36]

Former U.S. Health and Human Services secretary Donna Shalala became Miami's president in 2001, with a mandate from trustees to boost the university's endowment. She soon recognized that alumni discontent over admissions posed a potential stumbling block. When Miami launched a $1 billion fundraising campaign in 2003, it created a special admissions process for the children and grandchildren of alumni of its undergraduate college and graduate programs. The collaborative program between the admissions and alumni offices mollified alumni, and the campaign surpassed its goal, raising $1.4 billion.

Sullivan, whose title is "legacy admission coordinator," has headed the program since its inception. "We were going to have a $1 billion capital campaign," he recalls. "Your alumni are some of your best supporters. If they're not on board, we have an issue. We had to get this legacy thing going, and going right away. I became the face of the legacy program."

Sullivan identifies prospective legacy applicants through a sign-up page on the university's Internet site. "As we are increasingly more selective, it is important that we pay special attention to our relationship with alumni and take excruciating care in evaluating legacy applications," the text reads. "Legacy applications are encouraged and each is given very special consideration by our admission staff in the evaluation process."

That "special consideration" for legacies includes an admissions interview—not normally part of the application process. "No way we could interview 22,000 students," Sullivan says. During the interview, he advises legacies that they need a "strong B average" for admission, and that, if their high school record falls short, they may be able to enroll elsewhere for a year and reapply. Based on their applications and the knowledge he gleans from the interview, he personally advocates for legacy applicants before the university's admissions committee.

Legacies enjoy another perquisite at Miami—mid-year admission. This benefits the children of alumni with borderline credentials: they are placed on the university's waiting list. If the university cannot take them off the waiting list at the start of the academic year, it tries to find room for them in January. Typically, about one hundred freshmen enroll in January, of whom about half are legacies. Sullivan also has developed a "kinder, gentler" rejection letter for unsuccessful legacy applicants, acknowledging the value of alumni ties. He says the letter has cut down on indignant phone calls from alumni parents. If they do call him, he says, "I have the nicest way of saying no."

According to Sullivan, the admission rate for legacy applicants to Miami is only slightly higher than for other students. "The legacy admission process might help a student that's sick to get better," he says. "We don't bring the dead to new life." Switching metaphors, he adds, "It's not a golden pass. But it is indeed a card that legacies have in their deck that other students don't have."

About 180 alumni children matriculated at Miami in 2008, comprising 9 percent of the freshman class. The university continues to shower extra attention on alumni children after they enroll; since 2006, it has hosted an annual reception for freshman legacies and their alumni parents.

Sullivan believes that legacy preference "makes a lot of sense. A relative knocks on your door, you treat them differently than a complete stranger. Everybody gets the red carpet treatment when they come through admissions; for a legacy student, we'll vacuum the carpet, we'll get down and pick up the lint."

The Lack of Legacy Preference Abroad

Legacy preference in college admissions is an almost exclusively American custom. Foreign universities typically depend on government support, eliminating the financial incentive to admit alumni children. In some countries, admission or rejection is determined by performance on entrance exams. Although selective universities abroad are increasingly adopting the U.S. model of raising money from student tuition and private donors, particularly alumni, there is no evidence that they provide the type of systemic, open reliance on ancestry practiced by their American counterparts.

Alumni connections may play a role behind the scenes in admissions to foreign universities. "A question is whether it (legacy preference) comes into the process in the form of corruption, e.g. someone picks up the phone and has a chat with the admissions office," says Robin Matross Helms, founder of a consulting firm specializing in international higher education.[37] If so, such old-boy networks rarely see the light of a formal preference. In Western Europe, higher education is almost exclusively public; only 1 percent of students attend private institutions. In France and Germany, admission to college is based solely on entrance exams. In Eastern Europe, where all universities were government-funded in the Communist era, between one-quarter and one-half of students now go to private colleges. Yet those private schools, less prestigious and selective than their public counterparts, generally accept most applicants and thus are open to alumni children without any preference. India has hundreds of private colleges, which are notorious for selling admission slots for a "capitation fee" of several thousand dollars—to any buyer, not just alumni.[38]

Some private secondary schools around the world, such as United World College of Southeast Asia in Singapore,[39] give an admissions edge to alumni children. But the only country outside the United States where legacy preference has made any inroads in higher education is Japan. More than 70 percent of college students in Japan enroll at private institutions.[40] However, private colleges in Japan are more reliant on tuition than in the United States, and less reliant on private gifts. In 2005, private gifts and grants accounted for 2.9 percent of revenue of Japanese private universities, as against 13.6 percent of revenue of U.S. private universities.[41]

Asia University, a second-tier private university in Japan, introduced legacy preference about twenty years ago. A few other Japanese colleges, such as Otsuma Women's University, feature a special admissions process for alumni children.[42] Several of these schools, however, have virtually open admissions, and their legacy policy seems to be more of a marketing tactic to attract applicants than a criterion for entry.

At Japan's top private universities, alumni children do sometimes benefit from another admissions preference—given to graduates of affiliated high schools and primary schools. For instance, Keio University, Japan's oldest private university and one of the best, almost always accepts graduates of its affiliated high and primary schools. "Some alumni try very hard to prepare for entrance examination to this primary school as well as high schools," says Akiyoshi Yonezawa, associate professor at the Center for the Advancement of Higher Education at Tohoku University. "However, at least officially, these schools do not take legacy preference."[43]

Facing myriad budgetary pressures, governments throughout the world have struggled in recent years to afford rising higher education costs—for faculty salaries, scientific laboratories, and the like—and growing enrollment. Seeking to shift this burden, governments in the United Kingdom, Hong Kong, Singapore, and Ontario, Canada, among others, have encouraged alumni fundraising by offering to match private donations with public funds.[44] As a result, selective universities abroad increasingly have sought private funding, including student tuition and alumni donations. Emulating the U.S. model, foreign universities have expanded their development staffs, hired fundraising consultants, and opened offices in other countries to solicit alumni. "The interest in US development methods around the world is huge," says Professor Philip G. Altbach, director of the Center for International Higher Education at Boston College.[45]

The overseas expansion of the Council for Advancement and Support of Education (CASE), a U.S.-based organization that advises colleges on fundraising practices, tracks this trend. CASE opened a branch office in London in 1994, and in Singapore in 2007. Its annual United Kingdom conference drew 953 people from 20 countries in 2008—up from just 71 attendees at the first conference in 1990. In 2002, CASE also began hosting a weeklong course in the United Kingdom on educational fundraising. The eighth annual course, in

April 2009, attracted people from 15 countries, including Denmark, Poland, Nigeria, Tanzania, and South Africa. CASE plans to start a similar program for Asian-Pacific countries in October 2009.[46]

English universities, especially Oxford, are in the forefront of the shift to private funding. In 1996, Oxford named its new business school after Saudi entrepreneur Wafic Saïd, who donated £20 million.[47] In 2003, English universities began charging tuition. In 2008, Oxford launched a campaign to raise £1.25 billion, the biggest fund drive ever by a European university, reflecting "growing concern among leading British universities that they will have to find more money to compete with American rivals which charge much higher fees and enjoy multibillion dollar endowments boosted by their alumni."[48] It did not take long for Oxford's alumni donors to flex their muscles. That same year, Michael Moritz, a California high-tech tycoon who donated £25 million to Christ Church, his Oxford college, clashed with the university administrator leading the fund drive, apparently over Christ Church's handling of investments. The administrator, Jon Dellandrea, resigned.[49]

Asian universities are also increasingly soliciting alumni. In 2005, Nanyang Technical University in Singapore hired Marina Tan Harper, the former director of the development office at Northern Kentucky University, to head its fledgling fundraising effort. In two years, she boosted the number of alumni donors from 143 to more than 4,000. The National University of Singapore opened its development office in 2003.[50]

Even in mainland China, an ostensibly Communist country, universities are increasingly pursuing private gifts. For instance, Fudan University in Shanghai has announced several multimillion-dollar donations and established a nonprofit foundation in the United States to solicit gifts from alumni there. Tsinghua University in Beijing regularly sends promising members of its development staff to California to shadow Stanford fundraisers and learn their techniques.[51]

The University of Hong Kong, a public institution, is betting on the generosity of its graduates. Under its Stanley Ho Alumni Challenge, the Macao casino magnate agreed to match private donations dollar-for-dollar up to about \$75 million—\$15 million a year from 2005 to 2010. Donations reached the target in each of the first three years. In the first year, gifts soared 600 percent over the prior year. The "groundbreaking" challenge from Ho, himself an alumnus, has "inspired a new and unprecedented culture of alumni giving in Hong Kong."[52]

Hong Kong fundraisers and alumni apparently were undeterred by Ho's controversial reputation. His alleged links to cutthroat triad gangs that "use Macao's casinos to ply their loan-sharking trade, launder dirty money, and supply prostitutes and drugs to wealthy businessmen" have led the U.S. government to label him "a reputed organized crime figure." His plans to develop casinos in the United States, Canada, Australia, Singapore, and the United Kingdom have been stymied due to investigations into his alleged organized crime ties.[53]

As elite foreign universities that used to be sustained by taxpayer funding increasingly woo alumni, they are likely to face pressure to show their gratitude to private donors—and keep the spigot flowing—by admitting legacies. Most of these universities apparently have not anticipated this interference—the topic has not come up at CASE conferences overseas—and may be ill-prepared to resist. It seems likely that, in the near future, some colleges abroad may accommodate the new tide of private donors with legacy or development preference. "Can legacy preference be far behind? That's the question," says Altbach. "It's something the universities should be concerned about."[54]

The Legacy Establishment

Sheldon Whitehouse, whom Rhode Island elected to the U.S. Senate in 2006, is committed to broadening educational opportunity. "Today, more than ever, a college diploma is truly essential to a young person's success," the Democratic senator states on his website. "I'll keep fighting to make certain that all children and young people in America have a chance at the great education they deserve."[55]

Yet Whitehouse has never spoken out against one practice that arguably restricts educational opportunity: legacy preference. That reticence may be due to his family history. The senator graduated from Yale, as did his grandfather, his father, and his great-uncle.[56]

An uncle entered Yale but was killed in action in World War II before he could graduate. The senator's father and grandfather, both career diplomats, belonged to Skull and Bones, the controversial Yale secret society, as did his great-uncle.[57] Its members have included such prominent legacies as Presidents George H. W. Bush and George W. Bush, and Senator John Kerry, the 2004 Democratic presidential nominee. The senator's wife also graduated from Yale. Their double-legacy daughter is a member of Yale's class of 2011.

Whitehouse belongs to what has been termed the "Legacy Establishment": key officeholders in the executive, legislative, and judicial branches of government who are legacies themselves or sent their sons and daughters to their old schools.[58] The legacy establishment encompasses Democrats and Republicans, liberals and conservatives. Whether or not they or their children needed a boost in college admissions, their long-standing family affiliation to one institution inclines them to be sympathetic to the concept of legacy preference and helps explain why critics of the practice—most notably, former senators and presidential aspirants Bob Dole of Kansas and John Edwards of North Carolina—have made little headway.

Preferences for alumni children are unpopular with the American public. In a May 2004 poll by the *Chronicle of Higher Education*, 75 percent of respondents said they "strongly disagree" or "disagree" that "applicants to a college whose close relatives attended the same college should be given extra consideration for admission." Only 23 percent strongly agreed or agreed; the remaining 2 percent said they did not know. By contrast, 53 percent of respondents expressed support for giving "some preference . . . to minority candidates in order to ensure equal opportunity for a higher education in the U.S."[59] While the sympathetic tone of the statement ("to ensure equal opportunity") likely inflated the level of support for affirmative action, politicians who oppose race-based but favor ancestry-based preferences still risk alienating voters who may perceive them as inconsistent and elitist. Former president George W. Bush, an affirmative action foe and third-generation legacy at Yale, dodged this pitfall during the 2004 presidential campaign by telling an audience of black journalists that admissions should be merit-based and there should be "no special exception for certain people."

Yet the public disdain for legacy preference has not translated into legislative action. In 2003, for instance, a proposal to require colleges to disclose more information on legacy admissions failed in Congress. Ironically, the 2003 attack on legacy preference was spearheaded by a staffer for the late senator Ted Kennedy, a Harvard legacy. Charles Grassley, then chairman of the Senate Finance Committee, suggested at a 2006 hearing that alumni donations made in return for admissions preference for their children should no longer be treated as charitable gifts by the tax code. Grassley said he would ask the IRS to review the matter, but such gifts remain tax-exempt.

When the U.S. Supreme Court upheld the use of affirmative action in admissions to the University of Michigan in 2003, five of the nine justices or their children qualified for legacy preference. Former justice Sandra Day O'Connor, who wrote the majority opinion in the 5–4 decision, is a Stanford graduate and mother of two Stanford alumni, and has served on the university's board of trustees. Delivering Stanford's commencement address in 1982, she proclaimed that "there is no greater, more foresighted office in this land of ours than the admissions office of Stanford University." Her wish for the graduates, she said, was that "you will be lucky enough to have your children attend this paradise on earth . . . that we call Stanford." Justice Clarence Thomas, who has no legacy ties, suggested in an eloquent dissent that the majority was worried that outlawing affirmative action for minorities in college admissions would spur a reaction against legacy preference, which is often described as white affirmative action. "Were this court to have the courage to forbid the use of racial discrimination in admissions, legacy preferences . . . might quickly become less popular."[60]

At least one major-party candidate for president in each of the last three elections has had personal experience with legacy preference. Both George W. Bush and 2004 Democratic nominee John Kerry were mediocre students who entered Yale through the legacy door; each sent a daughter to Yale as well. Albert Gore, Jr., the Democratic nominee in 2000, graduated from Harvard, and so did his four children. John McCain, 2008 Republican nominee, followed his father and grandfather to the U.S. Naval Academy. "When that baby was born, I assumed he was going to go to the Naval Academy," his mother once said.[61] McCain himself "harbored a secret resentment that my life's course seemed so preordained."[62] The path of McCain's son, John McCain IV, also appears preordained; he graduated from the Naval Academy in 2009.

While President Barack Obama is not a legacy, and his daughters are not yet old enough for college, Vice President Joe Biden is a legacy parent. He and his older son, Beau, attorney general of Delaware, both attended Syracuse University's law school. Akin to legacy clout, alumni pull of a slightly different sort may have helped Biden's younger son, Hunter, get into one of the country's top law schools. When Hunter, then a senior at Georgetown University, applied to Yale Law School in 1993, then-dean Guido Calabrese was startled to receive a call from someone he identifies only as "a person of enormous authority."[63] The caller, Calabrese remembers, "asked me if I could do something to help" Hunter, whose father was then head of the Senate Judiciary Committee. In that era, Calabrese said, Yale Law "gave a very definite, very minor advantage to children of alums. If everything was even, they would be the first ones taken off the waiting list." But this was a different case altogether. Calabrese told the caller that he would not pressure Yale's admissions office, which rejected Hunter. But Calabrese agreed to meet with Hunter, and encouraged him to go to another law school for a year and reapply as a transfer student.[64] After a year at Georgetown Law School, Hunter transferred to Yale. According to two people familiar with the episode, the caller was Yale Law graduate Bill Clinton, then beginning his first term as president.

The legacy establishment continually replenishes itself. Including Senator Whitehouse, at least six legacies or alumni parents entered the U.S. Senate in 2006 or 2008. Among them: Pennsylvania senator Robert P. Casey, Jr., attended College of the Holy Cross in Worcester, as did his father, the late Pennsylvania governor Robert P. Casey, Sr. Like his father, son, and nephew, Maryland senator Benjamin Cardin went to law school at the University of Maryland.[65] Missouri senator Claire McCaskill was a double legacy at the University of Missouri.[66] Minnesota senator Al Franken and his daughter are Harvard graduates. These Senate newcomers joined longer-serving members of the legacy establishment, including Kerry, McCain, and Charles Schumer of New York, who is an alumnus of Harvard, where both of his daughters matriculated.

Numerous state officials also enjoy legacy ties. Richard Blumenthal, a Democrat, has been Connecticut attorney general since 1990 and is running for the U.S. Senate in 2010. Blumenthal has brought high-profile cases against environmental polluters and unscrupulous mortgage lenders. But the noted consumer advocate has not challenged legacy preference, which limits consumers' access to the colleges of their choice. In fact, he is part of a Harvard dynasty that has parlayed a combination of academic achievement, wealth, and legacy status into consistent admissions success.

The paterfamilias of the clan is Peter Malkin, who graduated from Harvard in 1955 and Harvard Law School in 1958. Malkin married Isabel Wien, the daughter of the late magnate Lawrence Wien, who pioneered real estate syndication in the 1930s. Malkin joined his father-in-law's real estate business, which invested in many premier office towers, including the Empire State Building.[67] As his fortune flourished, Malkin became a major supporter of his alma mater. He became a member of fifteen Harvard committees, including the board of overseers and the Committee on University Resources, which is composed of the university's four hundred or so biggest donors. In 1985, the university's indoor athletic facility was renamed the Malkin Athletic Center in his honor.[68]

Malkin's three children all went to Harvard. One son runs the family firm with his father, and also became a member of the Committee on University Resources. Malkin's daughter is married to Richard Blumenthal, who graduated from Harvard in 1967.

Now the next generation is beginning to apply to college. As Malkin reported at his fiftieth class reunion in 2005, "We have three wonderful children, all graduates of Harvard College, who have wonderful spouses, one each a graduate of Harvard, Wellesley and Princeton. They have given us 10 grandchildren, five girls and five boys, the eldest is Harvard class of '08."[69]

By the fall of 2009, five of the six Malkin grandchildren old enough for college had enrolled at Harvard (one grandson broke family tradition, opting for Stanford).[70] One grandson at Harvard said that the family's connection to the university "is a part of my history that I appreciate and know about."

Before enrolling at Harvard, Blumenthal's two older sons attended the Brunswick School, a private school for boys in

Greenwich, Connecticut. Each was one of only two students in his high school class to go to Harvard. A person familiar with their Brunswick records said that both were "very serious students" in the top 10 percent of their class rank, with "very, very good" test scores. "I've always felt, these guys did a good enough job. I can't honestly tell you if the Malkin factor was 1% or a huge percent. And their dad is a person of note."

"Most of these better schools, even in a legacy situation, clearly require strong academic performance and involvement. You better have the record to back up whatever legacy you have."[71]

Dropping Legacy Preference

As Justice Thomas observed, bans on affirmative action for minorities typically spur counterattacks on legacy preference. The University of California, which had favored children of out-of-state alumni by treating them as in-state students, eliminated the practice after California voters outlawed affirmative action in 1996. When a federal appeals court in 2001 struck down minority preference at the University of Georgia, that school scrapped legacy preference as well.

By the reasoning of the higher education lobby, which argues that legacy preference is essential to fundraising, the University of California system and the University of Georgia should have suffered a financial penalty for abandoning it. Surprisingly, that did not happen. Instead, a 2009 study found that, after dropping legacy preference, six University of California campuses and the University of Georgia enjoyed an increase in gifts. "The data that is currently publicly available refutes the received wisdom that the preferences result in increased private giving," the study concludes.[72]

One reason why eliminating legacy preference does not appear to deter giving is that many alumni do not have much faith in it anyway. As mentioned earlier, alumni increase donations to their old school as their children approach college age and plan to apply. This finding implies a realization on the part of legacy parents that, despite the pablum dished out by college officials about perpetuating tradition, alumni status alone is not enough to assure admission. With or without legacy preference, it helps to donate.

There is no doubt that some alumni complain loudly and curtail their giving if their children are rejected—a more likely eventuality without legacy preference. One Princeton alumnus poetically likened its rejection of his daughter to a fatal disease: "A cancer creeps insidiously here/Within our midst and masquerades about/Destroying as it does the very dear attachment/We can't bear to be without." But most alumni take such rebuffs in stride. After his grandson was turned down, one Harvard graduate and major donor told a school admissions official, "I couldn't agree with you more."[73] Moreover, one college's loss may be another's gain: alumni who write smaller checks to their alma mater after a son or daughter is rejected often shift their philanthropy to the school where the child does enroll.

Like the state universities of California and Georgia, another selective public institution, Texas A&M, learned that there is life after legacy preference. In January 2004, Texas A&M eliminated its policy of giving legacies four points on a one-hundred-point admissions scale, yielding to pressure from legislators, civil rights activists, and the media. They were upset that Texas A&M had decided not to restore consideration of race as a factor in admissions in 2003 following the Supreme Court decision upholding affirmative action at the University of Michigan, which reversed a 1996 lower-court decision banning preference for minorities at public universities in Texas. Texas A&M, the *Houston Chronicle* reported, had admitted 349 students in 2002 as a result of legacy points; 321 were white, 25 Hispanic, and 3 black.[74]

At first, giving to the Texas A&M foundation, the university's principal fundraising arm, dropped slightly, from $65.6 million in fiscal 2003 to $61.9 million in fiscal 2004. But then donations soared to $92 million in 2005, $95.2 million in 2006, and $114 million in 2007.[75] A university campaign, which ran from 2003 to 2007, raised $1.5 billion, surpassing its $1 billion target. Participation rates—the proportion of graduates who contribute to the university—also increased. "We've had grumbles" from alumni over the loss of legacy preference, "but it hasn't hurt fundraising in sheer numbers," says Kathy McCoy, director of marketing for the foundation. Adds Alice Reinarz, assistant provost for enrollment, "Anecdotally, we hear about these family members who are aggrieved: 'My son or daughter didn't get admitted and you'll never get a cent from me.' In most instances, they've never given a cent anyway."[76]

It is not entirely clear how strictly Texas A&M abides by its ban on legacy preference. Kathryn Greenwade, vice president of the university's alumni association, says she encourages legacies to describe their family ties to Texas A&M in their application essays. "We always tell our former students, there is still an opportunity in the application process to convey that Aggie connection and that legacy connection through the essay," she says. "They can talk about, 'I'm a third generation Aggie." Reinarz says such stratagems do not work: "Occasionally, a student will write in an essay, 'I really want to come to Texas A&M because my father and grandfather went there.' We instruct the reviewer to ignore it." She adds, however, that a new criterion for admission—"academic association"—tends to benefit alumni children. Students who have met with an academic adviser, joined a campus tour, or shown other signs of interest in Texas A&M gain a slight edge. "When we get to those final decisions, if we have a number of students who to all intents and purposes are the same, except that some of them have high academic association with the university, they get the nod." In some instances, she adds, "there is a correlation between high academic association and legacy status. Sons and daughters of former students know that academic association is the replacement for legacy. They work the system in that way."[77]

Reinarz believes that the Texas A&M administration also has defused alumni anger by persuasively communicating the reasons for the decision to jettison legacy preference. She recalls attending a speech that Robert Gates, then president of the university and now U.S. secretary of defense, gave defending the move to a potentially hostile audience—the Federation of Texas A&M University Mothers' Clubs. "You'd assume that Aggie moms, who are drawn together by connectedness by family, would be very unhappy," she says. Gates, who put himself through college with jobs and scholarships, told the mothers how hard he, his father, and his grandfather had worked for their educations. "Texas A&M was built by men who had rough hands," she recalls him saying.

"There were tears in the audience," Reinarz says. "When he was done, there was a standing ovation." Alumni now appreciate, she adds, that Texas A&M aspires to be elite, but not elitist.

With a similarly egalitarian spirit, the University of Illinois flagship campus at Urbana-Champaign started down the same road as Texas A&M—but quickly turned back. Without outside pressure from civil rights activists or lawmakers, or forceful leadership like Gates's on the issue, Illinois was not willing to try to change the hearts and minds of its alumni.

Until 2007, Illinois regarded legacy status as a "plus factor, one of many things one could take into consideration" in admissions, according to Keith Marshall, associate provost for enrollment management.[78] That year, the university eliminated legacy preference, deleting questions about parental education from its application form.

The move was not prompted by an affirmative action ban; Illinois still gives an edge in admissions to members of underrepresented minorities. Instead, the idea came from Illinois's own admissions staff. "It was the admissions office that recommended, 'We don't need this bit of data,'" Marshall says. "It wanted to base the decision on merit, on the quality of the individual."[79]

It proved to be a "short-lived experiment," Marshall says. For university higher-ups, the timing was unfortunate. That same year, the university launched a four-year $2.25 billion fundraising campaign, with a $1.5 billion goal for the Urbana-Champaign campus. "Because of the commitment of our alumni and friends . . . Illinois will be counted among the greatest public research universities in the nation," Chancellor Richard Herman promised at the June 2007 kick-off event.[80]

With so much at stake, Illinois could not afford to alienate alumni. After only a year, the university reversed its decision and restored legacy preference. Herman "does periodically say—we need to be paying attention to legacy," Marshall says. "The chancellor wants good relations with alumni. We at public institutions understand how to build alumni loyalty and how it translates into fundraising." Marshall says the university now uses the information on parental education to give a boost both to alumni children and to applicants who are the first in their family to go to college. The two preferences balance each other, he says: "Legacy can in some ways be perpetuating the stratification in the system, whereas first-generation can help you identify students that may have had all the opportunities." Besides restoring legacy preference, Illinois fostered "stratification" through other admission policies as well. The *Chicago Tribune* reported in May 2009 that the university placed applicants who were relatives, friends, or neighbors of lawmakers and trustees in a special category, accepting them at a higher rate than unconnected candidates and letting in some students with sub-par credentials.[81] In the wake of the scandal, Chancellor Herman resigned in October 2009.

Few if any selective private colleges have scrapped legacy preference in recent years. Since bans on affirmative action have generally applied only to public institutions, private schools haven't faced the countervailing pressure against legacy preference. Also, while state schools can risk a downturn in alumni support because they mainly rely on government funding, private colleges that depend on alumni donors are afraid to alienate them.

Still, respected private colleges, such as California Institute of Technology (Caltech), Berea College, and Cooper Union for the Advancement of Science and Art, pay virtually no attention to legacy status. All three schools evaluate applicants based on merit as they define it, while also taking into account socioeconomic disadvantages, such as coming from a single-parent family. As a result, they enroll a high proportion of low-income students. Yet they raise enough money to maintain academic quality and meet students' financial need. Their fundraising success undercuts the view that colleges need legacy preference to thrive financially.

At Caltech, faculty and students are deeply involved in admission decisions, ensuring high scientific standards and a meritocratic ethic. "Anyone who tried to use wealth and pull strings at Caltech would be laughed out of the room," observed one student on Caltech's freshman admissions committee. "It's how smart you are that counts."[82] Admissions director Richard Bischoff says that legacies "move through the process exactly like everybody else," and that he has never made nor changed an admissions decision based on alumni status. He does track applications from children, grandchildren, and siblings of alumni. "We want to know if we're disappointing somebody," Bischoff says, so that Caltech fundraisers are not placed in the awkward position of asking for money from an alumnus whose son or daughter was just rejected.[83] Bischoff left Caltech in 2009 to become vice president of enrollment management at Case Western Reserve University.

Caltech has amassed a $1.4 billion endowment, thirty-seventh largest among U.S. colleges. Alumni gave $71 million to Caltech in 2007, almost equaling the $77 million that MIT graduates donated to their alma mater, even though MIT has legacy preference and its pool of alumni is almost five times as large as Caltech's.[84] Caltech compensates for lacking legacy preference with creative approaches to fundraising. Gordon Moore, co-founder of Intel Corporation, who earned his doctorate at Caltech, gave $600 million to the institute in 2001, the largest gift ever to a U.S. college, in gratitude for what he calls its "fantastic intellectual climate." Moore's two sons did not go there, but he savored a different reward: Caltech named an asteroid after him.[85]

At Berea College in Kentucky, all students receive full tuition scholarships and hold campus jobs; applicants must meet not only academic but also financial eligibility guidelines. In general, students from households earning $60,000 or more are ineligible, ruling out children of successful alumni.[86] Yet Berea's endowment, nearly$800 million, exceeds that of better-known liberal arts colleges such as Middlebury, Oberlin, Vassar, and Bowdoin. It attracts much of its support from people who have no relation to the college but admire its progressive mission, as well as from affluent alumni children and grandchildren who attended other colleges themselves but recognize their family's debt to Berea. "Berea ought to reserve its places for children who couldn't be educated otherwise," said one such donor, a mutual fund analyst whose father emerged from rural poverty with the help of a Berea education. "If it made room" for rich students, "maybe my dad wouldn't have been able to go there."[87]

Applicants to Cooper Union, New York City's top art school, often enlist the rich and famous to recommend them. But connections do not help at Cooper Union; only talent matters. As at Berea, every Cooper Union student receives a full tuition scholarship. More than one-third of its students were born outside the United States.[88] Cooper Union's endowment ($600 million) ranks 124th, ahead of Bucknell, Haverford, and Davidson.

It can be argued that Caltech, Berea, and Cooper Union are atypical of American private higher education. Two of them enjoy significant revenues from sources other than private donations: Caltech from federal research grants, and Cooper Union from real estate holdings, including the landmark art deco Chrysler Building. Still, their ability to attract donors, along with the fundraising success of Texas A&M and the University of California, and the rise in private donations to universities overseas that do not practice legacy preference, all suggest that schools can prosper without compromising admission standards for alumni children.

Conclusion

When Texas A&M abandoned legacy preference, it did not entirely eliminate wealth as a factor in admissions, nor end special treatment for all alumni children. Reinarz acknowledges that the foundation, the university's fundraising branch, passes along names of applicants from big-donor families—alumni and non-alumni alike—and that the president's office encourages the admissions staff to view them favorably. "There is a conversation once a year to find out if the administration might want to put in a good word for a very modest number of students," she says. "Typically that's authorized by the president only." She adds that Texas A&M "has only a handful that I would call special admits. The notion that the foundation can get a bunch of people in is really an urban myth."

Such "special admits"—or "development cases," as they often are known—are not limited to Texas A&M. Though less discussed than legacy preference, development preference is equally prevalent in higher education—with Caltech, Berea, and Cooper Union again among the rare abstainers. At most colleges, anywhere from half a dozen to more than one hundred applicants are recommended by the development office or the president because major gifts may hinge on their enrollment. They are held to a lower standard than ordinary legacies, and the admissions staff rejects them at its peril. Besides relatives of big donors, children of politicians and entertainment/media celebrities are often treated as development cases because their enrollment indirectly enriches the university. Well-disposed politicians can earmark public funding to an institution for laboratories or other projects, while celebrities bring attention and buzz that can translate into more applicants and ultimately more donations. As with legacies in general, most development cases are white.[89]

Without the veneer of tradition and loyalty attached to preference for alumni children, development preference represents a more blatant swap of admissions for donations. It also may be more crucial to an institution's fundraising. While universities need the loyalty of a broad swath of graduates for many other reasons, including educational rankings—the alumni giving rate makes up 5 percent of the *U.S. News & World Report* score[90]—they derive the bulk of private donations from a small number of big givers. The top 1 percent of gifts constitute 70 percent of the total value of alumni contributions. "Alumni who make gifts of that magnitude are not dependent on legacy preferences to get special consideration for their children."[91]

Because it is limited to a smaller number of students and is explicitly intended to reap a huge financial windfall, development preference in some ways is more defensible than legacy preference. By heeding fundraising imperatives in a few cases, one could argue, Texas A&M cushioned the financial risk of eliminating an unfair edge for hundreds of alumni children.

Still, the Texas A&M solution—development but not legacy—carries its own set of problems. Preference for children of the rich and famous undermines the egalitarian, elite-but-not-elitist rationale for eliminating legacy preference. Moreover, because the Texas A&M approach grants an edge to a few legacies, while ignoring the rest, and rewards children of families with no prior connection to the institution, it is likely over the long run to stir up more grumbling among alumni than would a no-preference system like Caltech's.

Although ending legacy preference does not necessarily guarantee a wealth-blind process, it is an important step toward fairer admissions, one that more colleges could take without imperiling their prosperity. As Texas A&M, the University of California, and Caltech illustrate, legacy preference is by no means essential to fundraising. Unfortunately, the current economic downturn is likely to discourage most colleges from discarding the preference—and may tempt them to admit more alumni children in the hope of replenishing diminished endowments. As Northwestern University president Morton Schapiro recently noted, college applicants have "always been in an advantaged position to be rich and smart. Now you're at an even greater advantage."[92] Thus, even though legacy preference runs contrary both to public opinion and the national ethos of meritocracy, and is unheard-of in countries otherwise far less democratic than the United States, it remains firmly entrenched in American higher education.

5

An Empirical Analysis of the Impact of Legacy Preferences on Alumni Giving at Top Universities

Chad Coffman, Tara O'Neil, and Brian Starr

Introduction and Summary of Findings

A great debate is taking place about the application of legacy preferences in American colleges and universities. A primary justification often cited in favor of granting legacy preferences is that such policies have a positive impact on the amount of alumni giving.[1] The corollary proposition is that elimination of such policies would restrict an important source of funding for higher education. As far as we can tell, since these claims seem never to have been documented empirically, it is time to bring empirical data to the debate and test the claim of a link between legacy preference policies and alumni giving.

Our primary finding is that, after inclusion of appropriate controls, including wealth, there is no statistically significant evidence of a causal relationship between legacy preference policies and total alumni giving among top universities. Using annual panel data covering 1998 to 2008 for the top one hundred universities, we show that, after controlling for year, institution size, public/private status, income, and a proxy for alumni wealth, more than 70 percent of the variation in alumni giving across institutions and time can be explained. The coefficients all have the expected signs and there is no statistically significant evidence that legacy preferences impact total alumni giving.

These results should not be surprising. Legacy preference policies, in their pure form, do not purport to reward alumni donations with a greater chance of acceptance; they purport to give a greater chance of acceptance to all alumni, regardless of whether they donate. Therefore, there is no a priori reason to believe legacy preference policies themselves provide incentives for greater alumni giving.

Prior to controlling for wealth, however, the results indicate that schools with legacy preference policies indeed have much higher alumni giving. These combined results suggest that higher alumni giving at top institutions that employ legacy preferences is not a result of the preference policy exerting influence on alumni giving behavior, but rather that the policy allows elite schools to over-select from their own wealthy alumni. In other words, the preference policy effectively allows elite schools essentially to discriminate based on socioeconomic status by accepting their own wealthy alumni families rather than basing admissions on merit alone.

Literature Review

As mentioned, to our knowledge, there is no well-accepted systematic empirical analysis that establishes a causal relationship between legacy preferences and alumni giving behavior. A 2008 study by Steve D. Shadowen, Sozi Tulante, and Shara L. Alpern attempted to address the issue directly; it finds no evidence of a significant relationship between alumni giving and legacy preferences.[2] Those authors employ a cross-sectional multiple regression at the school level to test whether legacy preference policy is correlated with alternative measures of private giving.[3] Their data include information for the top seventy-five national universities and the top seventy-five liberal arts colleges from 1992 to 2006. They acknowledge that there are serious weaknesses in the data employed because it could not distinguish between alumni donations versus grants and contracts.[4] Our study seeks to expand and improve upon the work done by Shadowen and his colleagues by employing more robust data and econometric models. For example, our data isolate alumni giving from other forms of giving, and we introduce additional variables that generate greater explanatory power.

The 2008 study also investigates, in a cursory way, whether there is a change in total alumni giving after the abolition of legacy preferences at certain schools; they find no evidence of a decrease. We also expand upon this analysis and report the results of a more formal model of the change in alumni giving attributable to observed changes in legacy preference policies.

A 2003 study by Charles T. Clotfelter uses data from two cohorts of college graduates to explore the determinants of alumni giving.[5] Clotfelter identifies a number of determinants of alumni giving, including satisfaction with the institution, income, and obtaining a graduate degree, as well as other factors. While the purpose of the study was not to identify the impact of legacy preferences, for a subset of his data he had an indicator of whether a relative attended the institution. Clotfelter finds that alumni giving is correlated positively with having a relative that attended the school. Note, however, that Clotfelter's interpretation of this finding is not that legacy preferences result in greater giving, but that having a relative that previously attended the institution is a proxy for unmeasured wealth. Indeed, it is not even clear if the schools Clotfelter examined employed legacy preferences.

Two 2009 studies by Jonathan Meer and Harvey Rosen—one on altruism and one on family bonding with universities—attempt to analyze the impact on alumni giving of admitting alumni's children (and other relatives, in the case of the family bonding study).[6] Both of these studies rely on data from a single anonymous "selective research" institution—presumably one that employs legacy preferences. As a result, their analysis does not allow for a direct comparison of aggregate giving behavior between legacy granting and non-legacy granting schools. Rather, their study focuses on micro data and the determinants of giving behavior.

Meer and Rosen's study of altruism documents that, at least within this single institution, there was an increase in giving as alumni children approached admission age. There is no reason to believe, and Meer and Rosen certainly do not show, however, that these apparent "bribes" are a function of legacy preference policies. In other words, if parents believe (true or not) that donations increase the likelihood of admission, there is no reason to believe this effect would be limited to schools with legacy preferences. Recall that even within schools that employ legacy preference policies, the admissions decision is supposedly independent of prior giving.

Not surprisingly, Meer and Rosen's study of altruism also shows that alumni whose children are rejected give less than those whose children were accepted. One might try to bootstrap this finding into an argument that legacy preference policies, by simply rejecting fewer alumni children, must significantly increase alumni giving. This argument is speculative for a number of reasons. First, Meer and Rosen do not attempt to disentangle the effects of the preference policy on the applications process itself. In other words, in the absence of legacy preference policies, it is likely that fewer unqualified alumni children would apply in the first place—thus sparing them the rejection that Meer and Rosen demonstrate has a deleterious effect on future giving (relative to those that never apply). In addition, the reduction in giving by those rejected may be a function of the preference policy itself; in other words, alumni could be particularly offended by having their children rejected from a school they know has a legacy preference policy. Third, this study is done at the micro-level. While they may find differences in propensities to give at that level, total alumni giving, as they acknowledge, is driven in large part by a small number of very large donations,[7] which they find, in their study of family bonding, to be unrelated to whether other family members attend the school. Therefore, it would not be at all surprising to find that legacy preferences have little or no impact in the aggregate.

In the analysis of bonding, Meer and Rosen attempt to test the proposition that legacy preferences "bind entire families to the university" and thereby increase donations from these families. They perform regression analyses that purport to show greater giving by alumni when their children, and to a lesser extent, other descendants and previous generations (for example, children-in-law, nieces and nephews, aunts and uncles, and so on) are admitted to the institution.[8] Their regression is essentially testing for the marginal giving associated with having a relative that attended the institution. As suggested by Clotfelter, Meer and Rosen's findings could be largely a function of unmeasured wealth. One would expect that a family that has multiple generations that have attended a "selective research institution" has different levels of wealth than those that do not. Indeed, the authors raise that specific possibility and attempt to control for it to the extent their data allow (by controlling for SAT and excluding the largest gifts), but they admittedly do not employ a direct measure of family wealth. Their controls for current income also are limited to dummy variables for degree, time since graduation, and occupations in which the alumnus has worked during his career. While these variables are likely somewhat correlated with income and wealth, they cannot tell the whole story.

In summary, the Meer and Rosen studies highlight a number of interesting relationships within an example institution, but their analyses fall far short of a direct test of the aggregate impact of legacy preference policies—either within the institution they study or the higher education system more broadly. The authors specifically caution again at the end of their study that the results are based on a single institution and their findings may not be applicable to other institutions.

There are a number of other studies that analyze the determinants of alumni giving, but do not focus on the impact of legacy preferences. For example, James Monk investigates the influence of individual characteristics on alumni giving from twenty-eight institutions.[9] He specifies a linear regression model conditional on some level of giving with the natural logarithm of total giving as the dependant variable. Consistent with other studies, he finds a significant link between alumni income and giving (he specifies a model that has linear and quadratic income terms). He also finds a negative correlation between student loans and later alumni giving. The amount of debt is likely a proxy for family wealth—thus further supporting wealth as an important determinant of giving. Similar to other researchers, Monk also finds a very significant relationship between satisfaction with the undergraduate institution and later giving.

In a 2001 study, Phanindra V. Wunnava and Michael Lauze analyze determinants of alumni giving at a small liberal arts college.[10]

Their study is interesting for our purposes because they include a variable that indicates whether a "RELATIVE" attended the school and find that there is a statistically significant positive relationship between giving and whether a relative attended the school. The authors do not discuss what mechanism may account for this; moreover, their model does not include any controls for wealth or income. As a result, like Clotfelter concluded for his own study, we believe that RELATIVE could simply be a proxy for family wealth. Moreover, it is not even clear whether the school studied by Wunnava and Lauze employed legacy preferences. Therefore, their findings cannot be interpreted as support for legacy preferences exerting an influence on alumni giving.

Data

The schools in our data-set are the top one hundred national universities as of August 27, 2007, according to *U.S. News and World Report*.[11] For each of these schools, we analyze data for the period 1998 through 2008. The data were gathered and assimilated through a variety of sources.

First, the Council for Aid to Education, which represents roughly a quarter of the four thousand colleges and universities in the United States, administers the annual Voluntary Support for Education (VSE) survey.[12] Each year the VSE collects and reports a multitude of information related to giving for each school such as alumni giving, athletic giving, corporate giving, religious organization giving, bequests and deferred gifts, property gifts, endowments, expenditures, and so on. This survey is entirely voluntary, but schools have an incentive to participate because it "provides an institution a structure for summarizing its fundraising results,"[13] allowing it to see where strengths and weaknesses are in fundraising and support to the institution, as well as the ability to benchmark itself against similar schools.

We also used data from the Integrated Postsecondary Education Data System (IPEDS), which gathers data from all institutions participating in federal student financial aid programs. Participation in the IPEDS survey is mandatory for the institution to continue participation in the federal programs. The data gathered by the IPEDS survey, for purposes of our analyses, primarily deal with Pell Grants and aid for students. The primary publisher of IPEDS data is the National Center for Education Statistics, which conducts the IPEDS survey and is a part of the U.S. Department of Education.

The IPEDS data are important because for each institution they allow use of Pell Grants per undergraduate as a proxy for the wealth of student families—an important determinant of giving often discussed but rarely measured in the previous literature. In order to qualify for the federal Pell Grant, a student must fill out the Free Application for Federal Student Aid (FAFSA) form. Current and prospective college students fill it out to determine their eligibility for federal student financial aid. The FAFSA asks a series of questions regarding the student's finances (and parents' if the student is a dependent) to determine his or her Expected Family Contribution (EFC). Some of the many factors that are used to determine the EFC are family income, family assets, household size, and the number of household members in college. The EFC will, ultimately, determine what type of federal financial aid (grant, loan, work study) a student is eligible for and the amount for which he or she is eligible.[14]

Previous research also has indicated income is an important determinant of alumni giving. Data on the salaries of alumni by school was gathered from PayScale.com. (PayScale.com data has been used extensively by outside researchers and news organizations such as *Forbes* magazine.[15]) The salaries in our analyses include base salary or hourly wage in addition to commissions, bonuses, overtime compensation, and profit sharing. We use the median salary reported by PayScale.com members who are considered mid-career or "full-time employees with at least 10 years of experience in their career or field who hold a Bachelor's degree and no higher degrees."[16] We chose to use the mid-career salary as opposed to starting salary because it is a better indicator of the financial resources the parents of alumni have if and when their children apply to college. We were able to identify the median mid-career salary for nearly 80 percent of the schools in our dataset. It is important to highlight that the income measure from PayScale.com is an indicator of the median income of the *entire alumni population,* while the wealth measure we have (Pell Grant per undergraduate) is of the *admitted student population.*

Data regarding legacy preferences for applicants was gathered a number of ways. First, we e-mailed the majority of schools inquiring about legacy preference directly.[17] We also consulted the Common Data Set (CDS) provided on each institution's website. The CDS initiative is "a collaborative effort among data providers in the higher education community and publishers as represented by the College Board, Peterson's, and *U.S. News & World Report*. The combined goal of this collaboration is to improve the quality and accuracy of information provided to all involved in a student's transition into higher education, as well as to reduce the reporting burden on data providers."[18] In addition to admission requirements data, the CDS also contains information and statistics on enrollment; transfer admissions and policies; academic offerings and policies; student life/activities; annual expenses; financial aid; faculty and class size; and degrees offered. One area of the survey requires institutions to rank the importance of various factors for admission, including alumni relations. The school must then mark one of: "not considered," "considered," "important," or "very important."[19]

In some instances, if a school did not have their CDS available for 2008, the data was taken from collegedata.com. Collegedata.com has a similarly structured chart also containing *alumni/ae relations* as a factor. To further verify their status on legacy preferences, we looked directly on the application provided on the institution's website, if it was provided online. If it asked whether or not the student was related to an alumnus, we considered that to be showing preference for legacy applicants.

In order for us to consider an institution to be applying legacy preferences, two sources had to agree that they did. If one source conflicted with the others, then we marked the indicator as missing. That is, if a school did not ask an applicant about her relation to alumni, and on their CDS they said that alumni relations were "considered," but replied in an e-mail to us that they did not have legacy preferences, we marked that as missing, since the CDS and the e-mail response conflicted.

Table 5.1 presents a distribution for variables relevant to our analysis. LEGPREF is an indicator variable for whether an institution employed legacy preferences in that year. LEGPREF has a mean value of 0.764, indicating that legacy preferences were applied for 76.4 percent of the SCHOOL-YEAR combinations in our data. Appendix 5.1 (see page 119) shows the list of schools with and without legacy preferences as of 2007. Private schools are much more likely to practice legacy preferences. Private schools make up 52.3 percent of the top one hundred universities, but 94 percent of those schools employ legacy preferences as opposed to 50 percent for public universities.

Table 5.1 Distribution of Relevant Variables

Variable	N	Mean	Std. Dev.	Min	Max	P10	P25	P50	P75	P90
GIVINGPERALUM	1,040	$265.35	$376.93	$4.83	$4,898.69	$36.71	$77.96	$145.03	$298.45	$577.76
LEGPREF	1,000	0.764	0.425	0	1	0	1	1	1	1
PGRANT_UG	984	$394.33	$208.59	$49.00	$1,400.00	$187.00	$250.50	$340.00	$475.50	$696.00
ALUMREC	1,099	160,247	107,666	12,089	532,923	42,227	77,869	129,890	223,486	324,271
CAREERSAL	946	97,076	13,501	74,600	134,000	82,700	85,900	95,200	106,000	116,000
PSOLIC	1,085	0.861	0.153	0.146	1.000	0.650	0.810	0.909	0.974	1.000
PUBLIC	1,166	0.462	0.499	0	1	0	0	0	1	1
SAT	711	1,266	106	1,040	1,525	1,140	1,185	1,245	1,335	1,425

TOTALALUMGIVING comes from the VSE data and represents the total alumni giving in each year.[20] This value is obviously greatly dependant on school size, therefore we either include a measure of the alumni population (ALUMREC) in our models or use GIVINGPERALUM, which is the ratio of the two variables.[21] Table 5.1 shows that the mean giving per alumni is $265 per year but that there is significant variance across schools since there are values as low as $4.83 and as high as $4,898.69 even within the top one hundred universities. Unconditional on any controls, schools with legacy preferences have a much higher giving per alumni ($317.14 versus $201.04).

Alumni giving also varies substantially between public and private institutions—giving per alumni is 221 percent[22] higher at private schools versus public schools. The reasons for this are not entirely clear, although one could speculate that public universities exhibit much more diversity in terms of socioeconomic status, are larger, and that public funding makes them less dependent on alumni giving. Whatever the reason, it is clear that PRIVATE/PUBLIC is an important determinant of alumni giving.

The VSE data includes an indicator of the number of alumni that were solicited for donation so we can measure the fraction (or probability) solicited (PSOLIC). Clearly we would expect schools that expend more resources soliciting their alumni to have higher giving after controlling for other factors. Table 5.1 shows that the average school solicits 86.1 percent of its alumni, but this ranges from 14.6 percent to 100 percent. While this measure is somewhat crude because it does not measure the intensity with which alums are solicited, it provides a good first-order measure of effort.

CAREERSAL measures the midlife median earnings for alumni of each school. The mean of this variable is roughly $97,000 and ranges from $74,600 to $134,000. This measure of income likely understates the disparities in earnings across schools. First, it is a median measure of income, which necessarily lessens the influence of outliers. Second, the economic literature clearly documents that the distribution of earnings exhibits a long right hand tail. As a telling example, there was a recent report that Harvard has more than double the number of billionaires as its next closest rival.[23] More detailed alumni earnings measures would likely increase the explanatory power of our models.

PGRANT_UG measures the amount of Pell Grants per undergraduate. Pell Grants, as explained earlier, are provided based on need, and overall family wealth is considered in the application process. Therefore, PGRANT_UG serves as an important proxy for wealth. Table 5.1 shows that the average Pell Grant per undergraduate is $394, with a range of $49 (Harvard University) to $1,400 (Howard University). These statistics demonstrate the remarkable range of family wealth of admitted students across institutions.

Our proxy for family wealth is highly negatively correlated with legacy preferences. The average Pell Grant per undergraduate for institutions with legacy preferences is $329, while the same figure for institutions without legacy preferences is $559. Thus, students at non-legacy preference institutions qualify for almost 70 percent more in government grants than those at legacy preference institutions.

Finally, SAT measures the midpoint of the 25th and 75th percentile of SAT score for each school.[24] The average SAT across schools is 1266 and the range is from 1040 (University of California–Riverside) to 1525 (California Institute of Technology). The average SAT is higher for legacy preference schools (1295) than for non-legacy preference schools (1202). It is interesting to note, however, that this difference reverses and is insignificant after controlling for PUBLIC/PRIVATE.

Description of Models and Results

In the statistical models we employ to analyze the relationship between legacy preference policies and alumni donations, we control for a number of school characteristics (size, public/private, alumni solicited), year, characteristics of the total alumni population (income), and characteristics of the admitted population (wealth).

We use multiple ordinary least squares regression with the log of TOTALALUMGIVING as the dependent variable.[25] Since we have panel data with each institution appearing multiple times in the dataset, we cluster by institution to obtain robust standard errors. Table 5.2 provides the formal results.

Table 5.2 OLS Regression Analysis Testing the Claim that Legacy Preferences Increase Aggregate Giving by Alumni (control for wealth removed)

lnTOTAL ALUMGIVING	β	Robust Std. Err.	t-stat
LEGPREF	0.058	0.201	0.29
PGRANT_UG	-0.002	0.000	-3.16**
lnNALUMREC	1.067	0.112	9.54**
CAREERSAL	0.000	0.000	-1.70
CAREERSAL^2	0.000	0.000	2.48*
PSOLIC	0.993	0.326	3.05**
PUBLIC	-0.179	0.184	-0.97
1998	-0.200	0.094	-2.12*
1999	-0.072	0.077	-0.94
2000	-0.039	0.072	-0.55
2001	-	-	-
2002	-0.130	0.074	-1.76
2003	-0.082	0.090	-0.91
2004	-0.056	0.085	-0.67
2005	0.018	0.095	0.19
2006	0.148	0.093	1.58
2007	0.139	0.094	1.47
2008	-	-	-
_CONS	7.410	3.871	1.91
R^2:	0.721		
N:	669		

* Robust standard errors were used in order to account for clustering and correlation of the error term.
* p <= .05
** p <= .01

The first thing to note is that the coefficient on LEGPREF is slightly positive (0.058), but statistically insignificant (t-stat=.29). This indicates that after controlling for the other factors in the model, the presence of a legacy preference policy does not have a statistically significant impact on alumni donations. Using the point estimate of 5.8 percent and the mean value of giving per alumni ($265.35), it would imply that schools with legacy preference policies collect, on average, only $15.39 more per alumni than non-legacy preference schools after the relevant controls. This $15.39 per alumni is sufficiently small that we cannot reject simple randomness as the cause.

The other variables have the expected signs and the adjusted R-square is quite high at 0.72—indicating that our independent variables can explain 72 percent of the variation in alumni giving across schools and time. We would expect the coefficient on size (lnNALUMREC) to be close to one. In other words, for every one percentage point rise in size of institution, there is a one percentage point increase in alumni giving. The coefficient is 1.06, and we cannot reject the null hypothesis the true parameter is different from one.

Our measure of family wealth within the admitted student population (PGRANT_UG) is statistically significant and has the expected negative sign (Pell Grants are inversely related to wealth). Consistent with other studies, we include linear and quadratic terms for income (CAREERSAL and CAREERSAL2). Inclusion of each variable adds explanatory power. The insignificance of LEGPREF is not influenced by inclusion or exclusion of quadratics for PGRANT_UG or CAREERSAL.

As expected, the rate of solicitations (PSOLIC) is positively related to giving and is statistically significant. The coefficient of 0.996 implies that, at the margin, increasing the number of alumni solicited by 1 percent increases alumni giving by 1 percent. PUBLIC is negative as expected, but is not statistically significant. It is possible that the size and wealth variables account for the true underlying factors causing PUBLIC/PRIVATE differences in giving. We also include a set of YEAR dummies which are generally increasing over time, except for the post-recession year of 2002.

SAT is available for just slightly more than half the observations; therefore, we do not include it in Table 5.2. Running a separate regression that includes SAT shows it is significant and positive, but it has no influence on the LEGPREF coefficient.

In summary, after controlling for a reasonably narrow and intuitive set of factors, there is no evidence that legacy preference policies themselves exert an influence on giving behavior.

The more insidious result masked by Table 5.2 is the importance of wealth in explaining the coefficient on legacy preferences. Table 5.3 shows the same regressions but removes the wealth variable.

Table 5.3 OLS Regression Analysis Testing the Claim that Legacy Preferences Increase Aggregate Giving (control for wealth removed)

lnTOTAL ALUMGIVING	β	Robust Std. Err.	t-stat
LEGPREF	0.357	0.217	1.64
lnNALUMREC	1.084	0.114	9.48**
CAREERSAL	0.000	0.000	-1.33
CAREERSAL^2	0.000	0.000	2.04*
PSOLIC	0.951	0.326	2.92**
PUBLIC	-0.271	0.201	-1.35
1998	-0.042	0.064	-0.66
1999	-	-	-
2000	0.095	0.047	2.04*
2001	0.108	0.057	1.88
2002	-0.090	0.066	-1.35
2003	-0.121	0.055	-2.22*
2004	-0.102	0.062	-1.66
2005	-0.036	0.062	-0.59
2006	0.135	0.075	1.79
2007	0.126	0.065	1.96
2008	0.187	0.083	2.26*
_CONS	5.898	4.383	1.35
R^2:	0.68		
N:	807		

* Robust standard errors were used in order to account for clustering and correlation of the error term.
* p <= .05
** p <= .01

The coefficient on LEGPREF in this regression is a positive 0.357 and statistically significant at the 10 percent level. The coefficient of 0.357 implies that schools with legacy preferences, on average, have 35.7 percent higher alumni giving than non-legacy preference schools before controlling for wealth. What does this tell us? This suggests that schools with legacy preferences have higher alumni giving, but it can be explained entirely by the wealth of their *admitted* students. The fact that legacy preference schools, on average and holding all else equal, have wealthier admitted students is consistent with the notion that elite schools achieve higher giving simply by selecting disproportionately from families of their own wealthy alumni—not that giving legacy preferences somehow changes giving behavior.

To make this point abundantly clear, take two elite schools and assume that they are comparable in all relevant ways, including the demographics of their applicant pools. If admission were based purely on merit, we would expect the resulting student populations to be similar in terms of ability, income, and wealth. Now assume one of the schools has a legacy preference policy and that its own alums (because they are graduates of an elite institution) have higher income and wealth than the general population. By giving preference to and selecting a disproportionate number of applicants from alumni families, the legacy preference school will have higher wealth families (and thus donations). Thus, it is not that these elite institutions are simply lucky enough to have wealthier families in their student body. Instead, the preference policy itself allows, contributes to, and perpetuates over-selection from the upper class. Once we control for whatever wealth differences there are (whether endogenous to the selection process or exogenous to the applicant pool), there is no evidence suggesting legacy preference policies contribute to greater giving.

What does this imply about the impact of abolishing legacy preferences? Would it have an immediate deleterious impact on the finances of elite institutions because they would start selecting from "poorer" populations? While our models certainly suggest that abolishing legacy preferences would have an effect on the elite institutions as a result of selecting from less wealthy populations and rejecting more of their alumni's children, this impact would occur over a long time horizon. Consider the impact of admitting a less wealthy student populace in 2011. This would only change the demographics of one class out of the many legacy classes. In other words, it would take a generation or more for the full impact to be felt. This at least partially explains why Shadowen, Tulante, and Alpern find no immediate impact of changing legacy preference policies at certain schools.[26]

To explore this notion, we empirically test whether we observe a significant change in alumni giving for schools that have given up legacy preferences during the time period covered by our data. The procedure we employ is to create a dichotomous variable (LEGPREF_DROPPED) that is set to one in each year after a school dropped legacy preferences and zero otherwise. We then estimate a model of lnTOTALALUMGIVING that controls for LEGPREF_DROPPED, size, income, wealth, solicitation percentage, public/private, year, and school.[27] If the change in legacy preference policy caused a reduction in alumni giving, then we would expect to observe a negative coefficient for LEGPREF_DROPPED. The results of this regression are summarized in Table 5.4 and show the coefficient on LEGPREF_DROPPED is slightly positive and statistically insignificant. Unsurprisingly, the model suggests there is no short-term measurable reduction in alumni giving as a result of abolishing legacy preferences.[28]

Moreover, any loss in alumni giving at the elite institutions would presumably be at least partially, if not fully, offset by additional giving to alternative institutions where parents of wealthy students might donate as an alternative, and the wealthy students themselves would become alumni.

The importance of alumni giving should also be placed in the context of the total financial resources of the top one hundred universities. We constructed a variable called BUDGET_FRACTION which represents annual alumni giving as a fraction of annual total expenditures.[29] The mean of BUDGET_FRACTION in our data-set is 0.051 and the median is 0.035. This suggests that alumni donations make up roughly 5.1 percent of total expenditures on average and it is only 3.5 percent for the median institution. The ninety-fifth percentile is 14.8 percent. Therefore, while there is no denying that alumni donations play a significant and important role in funding higher education, once one combines the lack of empirical evidence that legacy preference policies play a substantial role in total giving with the fact that alumni donations make up a relatively small fraction of expenditures for the vast majority of institutions, it is difficult to see how the abolition of legacy preferences would have a major deleterious impact on the funding of higher education.[30]

Table 5.4 OLS Regression Analysis Testing the Claim that Ceasing the Practice of Legacy Preferences Results in Lower Aggregate Giving by Alumni

lnTOTAL ALUMGIVING	β	Robust Std. Err.	t-stat
LEGPREF_DROPPED	0.042	0.134	0.32
PGRANT_UG	0.000	0.000	-0.23
lnNALUMREC	0.208	0.161	1.29
CAREERSAL	0.000	0.000	1.11
CAREERSAL^2	0.000	0.000	0.02
PSOLIC	-0.026	0.170	-0.16
PUBLIC	0.562	0.219	2.57*
1998	-0.236	0.069	-3.4**
1999	-0.132	0.057	-2.32*
2000	-0.025	0.053	-0.47
2001	–	–	–
2002	-0.169	0.063	-2.68**
2003	-0.154	0.069	-2.22*
2004	-0.122	0.065	-1.87
2005	-0.005	0.070	-0.08
2006	0.151	0.074	2.03*
2007	0.176	0.067	2.62*
2008	–	–	–
_CONS	11.276	1.555	7.25**
78 categories absorbed for ID			
R^2:	0.943		
N:	669		

* Robust standard errors were used in order to account for clustering and correlation of the error term.

* $p <= .05$

** $p <= .01$

Conclusion

Our findings cast serious doubt on the financial justification for legacy preference policies. Using an OLS regression model with controls for size, public/private, income, wealth, year, and fraction of alumni solicited, we show that the presence of legacy preference policies does not result in significantly higher alumni giving. Moreover, we show that prior to controlling for wealth, there is a strong correlation between alumni giving and legacy preferences. This suggests that greater alumni giving at elite schools with legacy preferences is driven by the school's ability to over-select from their own wealthy alumni populations—not a result of the preference policies themselves inducing additional giving.

Appendix 5.1
Legacy Preference Status as of 2007

Schools with Legacy Preferences	Schools without Legacy Preferences
Auburn University	Brigham Young University
Baylor University	California Institute of Technology
Boston College	Colorado School of Mines
Boston University	Georgia Institute of Technology*
Brandeis University	Iowa State University
Brown University	Ohio State University
Carnegie-Mellon University	Rutgers University
Case Western Reserve University	Texas A&M University*
Clemson University	University of Arizona *
College of William and Mary	University of California, Berkeley*
Columbia University	University of California, Davis*
Cornell University	University of California Irvine*
Dartmouth College	University of California, Los Angeles*
Duke University	University of California, Riverside*
Emory University	University of California, San Diego*
Fordham University	University of California, Santa Barbara*
George Washington University	University of California, Santa Cruz*
Georgetown University	University of Georgia*
Harvard University	University of Iowa*
Indiana University	University of Kansas

Continued on next page

Schools with Legacy Preferences	Schools without Legacy Preferences
Johns Hopkins University	University of Massachusetts, Amherst*
Lehigh University	University of Nebraska, Lincoln*
Marquette University	University of Pittsburgh
Massachusetts Institute of Technology	University of Texas at Austin
Miami University	Vanderbilt University**
New York University	
North Carolina State University at Raleigh	
Northeastern University	
Northwestern University	
Pennsylvania State University	
Pepperdine University	
Princeton University	
Purdue University	
Rensselaer Polytechnic Institute	
Rice University	
Southern Methodist University	
Stanford University	
Stevens Institute of Technology	
Syracuse University	
Tufts University	
Tulane University	
University of Alabama	
University of Chicago	
University of Colorado	
University of Connecticut	
University of Delaware	
University of Florida	

Schools with Legacy Preferences	**Schools without Legacy Preferences**
University of Illinois—Urbana-Champaign	
University of Maryland College Park	
University of Miami	
University of Michigan	
University of Minnesota	
University of North Carolina at Chapel Hill	
University of Notre Dame	
University of Pennsylvania	
University of Rochester	
University of Southern California	
University of Tennessee	
University of the Pacific	
University of Vermont	
University of Virginia	
University of Washington	
University of Wisconsin	
Virginia Polytechnic Institute	
Washington University	
Worcester Polytechnic Institute	
Yale University	

*Denotes change in legacy preference policy over the time span our study encompassed. For the University of Nebraska in particular, although it asks applicants for information about their parents' college, the evidence nevertheless suggests that the university does not use legacy preference.

** Our evidence suggests Vanderbilt originally had legacy preferences and then dropped them. Recent evidence that post-dates the time period of study suggests they now employ legacy preferences.

The legacy preference information was not available for the following schools: American University, Clark University, Howard University, Illinois Institute of Technology, Michigan State University, Saint Louis University, SUNY-Binghamton, SUNY-College of Environmental Science–Forestry, SUNY-Stony Brook, University of Denver, University of Missouri-Columbia, University of Tulsa, Wake Forest University, Yeshiva University.

6

Admitting the Truth: The Effect of Affirmative Action, Legacy Preferences, and the Meritocratic Ideal on Students of Color in College Admissions

John Brittain and Eric L. Bloom

In 2004, the *Economist* blasted America for its frequent departures from the meritocratic ideal of the Founding Fathers. Despite their vision of a society that embodies the spirit of meritocracy where all people are judged not on their progenitors but upon their individual abilities, the editors opined, modern Americans frequently overlook departures from that ideal. They went on to note that, "[t]he biggest insult to meritocracy . . . is found in the country's top universities. These institutions, which control access to the country's most impressive jobs, consider themselves far above Washington and its grubby spoils system. Yet they continue to operate a system of 'legacy preferences'—affirmative action for the children of alumni."[1]

At many elite post-secondary educational institutions, applicants with an alumni parent are accepted at two to three times the rate of those without, leading one commentator to label legacy preferences as "[t]he largest affirmative action program in American higher education. . . ."[2] In the early 1990s, more students gained admission to Harvard pursuant to preferences granted to the children of alumni than the total number of black, Hispanic, and American-Indian students combined.[3] Michael Dannenberg, the director of the Education Policy Program at the New America Foundation, has noted, "There are more white students admitted to top ten universities after having benefited from a legacy preference than African-American or Latino students admitted after having benefited from affirmative action policies. In some elite institutions of higher education, there are more white legacy students than African-American and Latino students combined."[4]

The special advantages bestowed upon them—whether by formal policy or by informal but equally effective means—insulates legatees from full competition with other applicants. And this advantage becomes increasingly important as intensified competition drives overall post-secondary admission rates lower.[5] A record number of graduating high school seniors—3.3 million in 2009—are heading off to college, just as some colleges and universities are capping or even rolling back enrollment.[6] The increase in applicants and reduction in available slots allows admission officers to become increasingly selective. Given these figures, it is not surprising that the number of students attending their first-choice college continued a recent decline, dropping from 63.9 percent in 2007 to a thirty-four-year low of 60.7 percent in 2008.[7]

Recent research shows that three out of four top national universities and more than nine of the nation's ten best liberal arts colleges currently grant legacy preference, which gives an advantage to alumni children equivalent to an extra 23 to 160 SAT points (on a 1600-point scale) at elite universities.[8] In many cases, they need the leg up. As the *Journal of Blacks in Higher Education* noted: "In recent years, legacy admits at Harvard had average SAT scores thirty-five points below those of non-legacies, lower grade point averages, and fewer extracurricular activities in high school than other admitted students."[9] An example that was well-publicized in 2000 involved then-presidential candidate George W. Bush, son of the forty-first president of the United States, a Yale graduate, and a grandson of a U.S. senator who himself was a Yale graduate and Yale trustee. George W. Bush's SAT scores (printed during the 2000 presidential campaign by the *New Yorker*) were 566 verbal and 640 math, 180 points below the median scores for students admitted to his class.[10] Other research concludes that legacies are similarly less qualified than their peers and, once admitted, perform poorly (at least initially) compared to their freshman peers.[11]

Despite this, the *Wall Street Journal* reported that in 2002 legacies were admitted at nearly twice the rate of other applicants at the University of Pennsylvania, three times the rate of other applicants at Princeton, and nearly four times the rate of other applicants at Harvard.[12] At those elite schools that grant preferences, legatees represent 10 to 15 percent of admitted students; conversely, at California Institute of Technology, which grants no preferences, they make up only 1.5 percent of admitted students.[13]

Media reports over the past decade indicate that:

- at the University of Chicago, as many as one in twenty-five students is a legacy;[14]
- at Northwestern, one in ten new students in 2003 was a legacy;[15]
- at Notre Dame, legatees make up one-quarter of students accepted;[16]
- at Dartmouth, which admitted only 13.2 percent of its applicants in 2008, legatees enjoy an acceptance rate consistently 2 to 2½ times higher than that, with 164 children of alumni accepted in 2008, the highest total in five years;[17]
- at Middlebury College, which admitted only 18 percent of applicants in 2008, a record low, its legacy acceptance rate that same year was almost 50 percent; and
- at Bowdoin College, which admitted only about 18 percent of applicants in 2008, the legacy admission rate has hovered above 40 percent in recent years.[18]

The precise definition of legacies has ebbed and flowed over time. The University of Virginia, for example, historically defined a legacy as the child of any student who had been enrolled at the university, regardless of degree status.[19] In 1979, the university's Admissions Policy Committee formalized its definition of "legacy" to exclude the stepchildren and grandchildren of alumni; moreover, the school restricted legacy designation to the children of degree recipients.[20] The University of Virginia has since retreated from its 1979 reforms and now awards legacy status to alumni stepchildren.[21] The University of Pennsylvania considers parents and grandparents for legacy status.[22] Duke University considers as legatees those applicants with parents, grandparents, or siblings who have attended or are attending Duke.[23]

The applications of legacy candidates are processed differently at different institutions. Until abolishing its legacy preference program in 2004, Texas A&M gave legacy status to children, grandchildren, and siblings of school alumni, providing legatees four points on a 100-point scale.[24] Similarly, the University of Michigan had a 150-point "Selection Index" for undergraduates, with 100 points usually enough to get in. The university awarded a four-point bonus to children and stepchildren of alumni, or one point to grandchildren, spouses, or siblings of alumni.[25]

Private colleges tend to couch the assessment of legacies in the context of a "holistic" review of an applicant's file. For example, the Brown University admissions website states that legacy candidates are held to high standards, but admits they are given a preference: "All other things being equal, qualified applicants from families that have a relationship with Brown may be at a slight advantage." Brown considers not only the legacy statues of the applicant but also "the degree to which the applicant's alumni relatives have remained active with Brown affairs." Thus, a Brown official conceded, "certain applications will stand out if a parent has maintained a relationship with Brown through activities like interviewing applicants." Brown feels a sense of loyalty to the children of individuals who have served Brown after their graduation; therefore, upon reviewing the application of a loyal alumni's legacy, as an assistant dean of admissions acknowledged, "I would definitely take an extra special look at that student."[26]

The Effect of Legacy Preferences on Students of Color

How do legacy preferences affect students of color? For the most part, legacy preferences are "proxies for privilege" as they favor children of white, well educated, presumably affluent families.[27] As of 1995, some estimated that an astounding "96 percent of all living Ivy League alumni [were] white."[28] This is so because the majority of students who benefited from integration began attending selective colleges and universities only in the 1960s and 1970s.[29] "Thus, for many years, admissions policies favoring children of alumni have provided an advantage to students from non-minority, non-immigrant families," as the "'established white admissions advantage replicates itself' through policies that favor children of alumni because the overwhelming majority of alumni from elite colleges and universities are white."[30] (See Figure 6.1.) Duke University researchers recently concluded that legacies "largely represent constituencies that monopolized higher education at the beginning of the twentieth-century: affluent white Protestants."[31]

Although legacy students are becoming more diverse, only 7.6 percent of legacy applicants accepted at Harvard in 2002 "were black, Hispanic or Native American, compared with 17.8% of all successful applicants."[32] "In fact, the number of legacy admits in the freshman classes at the nation's most prestigious colleges and universities is usually three or four times the number of the entire cadre of black students at the school."[33] In 2002, for example, Texas A&M, a school that has since abolished its legacy admissions policy, enrolled among 10,291 incoming freshmen: 321 white students via legacy preference who otherwise would not have been admitted, but only 3 black and 25 Hispanic legacies.[34] During the same year at the University of Virginia, 91 percent of legacy applicants accepted on an early-decision basis were white; 1.6 percent were black, 0.5 percent were Hispanic, and 1.6 percent were Asian.[35]

Even after a generation of affirmative action, underrepresented minorities remain underrepresented, which suggests that the negative effect of legacy preferences on students of color is likely to continue far into the future. A 2008 study by the American Council on

Figure 6.1. Under-Represented Minority Proportions of National Applicant Pool, Legacy Pool, and U.S. Population (2005)

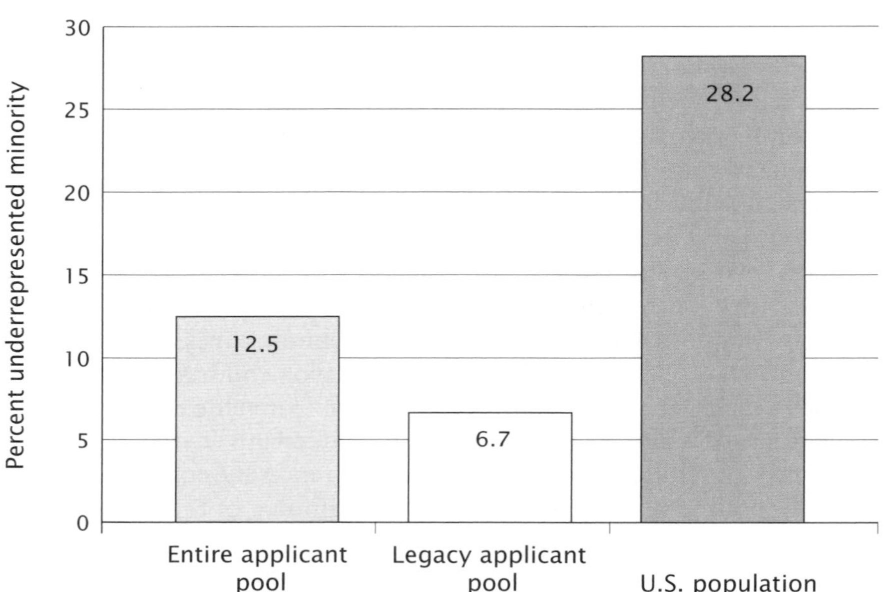

Source: William G. Bowen, Martin A. Kurzweil, and Eugene M. Tobin, *Equity and Excellence in American Higher Education* (Charlottesville: University of Virginia Press, 2005), 168 (underrepresented minority proportion of entire and legacy applicant pools); applicant pool data from all eighteen national schools for which authors had legacy data. U.S. Census Bureau, Population Division, Population Estimates Program, Vintage 2005, July 1, 2005 (underrepresented minority proportion of U.S. population).

Education (ACE), in fact, concludes that the trend of each succeeding generation in the United States attaining higher levels of education than the previous generation "appears to have stalled, and for far too many people of color, the percentage of young adults with some type of postsecondary degree compared with older adults has actually fallen." "It appears we are at a tipping point in our nation's history," said ACE president Molly Corbett Broad. "One of the core tenets of the American dream is the hope that younger generations, who've had greater opportunities for educational advancement than their parents and grandparents, will be better off than the generations before them, yet this report shows that aspiration is at serious risk."[36]

In its 2009 study, *State of College Admission,* the National Association for College Admission Counseling reported that as of 2007, "black and Hispanic persons constituted approximately 32 percent of the traditional college-aged population, but they represented only about 25 percent of students enrolled in postsecondary education."[37] Minority enrollment at four-year schools is even lower: blacks comprised 15.1 percent of the college-age population but only 11.2 percent of the enrollment at four-year public colleges and only 14.3 percent at four-year private colleges.[38] Hispanics comprised 17.3 percent of the college-age population but only 9.3 percent of the enrollment at four-year public colleges and only 7.6 percent at four-year private colleges.[39]

This underrepresentation is even more pronounced at selective institutions: in 2008, blacks accounted for just over 5 percent (instead of the expected 15.1 percent) of the enrollment at the top fifty colleges as ranked by *U.S. News & World Report.* Hispanics accounted for only 7 percent (instead of the expected 17.3 percent) of the enrollment. A look at the raw numbers is instructive: in 2008, just over one million (1,020,648, to be precise) students were enrolled in the nation's fifty most selective colleges (so deemed by *U.S. News & World Report*). If enrollment at these schools mirrored the racial mix of the population of students of college age, one would have expected to find 330,690 Hispanic or black students. But only 122,671 were enrolled.[40] (See Figure 6.2.)

But the problem is not limited to elite, private institutions; in fact, in many states, the selective private university is more diverse than its in-state public counterpart: according to a study published in 2010 by the Education Trust, twenty-two states have both a public flagship and a private university ranked in the top half of the *U.S. News & World Report* list of "national universities." The study found that in fifteen of those twenty-two states, "the top-ranked private institutions enrolled a higher proportion of minority students than the public flagship."[41] This flies in the face of the very purpose of public higher education as "an engine of social mobility."[42]

As the Education Trust has noted,

> Public higher education has a rich, proud tradition of serving as an engine of social mobility, and generations of striving Americans have long aspired to attend its institutions. State flagships sit atop this pyramid of opportunity, offering the hope that students from humble origins can learn alongside talented students from all backgrounds. This was America's promise: work hard, excel in school and you, too, could follow your dreams into your state's flagship university. Over time, however, that compact has been broken, and in its place has come something quite different: the relentless pursuit not of expanded opportunity, but of increased selectivity.[43]

These elite institutions' increased selectivity heightens the contrast between an applicant's qualifications and the institutional standards of admission. Race-sensitive admissions are used at most selective universities in the country.[44] In response to opponents of these admissionpolicies, Justice Ginsburg noted, "The rallying cry that in the absence of racial discrimination in admissions there would be a true meritocracy ignores the fact that the entire process is poisoned by numerous exceptions to 'merit.'" She pointed out that legacy preferences and other exceptions "to a 'true' meritocracy give the lie to protestations that merit admissions are in fact the order of the day at the Nation's universities."[45] But beneficiaries of affirmative action based on race are likely perceived much differently then beneficiaries of legacy preferences—and affirmative action does not offset the inequity of legacy preferences.

In *Brown* v. *Board of Education,* the Supreme Court reasoned that the racial segregation of African-American schoolchildren "generates a feeling of inferiority as to their status in the community that may affect their hearts and minds in a way unlikely ever to be undone."[46] That stigmatizing injury and the denial of equal opportunities that accompanies it, "deprives persons of their individual dignity and denies society the benefits of wide participation in political, economic, and cultural life."[47]

Affirmative action itself, of course, also imposes stigma harms.[48] As Justice Douglas noted in 1974, "A segregated admissions process can also create a suggestion of stigma and caste no less than a segregated classroom, and in the end it may produce that result despite its contrary intentions." He explained that such

Figure 6.2 Expected versus Actual Black and Hispanic Enrollment at Elite Colleges in 2008

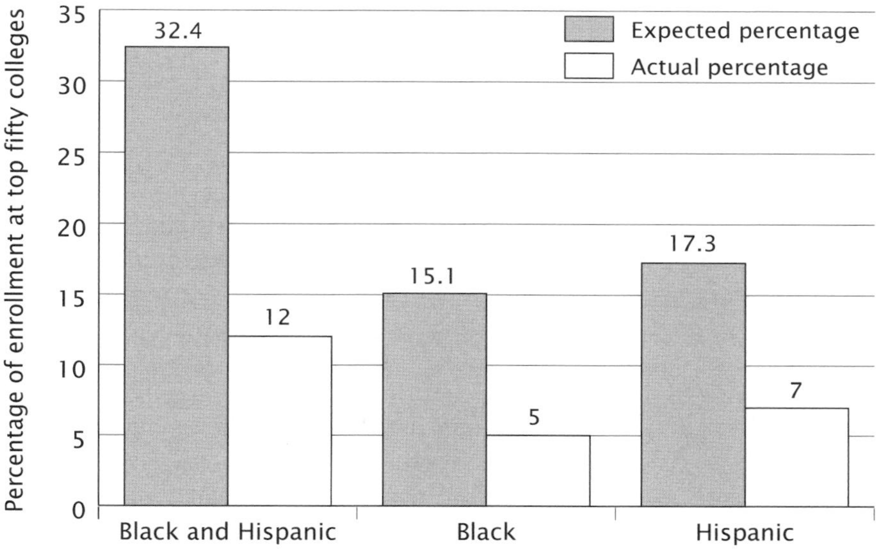

Note: Expected proportion is based on the demographic group's proportion of the traditional college-aged population. The "Top 50 Colleges" refer to the fifty national universities ranked highest by *U.S. News & World Report.*

Source: U.S. Department of Education, National Center for Education Statistics, IPEDS Peer Analysis System, 2008 Four-year, Not-for-profit and Public, Degree-Granting, Title-IV Participating Institutions; *U.S. News & World Report: Best Colleges 2008*; U.S. Department of Education, National Center for Education Statistics, *Digest of Education Statistics 2008*, Table 227.

a process is premised on the assumption "that blacks or browns cannot make it on their individual merit" and thereby places "a stamp of inferiority" on these students.[49]

There is no similar stigma attendant to legacy status, however. While both legacy-based and race-based affirmative action are exceptions to the paragon of meritocracy, "preferences for legacies do not inspire the same degree of animus as preferences based on race," perhaps because "class-based animus is less prevalent than racial animus in the United States."[50] So, although legatees in a given admission class might outnumber the population of black students at the school by a four to one ratio,[51] "preferences based on wealth and influence are covert"[52]; therefore, it is much easier to pick out the potential recipients of affirmative action racial preferences than of legacy preferences at the freshman matriculation ceremony.

Clearly, affirmative action does not offset legacy preference: the use of legacy preference, in fact, requires college admission officers to rely more heavily on affirmative action to attempt to ensure a diverse student population. Legacy-based affirmative action, therefore, may compound the stigma of race-based affirmative action. And even worse, public universities in three states continue to grant legacy preferences even though they no longer give preferences to racial minorities.[53]

Comparing and Contrasting Legacy Preferences with Affirmative Action

Although legacy preferences and race-based affirmative action are often lumped together as deviations from "merit," the justifications for each set of preferences are markedly different.

Race-conscious remedies explicitly utilize race to remedy both individual and systemic forms of discrimination. One of the fundamental purposes of the Civil War amendments was to raise African Americans "from that condition of inferiority and servitude in which most of them had previously stood, into perfect equality of civil rights with all other persons within the jurisdiction of the States. They were intended to take away all possibility of oppression by law because of race or color."[54] Thus, the Fourteenth Amendment provides, in relevant part, "No State shall . . . deny to any person within its jurisdiction the equal protection of the laws."[55]

Reconstruction Congresses utilized race-conscious remedies in passing myriad race-conscious statutes, including efforts to integrate schools.[56] Less than a year after passing the Fourteenth Amendment, for example, in an effort to establish an integrated higher education institution in Washington, Congress passed a charter incorporating Howard University.[57] "Congress considered such race-conscious means wholly permissible, and often necessary, to build a society without 'caste'—a society that was 'color-blind' in the sense that it allowed 'no superior, dominant, ruling class of citizens.'"[58]

Similarly, race-based affirmative action policies have been used in college admissions since the late 1960s as a way of remedying past discrimination against racial minorities and promoting the educational benefits of a diverse student body. In assessing the admissions practices that utilize classifications based on race or on national origin, the school bears the burden of demonstrating that its admissions policy serves a compelling governmental interest and is narrowly tailored to the achievement of that goal.[59]

In *Regents of the University of California* v. *Bakke*, a 1978 case challenging affirmative action, four members of the Supreme Court—Justices Brennan, White, Marshall, and Blackmun—found the University of California at Davis (UC–Davis) Medical School's admissions program lawful under both Title VI and the Constitution. Their reasoning was that government entities can adopt race-conscious policies to overcome the present effects of their own past discrimination or of societal discrimination, if the program is reasonable in light of this objective and does not stigmatize any group or disadvantage groups relatively unrepresented in the political process.[60]

Justice Powell, the swing vote on the Court, rejected efforts to combat societal discrimination as a rationale for affirmative action but found that the object of attaining a diverse student body "clearly is a constitutionally permissible goal for an institution of higher education. Academic freedom, though not a specifically enumerated constitutional right, long has been viewed as a special concern of the First Amendment."[61] Justice Powell noted that a university seeks "to provide that atmosphere which is most conducive to speculation, experiment and creation."[62]

The Court found diversity a compelling state interest: "An otherwise qualified medical student with a particular background—whether it be ethnic, geographic, culturally advantaged or disadvantaged—may bring to a professional school of medicine experiences, outlooks, and ideas that enrich the training of its student body and better equip its graduates to render with understanding their vital service to humanity."[63] Despite this, the Court rejected UC–Davis's argument that reserving a specified number of seats in each class for individuals from the preferred group is the only effective means of serving the interest of diversity. The Court characterized this approach as "seriously flawed" because "the diversity that furthers a compelling state interest encompasses a far broader array of qualifications and characteristics of which racial or ethnic origin is but a single though important element."[64] The Court pointed to Harvard's admission standards[65] as an example: "In recent years Harvard College has expanded the concept of diversity to include students from disadvantaged economic, racial and ethnic groups. Harvard College now recruits not only Californians or Louisianans but also blacks and Chicanos and other minority students."[66] In such an admissions program, Justice Powell wrote, "race or ethnic background may be deemed a 'plus' in a particular applicant's file, yet it does not insulate the individual from comparison with all other candidates for the available seats."[67]

Justice Powell explained that the file of a particular applicant may be examined for qualities more likely than race or ethnicity to promote beneficial educational pluralism: "Such qualities could include exceptional personal talents, unique work or service experience, leadership potential, maturity, demonstrated compassion, a history of overcoming disadvantage, ability to communicate with the poor, or other qualifications deemed important" in any given year, depending upon the "mix" both of the student body and the applicants for the incoming class.[68]

Because *Bakke* was a 4–1–4 decision, the precise holding of which was the subject of much debate, and perhaps because the Supreme Court grew more conservative in the intervening two decades, opponents of affirmative action subsequently challenged racial preference policies in a number of cases, including two involving the University of Michigan. In 2003, the Supreme Court in *Grutter* v. *Bollinger*[69] upheld the use of race in admission decisions by the University of Michigan Law School; however, the Court simultaneously struck down as unconstitutional the university's undergraduate affirmative action program in *Gratz* v. *Bollinger*.[70]

In the Michigan Law School case, in a 5–4 vote, the Supreme Court endorsed Justice Powell's view that student body diversity is a compelling state interest that can justify the use of race in university admissions.[71] The majority deferred to the law school's educational judgment that diversity is essential to its educational mission, as it promotes cross-racial understanding, promotes learning outcomes, and better prepares students for an increasingly diverse workforce and society.[72] The Court found diversity particularly important in legal education, "so that all members of our heterogeneous society may participate in the educational institutions that provide the training and education necessary to succeed in America.[73]

Having found a compelling state interest, the Court turned to whether the admissions program was narrowly tailored and was "flexible enough to consider all pertinent elements of diversity in light of the particular qualifications of each applicant, and to place them on the same footing for consideration, although not necessarily according them the same weight."[74] The Court found that the Michigan Law School's admissions program bore the hallmarks of a narrowly tailored plan in that it used race in a flexible, non-mechanical way; it did not establish quotas for members of certain racial groups or put members of those groups on separate admission tracks; and it did not insulate applicants who belong to certain racial or ethnic groups from the competition for admission.[75] "So long as a race-conscious admissions program uses race as a 'plus' factor in the context of individualized consideration," concluded the Court, "a rejected applicant 'will not have been foreclosed from all consideration for that seat simply because he was not the right color or had the wrong surname . . . . His qualifications would have been weighed fairly and competitively, and he would have no basis to complain of unequal treatment under the Fourteenth Amendment.'"[76] The Court concluded, "We expect that 25 years from now, the use of the racial preferences will no longer be necessary to further the interest approved today."[77]

In *Gratz*[78] the undergraduate case, by contrast, the Supreme Court reached the opposite conclusion it reached in *Grutter*. Unlike the Michigan Law School, the undergraduate admissions office used a "selection index," on which an applicant could score a maximum of 150 points; the system automatically awarded every applicant from an underrepresented racial or ethnic minority group 20 of the 100 points required to guarantee admission.[79] The Court invalidated as not "narrowly tailored" an admissions policy that automatically distributed 20 percent of the points needed to guarantee admission to every single underrepresented minority applicant solely because of the applicant's race.[80]

While race-based affirmative action barely has hung on by a 5–4 majority, the policy and legal arguments in favor of ancestry-based affirmative action—legacy preferences—are much weaker.

First, legacy preferences are not aimed at remedying historical discrimination; conversely, in fact, the origins of the practice were clearly discriminatory. If affirmative action is aimed at opening the doors to excluded minorities, legacy preferences were designed to slam those doors shut. The notion of "selectivity" in post-secondary education is recent: in 1920 only about a dozen elite American colleges and universities turned away any applicants and as late as 1951, Stanford admitted 85 percent of all who applied.[81]

Preferences for children of alumni find their origin in the 1920s, a result of anti-Semitism and xenophobia at Harvard, Yale, and Princeton, which attempted to stem an influx of the "wrong" types of students.[82] At the turn of the twentieth century, "Harvard College adopted the College Entrance Examination Board tests as the principal basis for admission, which meant that virtually any academically gifted high-school senior who could afford a private college had a straightforward shot at attending." The switch to standardized testing threw the doors to the college open: "By 1908, the freshman class was seven percent Jewish, nine percent Catholic, and forty-five percent from public schools, an astonishing transformation for a school that historically had been the preserve of the New England boarding-school complex known in the admissions world as St. Grottlesex." By 1922, Jews made up over 20 percent of Harvard's freshman class.[83]

Alarmed by this increase, Harvard's president, A. Lawrence Lowell, devised a plan "[t]o prevent a dangerous increase in the proportion of Jews," whereby admission decisions would be based on "a personal estimate of character on the part of the Admissions authorities."[84] Shifting reliance from academic merit as measured by test results to this "personal estimate of character" as measured by recommendation letters allowed these schools to curtail the representation of Jews, Catholics, and other groups that Harvard deemed undesirable.

The implementation of the legacy preference program worked as designed. By 1933, the percentage of Jews at Harvard was back down to 15 percent.[85] And the sons of St. Grottlesex continued to reassert their numbers at elite Ivy League schools. "By 1951, 73 percent of legacies were admitted at Yale, 79 percent at Princeton, and 94 percent at Harvard."[86]

Second, as noted above, legacy preferences do not enhance racial, ethnic, and economic diversity on campus; they do the opposite, favoring white and wealthy applicants who are already over-represented at selective institutions of higher education.

Third, legacy preference advocates argue that legacy preferences enhance the fundraising ability of colleges and universities. But as is discussed in Chapter 5 of this volume, the empirical basis for this claim is very shaky. Moreover, the argument—even if it were empirically sustainable—simply is not legally cognizable, because "the law cannot recognize the receipt of revenue from the discrimination's beneficiaries as a legitimate interest."[87]

What Happens to Legacy Preferences if Affirmative Action Is Outlawed?

Proponents of affirmative action argue that if the policy's opponents truly believe in the meritocratic ideal, then legacy preferences cannot stand. As noted civil rights author and activist Theodore Cross has argued, "in a post-*Bakke* race-blind admission environment, the traditional legacy system favoring children of graduates would reinforce the college admission advantage of whites since at most institutions there are so few legacies who are black."[88]

Some public universities that have banned the use of race in admissions—in California and Georgia—also have eliminated legacy preferences. Likewise, the experience of Texas A&M—in which one of us (John Brittain) was intimately involved—underscores the intense pressure that universities could face to eliminate legacy preferences in the event that affirmative action is banned or curtailed throughout the country.

In 1996, the Fifth Circuit Court of Appeals decided *Hopwood v. Texas*, which barred race-based affirmative action in Texas, Louisiana, and Mississippi.[89] Reaction to the opinion was swift and dramatic, typified by University of Texas's president Robert Berdahl's contention that "[t]he *Hopwood* decision has serious implications for Texas, including the virtual resegregation of higher education."[90] Texas A&M system chancellor Barry Thompson noted, "This ruling was so pervasive of all higher education that it will have more impact than any education opinion of the last 20 years."[91] Public universities in Texas were directed by Texas attorney general Dan Morales to no longer consider an applicant's race during the admissions process.[92]

After *Hopwood,* the percentage of black and Hispanic residents of Texas in the freshman classes admitted dropped immediately.[93] At Texas A&M, for example, the Hispanic share of first-time freshmen fell from 14.7 percent in the fall of 1996 to 9.7 percent in the fall of 1997.[94] In response, the Texas legislature enacted the Ten Percent Plan, which provided that Texas residents graduating in the top 10 percent of their high school class—public or private, suburban or urban—are admitted automatically to the Texas university of their choice.[95]

"Many high schools in Texas are either nearly all-white or all-minority. So basing admissions on class rank ensures that every Texas high school can send top graduates of all races to UT, A&M and other selective state colleges."[96] In 1996, the last year of affirmative action, 50 percent of the University of Texas's entering class came from only 64 high schools; the other half came from another 500 schools, and about 900 Texas high schools sent no students to the university.[97] Thus, the Top Ten Percent Plan took advantage of the lack of integration at many Texas high schools, which resulted in a top 10 percent in some schools composed predominantly of minorities.[98]

Since the 1996 *Hopwood* ruling, high-achieving minorities left Texas for other states offering race-conscious scholarships in such great numbers that a Texas A&M University "internal report in 2002 described the university as 'an enclave for the education of White students.'"[99] When the Supreme Court in 2003 clarified its position regarding affirmative action admission programs in the *Grutter* and *Gratz* cases, schools affected by the *Hopwood* decision had a chance to reevaluate their admission policies.

Texas A&M president Robert M. Gates (who spent his entire career before coming to Texas A&M working for the Central Intelligence Agency, including a stint as director of the agency from

1991 to 1993) had to decide whether to reinstate race- or ethnicity-based admissions. As of the fall 2003 semester, "82 percent of Texas A&M's undergraduates were White, two percent Black, nine percent Hispanic and three percent Asian American."[100]

Despite the exodus of minority students to other states, in late 2003, Texas A&M system regents approved a race-blind admissions plan.[101] The regents explained that the school's new plan would continue to make attracting minorities a top priority through a variety of initiatives, including increased outreach efforts in predominantly minority areas.[102]

Despite refusing to reinstate a race-based affirmative action plan, Texas A&M did not announce any similar plan to eliminate its legacy preference program. By some estimates, 1,650 to 2,000 legatees benefited from the addition of four points on a hundred-point scale used in the admissions process.[103] In 2003, 312 white applicants who otherwise would not have made the cut were admitted to Texas A&M solely because of those four legacy points. In 2002, that figure was 321. The program was the difference for six blacks and twenty-seven Hispanics in 2003, and three blacks and twenty-five Hispanics in 2002.[104]

Criticism of the intellectual inconsistency in refusing to implement affirmative action for underrepresented minorities while maintaining an affirmative action program for those already privileged is not new. For example, in his concurring opinion in *Bakke* Justice Blackmun noted:

> It is somewhat ironic to have us so deeply disturbed over a program where race is an element of consciousness, and yet to be aware of the fact, as we are, that institutions of higher learning. . . . have given conceded preferences up to a point to those possessed of athletic skills, to the children of alumni, to the affluent who may bestow their largesse on the institutions, and to those having connections with celebrities, the famous, and the powerful.[105]

Despite this irony, an editorial in the *Houston Chronicle* pointed to Gates's confession to a Houston reporter "that he hadn't given much thought at all to legacy admissions, which give preferential treatment to the children, grandchildren and siblings of A&M alumni, even by admitting some who otherwise would have been rejected."[106] Texas

A&M's abandonment of affirmative action while leaving legacy preferences intact had "left it in the unusual position of rejecting race as a factor while still allowing family ties to influence the admissions process."[107] "There was an uproar from some faculty members—a Hispanic professor wrote Gates that he was perpetuating the image of Aggieland as 'Crackerland'—but Gates didn't budge."[108]

The *Houston Chronicle* editorial blasted Gates's assertion that he wanted "every student at A&M to be able to look at every other student and know that they all got in on the same basis, on the basis of personal merit, personal achievement, qualities of their person, because of who they are rather than what they are." The editors pointed out that this purportedly strict merit system did not apply to the hundreds of applicants who depended upon extra legacy points to gain admission for the 2003–04 academic year. The *Houston Chronicle* opined that Texas A&M officials were "hypocritical . . . to endorse admissions of less qualified legacy applicants while touting academic meritocracy as the justification for rejecting student admissions via affirmative action. In reality, A&M's hang-up doesn't seem to be the admission of students of dubious academic achievement but the failure in its duty to taxpayers to cast its nets more diligently for black and Hispanic 'fish.'" The *Houston Chronicle* noted that "unlike with some of its legacies, such efforts would not require A&M to lower admission standards."[109]

Other Texas leaders agreed. State senator Rodney Ellis criticized Texas A&M's "hypocrisy" for being "so adamant about race not being a factor and then to have such a large legacy program. . . . It's just so blatantly inconsistent that it defies common sense."[110] Ellis pointed out that because "[r]ace was used in Texas over a long period of time to keep people of color, especially African-Americans, out of the higher education system. . . . [i]t only seems appropriate that race could be used as a factor, just as legacy is used."[111] Texas NAACP president Gary Bledsoe called the school's legacy preference program "'inherently discriminatory' because blacks didn't attend A&M until 1963, precluding the 'legacy' of many minority applicants, and some lawyers suggested they would file suit if the policy wasn't changed."[112]

Gates finally acted in late 2003 after intense public pressure by local lawmakers, members of Congress, and community groups who held news conferences across the state to denounce the university's preferential treatment of legacies.[113] Gates announced that Texas A&M would "no longer award points for legacy in the admissions review process." "In an admissions process based on individual merit and potential contribution to the university community," wrote Gates, "prior affiliation with Texas A&M should not be a criterion." Gates noted that public perceptions of the fairness and equity of Texas A&M's admissions process required "prompt action to deal with an obvious inconsistency in an admissions strategy based on individual merit."[114]

One admiring faculty member who heard Gates defend his decision to drop legacy preferences noted,

> It sent chills down my spine. He asked us to put ourselves in the mindset of a family who had never had the opportunity to send their kid to college. Ask yourself, "Is admitting legacies fair to that student?" If we're going to truly change the stereotype, we have to change our mind-set. And what is the stereotype? It's what you see on TV during Aggie football games. All male. All white. All military. All the time.[115]

In lieu of the prior quantitative method of assigning points for grades and test scores, Texas A&M implemented a new admissions system. Approximately two-thirds of the freshman class was made up of "automatic admits"—students who finish in the top 10 percent of their class or score higher than 1300 on the SAT. The remaining applicants received a "'holistic full-file review' . . . to identify 'students who have the propensity and capacity to assume roles of leadership, responsibility, and service to society.'" Admission counselors evaluate "academic achievement (grades and test scores), personal achievement (honors, extracurricular activities, community service), and distinguishing characteristics (educational level of parents, family responsibility and obligations, fluency in a second language, and overcoming adversity in the educational environment). Texas A&M's admissions officers never see any information about ethnicity, although 'distinguishing characteristics' is clearly a category that generally benefits minority applicants along with first-generation college students." The new admissions policy attracted students who are the first in their family to attend college; in fact, "For several years, including [2006], these students have made up at least a quarter of the freshman class."[116]

Although apparently forced by public outcry over the contradiction of ending race-conscious affirmative action policy in admissions while initially maintaining the legacy preference policy, Gates deserves praise for intellectual consistency in eventually dropping both preferences.

To be clear, civil rights activists do not endorse the Texas A&M model of eliminating both legacy and race preferences. At the point in history when universities, politicians, and civil rights groups rejoiced in the decision by the United States Supreme Court in 2003 to uphold race and ethnic-conscious affirmative action measures for admissions in a legal manner, Gates chose to abandon the most successful remedy for increasing diversity on campus.

If diversity is an academic freedom right—based upon the First Amendment for universities to create a sound and efficient educational program—then it must utilize race and ethnicity as a factor in admission preferences. By negating both legacy and race-conscious affirmative action preferences in the name of intellectual consistency of principles, Texas A&M's race-neutral admissions policy has done little to advance the values of diversity in the university.

But universities should be placed on notice that in the event affirmative action policies fall by the wayside—either because of judicial rulings or voter initiatives—the civil rights community is unlikely to let stand the hypocrisy of continued legacy preferences. As one commentator has pointed out, "Universities can't in good conscience tip the admission scales for the more privileged and then ask the less privileged to compete solely on merit. What's more, eliminating race while keeping legacies will make the admissions process less fair, not more fair, because it will open up minority slots to competition by whites but not vice versa."[117]

As Theodore Shaw, former director-counsel of the NAACP Legal Defense and Education Fund, has noted, "What does legacy preference do to advance fairness and merit?" He continued, "Why is it more defensible than an attempt to include people from minority groups that have been excluded in the past and are still underrepresented?"[118]

Legal and Policy Options for Curtailing Legacy Preferences

7

Legacy Preferences and the Constitutional Prohibition of Titles of Nobility

Carlton F. W. Larson

Legacy preferences are pernicious as a matter of public policy. When practiced by public universities, however, legacy preferences are not just harmful and unfair—they are grossly unconstitutional. Why? Because of two provisions in the Constitution that most Americans (and even most lawyers) have never heard of. These provisions, included in the original Constitution of 1787, are known as the Nobility Clauses. These clauses restrict both the federal government and the states. The "federal" clause provides that "No Title of Nobility shall be granted by the United States."[1] Similarly, the "state" clause provides that "No State shall . . . grant any Title of Nobility."[2]

My contention is that public universities violate the Nobility Clauses when they choose to prefer certain applicants over others

---

This chapter is a condensed and modified version of "Titles of Nobility, Hereditary Privilege, and the Unconstitutionality of Legacy Preferences in Public School Admissions," *Washington University Law Review* 84, no. 6 (2006): 1375–1440.

based on ancestry. I admit this argument may seem startling at first glance. How is granting a legacy preference the same as granting a title of nobility? After all, the state has not made anybody a duke. But this supposes that what constitutes a prohibited title of nobility is a relatively easy question to answer. No dukes, no kings—that's about it. But what if "titles of nobility" means more than that? What if "nobility" meant something quite different to the eighteenth-century Americans who enshrined the Nobility Clauses in our Constitution? I believe that it did. As this chapter will argue, the constitutional prohibition on titles of nobility is most properly understood as a prohibition on government-sponsored hereditary privileges.

The Nobility Clauses prohibit a particular type of substantive governmental action, not simply the use of certain distinctive words. Narrower readings of the clauses simply do not capture their significance. To see why, let us consider some alternative answers to the question, "What is a title of nobility?" First, one could argue that "title of nobility" is a technical legal term from English law and should be interpreted in accordance with English precedents. But this answer yields truly unacceptable results. Under English law, the "nobility" consisted of a narrowly defined and readily ascertainable class. As Sir William Blackstone, the leading eighteenth-century exponent of English law, explained in the 1760s, the titles of nobility then in use were limited to "dukes, marquesses, earls, viscounts and barons."[3] Significantly, the definition excluded royal titles as king or prince, as well as lesser figures such as knights, whose titles were not hereditary.[4]

There is no evidence whatsoever indicating that anyone in late-eighteenth-century America viewed the Nobility Clauses as reflecting only this limited, technical interpretation of nobility. Indeed, if we were to accept that interpretation, states could endow citizens with titles such as king, prince, or knight, as well as other titles unknown to England, such as czar, emperor, or sultan. Yet knighthoods, for example, have long been considered inconsistent with the prohibition on titles of nobility. In 1784, in referring to the prohibition of titles of nobility in the Articles of Confederation, George Washington wrote that "it appears to be incompatible with the principles of our national Constitution to admit the introduction of any kind of nobility, knighthood, or distinctions of a similar nature, amongst the citizens of our republic."[5] Obviously, the Nobility Clauses must extend beyond the narrow meaning of nobility under English law.

So let us try a broader answer: the Nobility Clauses may simply mean that a state may not bestow a title that has been used to denote some form of royalty or nobility in any country in the world. Yet a basic hypothetical should put that notion to rest. Suppose a state decided to create a title called "distinguished citizen." There would be one distinguished citizen in each county. The state would build each such person a large country estate and grant that person a distinctive coat of arms. Moreover, the state senate would be replaced with a Chamber of Citizens, composed solely of the distinguished citizens. Finally, the title and privileges of a distinguished citizen would be hereditary and would descend to the eldest child or other heir at law.

If the Nobility Clauses are simply about words, about the prohibition of certain distinctive terms from European aristocracy, this scheme would be unobjectionable. No formal "title" of nobility has actually been used. Yet such a scheme would replicate the English House of Lords in all but name, and would violate the Constitution only if the Nobility Clauses have some substantive content and are not simply about semantics and wordplay. It is the *substance* of nobility that the clauses primarily forbid, not just the forms in which nobility appears. Indeed, the fulsome praise of these prohibitions in the Revolutionary generation is inexplicable if they were meant to destroy only the outer trappings of nobility, but to leave its substance firmly in place. As Senator John Taylor put it in 1794, "Whilst the constitution inhibits a nobility even *nominally*, are its principles permissive of its erection *in reality*? Does it reject the *term* 'murder,' and yet allow the crime to be perpetrated?"[6] The government cannot create a nobility and evade the constitutional prohibition simply by blessing the practice with an innocuous name.

So what, then, is the substance of nobility? Two fundamental principles lie at the core of the Nobility Clauses: (1) a prohibition of hereditary privileges with respect to the institutions of the state; and (2) a prohibition on special privileges with respect to the institutions of the state. For our purposes, it is the first prohibition that is relevant. The Nobility Clauses squarely prohibit both the federal government and the states from granting hereditary privileges with respect to state institutions. This idea is anchored in the bedrock principle for which eighteenth-century Americans fought and died—the equality of all citizens before the law. Revolutionary Americans repeatedly and consistently denounced hereditary privileges of all forms, and they viewed the Nobility Clauses as performing a vital role in their elimination. In light of this Revolutionary heritage and the Constitution's square prohibition of hereditary privileges through the Nobility Clauses, legacy preferences in public university admissions fail miserably.

This chapter will focus heavily on important but largely forgotten aspects of the American Revolution—aspects that have much to teach us about the meaning of the Nobility Clauses. It begins by examining the Revolutionary era's rejection of nobility and hereditary privilege as inconsistent with republican ideals of equality and liberty. It focuses particular attention on the controversy surrounding the formation of the Society of the Cincinnati, a hereditary organization limited to Continental Army officers and their heirs. The legitimacy of this institution, in light of the ban on titles of nobility in the Articles of Confederation, became the subject of widespread popular debate. A close examination of this debate provides substantial evidence that contemporaries viewed prohibitions on titles of nobility as substantive bans on hereditary privileges. This understanding is reiterated in numerous speeches and writings surrounding the ratification of the U.S. Constitution.

The chapter then will analyze legacy preferences under the appropriate constitutional standards. Legacy preferences at exclusive public universities were precisely the type of hereditary privilege that the Revolutionary generation sought to destroy forever. The chapter concludes by considering and rejecting a variety of arguments that might be raised in defense of the constitutionality of legacy preferences.

The Rejection of Hereditary Privilege in the American Revolution

When the leaders of the American Revolution banned titles of nobility in the Articles of Confederation, in the earliest state constitutions, and in the U.S. Constitution, they sought to ensure one of the

Revolution's deepest principles—that hereditary privilege would have absolutely no place in the new American republic. Such distinctions were unthinkable in a nation founded upon principles of equality. The American Revolution, as historian Gordon Wood reminds us, was not simply about American independence, but about the replacement of the social order of monarchy with an order appropriate for a republic. As Wood notes, "Because the revolutionaries are so different from us, so seemingly aristocratic themselves, it is hard for us today to appreciate the anger and resentment they felt toward hereditary aristocracy."[7] Indeed, it has become easy to dismiss the Nobility Clauses, because we now take it for granted that a hereditary police chief or university president or general would be ridiculous. But the world of eighteenth-century Britain was a world in which positions of power and access to education were deeply tied to one's ancestry.[8] It is that British world of inherited privilege that the leaders of the American Revolution sought to overthrow forever.

As the crisis with Great Britain deepened in early 1776, Thomas Paine published his famous *Common Sense*, the most influential political pamphlet in the history of the world. Paine crystallized the exasperation so many Americans felt in the presence of a hereditary monarchy and a hereditary House of Lords. Although the supporters of monarchy invoked biblical authority, Paine argued that monarchy was "the most preposterous invention the Devil ever set on foot for the promotion of idolatry." Hereditary succession was "an insult and an imposition on posterity." "One of the strongest *natural* proofs of the folly of hereditary right in kings," Paine argued, "is that nature disapproves it, otherwise she would not so frequently turn it into ridicule, by giving mankind an *ass for a lion*." It opens the door to "the *foolish*, the *wicked*, and the *improper*." Indeed, he continued, "most wise men, in their private sentiments, have ever treated hereditary right with contempt; yet it is one of those evils, which when once established is not easily removed; many submit from fear, others from superstition, and the more powerful part shares with the king the plunder of the rest."[9]

When Americans turned to drafting their own constitutions, they quickly banished titles of nobility and any hint of hereditary privilege with respect to state institutions. The Virginia Declaration of Rights, for example, adopted on June 12, 1776, declared, "no man, or set of men, are entitled to exclusive or separate emoluments or privileges from the community, but in consideration of public services; which, not being descendible, neither ought the offices of magistrate, legislator, or judge, to be hereditary."[10] Similarly, the Maryland Declaration of Rights stated, "no title of nobility, or hereditary honours, ought to be granted in this State."[11] The New Hampshire Constitution declared that "no office or place, whatsoever, in government, shall be hereditary—the abilities and integrity requisite in all, not being transmissible to posterity or relations."[12] The North Carolina Declaration of Rights stated "that no hereditary emoluments, privileges or honors ought to be granted or conferred in this State."[13] The Massachusetts Constitution of 1780, largely drafted by John Adams, stated,

> No man, nor corporation, or association of men have any other title to obtain advantages, or particular and exclusive privileges, distinct from those of the community, than what arises from the consideration of services rendered to the public; and this title being in nature neither hereditary, nor transmissible to children, or descendants, or relations by blood, the idea of a man born a magistrate, lawgiver, or judge, is absurd and unnatural.[14]

Similarly, in a 1777 pamphlet, Benjamin Rush, a signer of the Declaration of Independence, denounced "hereditary titles, honour and power" and sought "to exclude them for ever [sic] from Pennsylvania."[15]

In 1777, the Articles of Confederation, America's first constitution, was sent to the states for ratification. The Articles provided, "nor shall the United States, in Congress assembled, or any of them, grant any title of nobility."[16] This provision was a significant restriction on the powers of the states. As Professor Akhil Reed Amar of Yale Law School points out, "Nowhere else had the Confederation so directly regulated states' internal governance."[17] The prohibition on titles of nobility in the Articles of Confederation is especially important because it was the direct predecessor of the Nobility Clauses of the U.S. Constitution. If we wish to understand the Nobility Clauses, we must understand what the predecessor provision meant in the Articles of Confederation. Did the Articles simply prohibit particular titles, formal words such as "duke" or "earl," or did they carry a more substantive meaning?

THE CASE OF THE SOCIETY OF THE CINCINNATI

Fortunately, we have surviving evidence of a highly probative nature. In the mid-1780s, Americans fiercely debated the legitimacy of the institution of the Society of the Cincinnati.[18] This debate provides significant evidence of the original meaning of the Titles of Nobility Clause in the Articles of Confederation. The thrusts and parries in this debate show that the subsequent Nobility Clauses of the U.S. Constitution were not solely a limitation of certain distinctive titles, such as "duke" or "earl." Rather, these prohibitions carried an important substantive component—a prohibition on hereditary privileges with respect to state institutions.

The story begins at the end of the Revolutionary War. In 1783, two years after the conclusion of open hostilities, a group of former officers in the Continental Army formed a private organization entitled the Society of the Cincinnati. The Society was named after the famous Roman general Cincinnatus, who had returned to his farm after his military campaigns were concluded. Membership in the Society was limited to men who had been officers of the Continental Army for a specified period of time, although the Society had the power to elect certain honorary members as well.[19] The Society was divided into separate state societies, loosely overseen by an overarching national organization.[20] There was also a French chapter for French officers who had served during the Revolution.[21] The purpose of the Society was to promote fellowship among former officers and, quite possibly, to ensure that promised salaries and benefits were paid by the often recalcitrant Continental Congress. All of this in itself would not have been particularly alarming, probably provoking as little objection as an alumni society for Harvard or Yale College.

There were two additional features of the Society, however, that immediately brought a torrent of criticism from outraged Americans. First, members wore a ribbon and a medal indicating their membership in the Society; such ribbons and medals were a common symbol of British nobility.[22] Second, and far more troubling, membership in the Society was made hereditary, passing to each member's eldest son or other heir at law. In short, membership, with the exception of the honorary memberships, was forever limited to the descendants of Continental Army officers. As word of these features spread, Americans responded with outright horror.

The first sustained attack came from the chief justice of South Carolina, Aedanus Burke. An emigrant from Ireland, Burke was a well-read lawyer who had risen rapidly in the South Carolina legal establishment.[23] Under the pseudonym "Cassius," he published a blistering pamphlet on the Society, arguing that it "creates a race of hereditary patricians, or nobility." As he explained, "it is in reality, and will turn out to be, an hereditary peerage; a nobility to them and their male issue, and in default thereof, the collateral branches: what the lawyers would call a title of peerage of Cincinnati to them and their heirs male." Such an institution, Burke contended, was a direct violation of the prohibition on titles of nobility in the Articles of Confederation. On this point, Burke's argument had to confront an obvious objection. The Articles prohibited the United States and the states from granting titles of nobility; the Society was simply a private organization, acting without sanction from any government. Burke argued that any state sanction of the Society would be an obvious violation of the Articles, noting that "the order cannot, at present, be sanctified by legal authority," and that creation of the Society "by Congress or our own Legislature" would be a "violation of the confederation and of our laws."[24]

Even as a private organization, however, the Society still violated the Articles. As Burke put it, "[T]he order of Cincinnati usurp a nobility without gift or grant, in defiance of Congress and the States." It was an "infringement of a general law of the Union" and would reduce the country in less than a century to "two ranks of men: the patricians or nobles and the rabble." The Society would "soon have and hold an exclusive right to offices, honors and authorities, civil and military." The Society therefore was "breaking through our constitution" and "turning the blessings of Providence into a curse upon us."[25]

Burke urged the legislature "to immediately enter into spirited Resolutions" against the Society. "Instituting exclusive honors and privileges of an hereditary Order, [was] a daring usurpation on the sovereignty of the republic." It was also a "dangerous insult to the rights and liberties of the people, and a fatal stab to that principle of equality which forms the basis of our government, to establish which the people fought and bled as well as the Cincinnati."[26]

It is important to note Burke's argument that legislative creation of the Society would have violated the prohibition on titles of nobility in the Articles of Confederation, even though no formal "titles" were used. The Society's medal, ribbon, and hereditary descent were sufficient to bring it within the prohibited category of nobility. If this argument were truly "off-the-wall," to use Yale law professor Jack Balkin's term for arguments outside the acceptable professional mainstream,[27] one would expect it to fall on deaf ears and be dismissed as the ravings of a paranoid lunatic. Yet nothing of the sort occurred.

Burke's arguments against the Society were instead enthusiastically embraced across the nation, and his pamphlet was published widely.[28] A popular convention in the state of Connecticut warmly recommended Burke's pamphlet "to the notice and perusal of the people at large."[29] It later issued a statement warning that "a new and strange order of men had arisen under the eye of Congress, by the name of the Society of the Cincinnati . . . to be distinguished from the rest of the citizens, wearing the badges of peerage."[30] A committee of the Massachusetts legislature was appointed to inquire into any associations "which may have a tendency to create a race of hereditary nobility, contrary to the confederation of the United States and the spirit of the constitution of this commonwealth."[31] The committee issued a scathing report on the Society in March 1784. The report, adopted in full by both houses of the legislature, stated, "hereditary distinctions and ostentatious orders, strike the minds of unthinking multitudes, and favour the views and designs of ambitious men, often issuing in hereditary nobility, which is contrary to the spirit of free governments, and expressly inhibited by an article in the confederation of the United States."[32] Although the men who fought in the Revolution were worthy of honor, there was a constant danger of "rewarding the families" of such men.[33] In short, the Society of the Cincinnati was "unjustifiable, and if not properly discountenanced, may be dangerous to the peace, liberty, and safety of the United States in general, and this commonwealth in particular."[34] Even Henry Knox, a founder of the Society, was forced to concede that in Boston, "the cool, dispassionate men seem to approve of the institution generally, but dislike the hereditary descent."[35]

On February 19, 1784, the governor of South Carolina addressed the state legislature and roundly denounced the Society of the Cincinnati as "dangerous" and as "generative of suspicion, jealousy, division and domestic discord."[36] The Society's assumption of the "power of creating orders descendable to the oldest male posterity" was "incontestably big with alarm."[37] A Boston newspaper reported on April 19, 1784, that the state of Rhode Island was determined "to disenfranchise any and every person who is a member [of the Society of the Cincinnati] and render them incapable of holding any post of honor and trust in that government."[38] Other writers argued that members of the Society should be barred from all civil and military offices in the United States.[39] Samuel Adams contended that the Society represented as "rapid a stride towards an hereditary military nobility as was ever made in so short a time"[40] and wondered how the Society could "imagine that a people who had freely spent their blood and treasure in support of their equal rights and liberties could be so soon reconciled to the odious hereditary distinctions of families."[41] The French minister to the United States reported in April 1784, "The institution of the Society of the Cincinnati gives every day more ombrage to the inhabitants of the North. They do not wish to suffer any distinctions to exist."[42] He continued, "They find them incompatible with republican government, dangerous to liberty, and I think their fears are not chimerical. . . . It is in effect an institution diametrically opposed to the principles of equality."[43]

Other writers emphasized the inconsistency between the Society and the principles of the Revolution. As Isaac Backus, a New England historian, wrote in 1784,

> And though the war was levied against hereditary claims of power over others, and to secure equity among all the inhabitants, and the articles of union and confederation between these States expressly forbid their granting any titles of nobility, yet in May following those officers presumed to incorporate a society among themselves, to have an hereditary succession, and each a golden medal and blue ribbon, with a large fund of money at command, and power to elect our chief rulers into their society. . . . The above proceedings have caused unspeakable difficulties through these States, which have been loudly complained of by multitudes.[44]

The hereditary aspect was easily the most grating. One opponent of the Society pointed out the significant differences between it and other fraternal organizations. The honors and privileges of Freemasons would "with their respective natural bodies, be laid in the dust,"[45] but the "honors and privileges of the *military* majority of the Cincinnati . . . are entended [sic] to descend, and like the nobility in monarchical and aristocratical governments, entailed to their male heirs forever."[46]

One of the more unusual sources of attack against the Society came from a French count. Drawing heavily on Burke's pamphlet and with assistance from Benjamin Franklin,[47] the Count de Mirabeau published a lengthy polemic that was widely reprinted in America. Mirabeau, writing in the voice of an American, reiterated many of Burke's arguments and contended that the formation of the Society was the "creation of an actual patriciate, and of a military nobility." Continuation of the Society risked "the total subversion of our constitution." The Society violated prohibitions in various state constitutions as well as the prohibition on titles of nobility in the Articles of Confederation, which Mirabeau described as "the fundamental law of the political existence of the American states." He asked, "Can it be doubted whether [the Society] violates the spirit of our laws? Whether it subverts the principles of that equality, of which we are so jealous? Whether it establishes, and eternally fixes in the state, an order of citizens distinct from their fellow-citizens?" The Society had "lain in ruins that beautiful, plain, and natural equality, which God created for our use and happiness, which philosophy contemplated with heart-felt pleasure, which our laws and government promised and ought to have secured to us."[48]

American ministers serving in France heartily agreed with Mirabeau. John Adams wrote to Lafayette in 1784, denouncing the Society as an "order of chivalry" and stating that it was "against our confederation, and against the constitutions of several States."[49] It was "against the spirits of our governments and the genius of our people."[50] Adams would later describe the Society as the "deepest piece of cunning yet attempted" and an "inroad upon our first principle, equality."[51] His fellow minister John Jay declared that if the Society "took well in the States he would not care if the Revolutionary War had succeeded or not."[52] Benjamin Franklin stated,

> I only wonder that, when the united Wisdom of our Nation had, in the Articles of Confederation, manifested their Dislike of establishing Ranks of Nobility, by Authority either of the Congress or

> of any particular state, a Number of private persons should think proper to distinguish themselves and their Posterity, from their fellow Citizens, and form an order of *hereditary Knights*, in direct Opposition to the solemnly declared Sense of their Country.[53]

Franklin hoped that "the Order will drop this part of their project, and content themselves . . . with a Life Enjoyment of their little Badge and Ribband, and let the Distinction die with those who have merited it. This I imagine will give no offence."[54]

Lafayette reported to Washington from Paris that "[m]ost of the Americans Here are indecently Violent Against our Association."[55] He expressed strong reservations about the hereditary component, suggesting that it "endanger[ed] the Free Principles of democracy."[56] Lafayette would later admit that he wished the Society "had not been thought of" and that his "principles ever have been against heredity."[57]

Thomas Jefferson was equally hostile to the Society. In a letter to George Washington, Jefferson advised Washington to distance himself from the Society and pointedly summarized the major objections: "That it is against the Confederation; against the letter of some of our constitutions; against the spirit of them all—that the foundation, on which all these are built, is the natural equality of man, the denial of every preeminence but that annexed to legal office, and particularly the denial of a preeminence by birth."[58] Jefferson reported that the Continental Congress would be "unfriendly to the institution" and that his private conversations with the delegates revealed almost unanimous opposition to the Society.[59] General Nathanael Greene echoed Jefferson on this point, observing "Congress has said nothing on the subject, but they are not less displeased with the order than other citizens."[60] Jefferson further reported that he had "hear[d] from other quarters that [the Society] is disagreeable generally to such citizens as have attended to it, and therefore will probably be so to all when any circumstance shall present it to the notice of all."[61] In Jefferson's view, making the Society "unobjectionable" would require abolition of hereditary membership.[62] Jefferson would later note that he was an "enemy of the institution from the first moment of it's [sic] conception."[63]

Placed in a deeply defensive posture by this barrage of criticism, supporters of the Society produced several supportive pamphlets that stressed the virtuous and pure motives behind its founding. When they engaged the arguments about prohibited titles of nobility, they primarily emphasized the Society's lack of connection with any institutions of the state. One supporter noted, "the Cincinnati have nothing but an empty title, exhibited, like the honors of masonry, on a parchment, a medal, and a riband."[64] They were entitled neither to estates nor offices. "From such a society of men as little is to be feared as from the order of masons, a convention of physicians, or a company of merchants and mechanics."[65] It was "ridiculous" to suggest that a "number of individuals combined merely for social purposes and those of the most benevolent kind, without any power annexed to the honours of the society, should be dangerous to a republican form of government."[66] One anonymous pamphleteer pointed to the failure of the Continental Congress to prohibit the organization, and emphasized that any distinctions created by the Society were "distinction[s] without power."[67] Simply put, "The institution of the order of the Cincinnati is back'd by no power, and consequently attended with no danger."[68] For another supporter, the Society was primarily a "charitable institution" with limited funds, making fears of nobility "extravagant."[69]

One member of the Society, in a reply to Burke, tartly stated, "I believe the military gentlemen approve, as much as you can do, of the article of our confederation, prohibiting the grant of titles of nobility; and probably may have as much interest in the preservation of a republic which they have sought to establish, as those who enjoy its blessings at a cheaper rate." But the Society simply was not a title of nobility, "its objects being of a private nature, and not interfering with the rights and privileges of any set of men." As he explained, "It certainly bears no resemblance to a city corporation of shop-keepers or tailors, or to any corporate body whatever. It has no charter; it has no privileges or immunities, but what arise from its own funds." As such it was no different than the Freemasons, and its members were "no longer military commanders, but private citizens, combined as friends, without any political weight or authority."[70]

These defenses are important both for what they say and what they do not say. If the prohibition on titles of nobility were simply a prohibition on words such as "duke" or "earl," there would have been no violation even if the Society had been created by the

Continental Congress or by an individual state. Burke's argument could have been quickly dismissed in a single paragraph, or indeed, a single sentence. But no defender appears to have made that argument. Rather, they focused their energy on repeatedly emphasizing the private nature of the Society and its lack of any connection to the state. Thus, at no point did they squarely rebut Burke's and other critics' contention that the Society, if created by Congress or an individual state, would constitute an impermissible title of nobility. The silence on this critical point is telling.

As criticisms mounted, the Society held its first general meeting in May 1784.[71] George Washington noted that the opposition of Virginia and other states to the Society had become "violent and formidable." Delegates from Connecticut, Massachusetts, and New Hampshire reported opposition in their states. The South Carolina delegate reported that "almost all the various classes" in his state "were opposed to the institution in its present form." The Pennsylvania delegate specifically noted the objection of the people to "the hereditary part."[72]

George Washington then delivered one of the most forceful speeches of his life. He insisted that the Society "discontinue the hereditary part in all its connections *absolutely*, without any substitution which can be construed into concealment."[73] Indeed, had he not feared alienating the French members of the Society, Washington stated he "would propose to the Society to make one great sacrifice more to the world [and] abolish the Order altogether." Washington then introduced a report of a committee of Congress providing that "no persons holding an hereditary title or order of nobility should be eligible to citizenship in the new state they were about to establish." Washington stated that he "knew this to be leveled at our Institution." If the Society did not abolish hereditary succession, "we might expect every discouragement and even *persecution* from them and the states severally . . . 99 in a hundred would become our violent enemies." Washington concluded by referring to a letter from Lafayette, "objecting to the hereditary part of the Institution, as repugnant to a republican system, and very exceptionable." The next day, Washington put his personal reputation directly on the line. He spoke against the hereditary provisions with "much warmth and agitation," noting that they were "peculiarly obnoxious to the people" and stating that unless they were abolished, he would resign from the Society.[74]

Yielding to Washington, and to overwhelming public pressure, the general meeting accordingly revised the founding document of the Society to eliminate all traces of hereditary succession. Shortly thereafter, the Society issued a circular letter under Washington's signature to the various state societies. Widely reprinted in American newspapers,[75] the letter explained that the Society had initially been created "in a hasty manner."[76] Because the "original institution appeared in the opinion of many respectable characters to have comprehended objects which are deemed incompatible with the genius and spirit of the confederation," the Society had abolished "the hereditary succession."[77] This succession would have drawn an "unjustifiable line of discrimination between our descendants and the rest of the community."[78] As one defender of the Society explained, "the exceptionable part was the hereditary descent; that was, to conform to the sentiments of the people, abolished."[79] Washington later contended, "if the first institution of this Society had not been parted with, ere this we should have had the country in an uproar, and a line of separation drawn between the Society and their fellow-citizens."[80] Even Nathanael Greene, who had initially supported the hereditary provisions, conceded his error. In a letter to Washington, he admitted, "The clamour raised against the Cincinnati was far more extensive than I had expected. I had no conception that it was so universal. . . . [B]ut I found afterwards our ministers abroad and all the inhabitants in general were opposed to the order."[81] He commended Washington for the measures he took, which "seemed to silence all jealousies on the subject."[82]

With this important modification, opposition to the Society of the Cincinnati largely faded away. Surprisingly, however, the abolition of hereditary succession never became formally effective, because it failed the necessary ratification by the state chapters of the Society.[83] In 1786, for example, Alexander Hamilton, who knew something about low birth, served on a committee of the New York Society of the Cincinnati. Although the committee rejected the proposed changes on the grounds that they provided no alternative mechanism for the Society to continue, it did note serious concerns with the hereditary succession, since it "refers to birth what ought to belong to merit only, a principle inconsistent with the genius of a Society founded on friendship and patriotism."[84] Most Americans were likely unaware that hereditary succession had not been formally abolished. In the mid-1790s, Edmund Randolph approvingly noted that the Society had abolished "hereditary succession" at the "first general meeting."[85] In 1797, another historian noted, "the Cincinnati afterwards expunged the exceptionable part of their constitution."[86] A modern historian points out that it "was not clear . . . how many state societies had to accept the amended institution before it became effective" and that "the question remained undecided for the next sixteen years."[87]

Reflecting on the dispute several years later, John Adams emphasized that "in America . . . legal distinctions, titles, powers, and privileges, are not hereditary." For Adams, there was no more "remarkable phenomenon in human history, nor in universal human nature, than this order." How could the army officers "voluntarily engaged in a service under the authority of the people" institute "titles and ribbons, and hereditary descents, by their own authority only?" Quite simply, the Society of the Cincinnati was "founded on no principle of morals, true policy, or our own constitution."[88] Similarly, in an article for a French encyclopedia on the controversy, Jefferson wrote, "Of distinctions by birth or badge, [Americans] had no more idea than they had of the mode of existence in the moon or planets. They had heard only that there were such, and knew they must be wrong."[89]

Throughout the controversy, prominent Americans, including well-trained lawyers, repeatedly referred to the prohibition on titles of nobility in the Articles of Confederation. This widespread popular deliberation over the meaning of this provision represents the best and most concrete evidence of how late-eighteenth-century Americans viewed constitutional prohibitions on titles of nobility. The Society was established as little more than a private fraternity of retired public officials with a hereditary right to wear a ribbon. Yet it was denounced as illegitimate and inconsistent with the Articles of Confederation by people who disagreed about almost everything else. On what other subject did John Adams, John Jay, Thomas Jefferson, Samuel Adams, Benjamin Franklin, and, I think we can safely say, George Washington, all agree? How would these Americans have reacted if the federal government or a state had opened and funded an exclusive university to which admission was linked, even in part, to hereditary privilege? I think the answer is obvious—they would have resisted it with every fiber of their being.[90]

Titles of Nobility and the Ratification of the U.S. Constitution

In 1787, there could be little doubt that the prohibition on titles of nobility would survive whatever revisions were made to the Articles of Confederation. A year earlier, Noah Webster praised the fact that "[n]ot a single office or emolument in America is held by prescription or hereditary right; but all at the disposal of the people."[91] Such principles, Webster explained, "form the basis of our American governments; the first and only governments on earth that are founded on the true principles of equal liberty, and properly guarded from corruption."[92] In an earlier work, Webster had emphasized that the "annihilation of all hereditary distinctions of rank" was necessary for the preservation of popular government, and he singled out for praise the provision of the Article of Confederation "barring all titles of nobility in the American states."[93]

The Nobility Clauses occasioned little debate in the Constitutional Convention itself; indeed, as carryovers from the Articles of Confederation they were unlikely to be the subject of much comment. It is not until the ratification period that we can find significant statements about the meaning of these clauses. Even then, however, explanations were often perfunctory. In *The Federalist*, James Madison simply stated, "The prohibition with respect to titles of nobility, is copied from the Articles of Confederation, and needs no comment."[94] His coauthor, Alexander Hamilton, was slightly more expansive, stating "Nothing need be said to illustrate the importance of the prohibition of titles of nobility. This may truly be denominated the corner stone of republican government; for so long as they are excluded, there can never be serious danger that the government will be any other than that of the people."[95] He emphasized that the Constitution's Nobility Clauses, along with the prohibition on ex post facto laws and the establishment of the writ of habeas corpus, "are perhaps greater securities to liberty and republicanism than any it contains."[96]

Nonetheless, there are enough statements in the ratification period to lend strong support to an interpretation of the Nobility Clauses as a substantive prohibition on hereditary privilege. Indeed, one Federalist writer in 1787 explicitly linked equivalent educational opportunities to the absence of a hereditary nobility. He argued that senators would "have none of the peculiar follies and vices of those men, who possess power merely because their fathers held it before them, for they will be educated (under equal advantages, and, with equal prospects) among and on a footing with the other sons of a free people."[97] A similar point was made in 1799:

> Since knowledge is the foundation of Republicanism, let us be careful to render the avenues to it easy and accessible. Let us put into the hands of the poor man, as well as the rich, the means of ennobling his nature. No hereditary distinctions, no titles of nobility, will ever be suffered to trample on our equal liberties. Genius and exalted abilities will always receive sufficient encouragement under a free government.[98]

Other Federalists stressed the broad egalitarian implications of the Nobility Clauses. The paradigmatic example was holding office. One Federalist emphasized that it was not "necessary to be of noble blood or of a powerful family" to hold office in America.[99] Rather, "it is declared that there shall be no titles, rank or nobility" and power is vested "in the people themselves."[100] In the Massachusetts ratifying convention, Isaac Backus praised the Constitution for "excluding all titles of nobility, or hereditary succession of power. . . . Such a door is now opened, for the establishing of righteous government, and for securing equal liberty, as never was before opened to any people upon earth."[101] But the scope of Nobility Clauses was not limited to holding office. It extended to any form of privilege provided by government. As another Federalist explained, under the Constitution there "never can be any nobility in the states, or person possessed of any rights or privileges but what are common to the meanest subject."[102]

The years following the ratification of the Constitution provided Americans an opportunity to look back at what the Revolution had accomplished. Not surprisingly, many of them pointed to the prohibitions on titles of nobility and the elimination of hereditary privilege as some of the Revolution's most significant achievements. An almanac pointed out that American government was not "committed to the weak and worthless, merely because they might boast an hereditary right."[103] South Carolina Federalist David Ramsay explained that the Revolution had changed monarchical subjects into citizens. "Subjects look up to a master, but citizens are so far equal, that none have hereditary rights superior to others."[104] The 1790 Pennsylvania Constitution declared that the legislature shall "not grant any title of nobility or hereditary distinction."[105] An identical provision appeared in the South Carolina Constitution of the same year,[106] and in the 1792 Kentucky Constitution.[107]

In 1791, the president of the Massachusetts Senate delivered an oration prior to Samuel Adams's inauguration as governor. He returned to the "first principles" of government, particularly the provision of the Massachusetts Constitution that explicitly stated, "the idea of a man born a magistrate, legislator or judge, is absurd and unnatural."[108] "May it not hence be inferred," he asked, "that claims to hereditary right, to shares in sovereignty, or in the administration of government, transmissible to children, or relations by blood are usurpations of the natural rights of men, as well as totally repugnant to the first principles of our free Constitution."[109] That same year Governor Thomas Mifflin of Pennsylvania argued that "[s]o many dangers attend the perpetuation of any office whatever, by hereditary succession, that the people of America ought to tremble at the idea of seeing a law passed to establish even hereditary bailiffs or constables."[110] A New Hampshire minister in 1792 preached, "While clouds of hereditary rights, shadows of aristocracy, and the darkness of monarchical governments involve other nations in slavery, we are free."[111] The next year, a newspaper writer argued, "Titles of nobility are properly discarded in the federal constitution, because they convey a legal right to hereditary rank and consequence."[112]

In the early 1790s, Thomas Paine published *The Rights of Man,* his famous defense of the French Revolution. Paine's work found a large American audience. At least four American editions were printed by 1791, each bearing praise from Thomas Jefferson, and the work was widely excerpted in newspapers across the country.[113] Paine's attack on hereditary privileges had lost none of its punch since *Common Sense*. Paine contended, "[T]he idea of hereditary legislators is as inconsistent as that of hereditary judges, or hereditary juries, and as absurd as an hereditary mathematician, or an hereditary wise man, and as ridiculous as an hereditary poet laureate." The "hereditary system" was as "repugnant to human wisdom as to human rights, and is as absurd as it is unjust." The "absurdity of hereditary government" was amply demonstrated by the "descendants of those men, in any line of life, who once were famous." "Is there scarcely an instance in which there was not a reverse of the character? It appears as if the tide of mental faculties flowed as far as it could in certain channels and then forsook its course, and arose in others."[114] In a published letter, Paine reiterated that the notion of hereditary succession was "the most base and humiliating idea that ever degraded the human species, and which, for the honor of humanity, should be destroyed forever."[115] In another letter Paine noted, "The system of government purely representative, unmixed with anything of hereditary nonsense, began in America."[116]

In 1794, in a speech to the Massachusetts legislature, Samuel Adams pointedly linked the Nobility Clauses to the Declaration of Independence's assertion that "all men are created equal."[117] The doctrine of "liberty and equality [was] an article in the political creed of the United States," and the framers of the Constitution had accordingly properly rejected titles of nobility as "introductory to the absurd and unnatural claim of hereditary and exclusive privileges."[118] Looking back on the American Revolution in 1798, the adventurer Stephen Burroughs recalled that the revolutionaries considered "a man's merit to rest entirely with himself, without regard to family, blood, or connection."[119] A grand jury charge the same year emphasized, "Hereditary succession being unknown in our government, there can be no danger that the right of birth will ever place those in office, under our constitution, who have no meritorious claims of their own, but what they derive from the rank and glory of their ancestors."[120]

In sum, there is significant evidence that the Nobility Clauses were widely understood at America's founding as vital components of America's commitment to the core principle of equality. This commitment to equality entailed a deep-rooted conviction that hereditary privileges with respect to state institutions were fundamentally wrong, both legally and morally. Americans of the founding era repeatedly linked their denunciations of hereditary privilege to the constitutional prohibition on titles of nobility. The debate on the Society of the Cincinnati shows that the idea of nobility was not confined to the granting of particular titles such as "duke" or "earl." Rather it was the substance of nobility—the unearned privilege that descends from parent to child—that grated on Revolutionary sensibilities most intently. [121]

Applying the Nobility Clauses to Legacy Preferences

So how do the lessons of the Revolutionary era apply to the modern case of legacy preferences? The basic constitutional rule is that hereditary privileges are impermissible.[122] Yet for many college applicants, access to significant higher educational benefits will turn, at least in part, on the simple fact of whether or not an ancestor attended the institution in question. It is a distinction that turns solely on ancestry, and bears no relationship to the individual merit of the applicant; it is hereditary privilege, pure and simple.

In this respect, legacy preferences bear a close relationship to one of the most repulsive creations of American law—the notorious grandfather clauses used in the American South to disenfranchise African Americans following the Reconstruction Amendments. As Akhil Amar of Yale Law School and Neal Katyal of Georgetown University Law School have pointed out, legacy preferences are "quite literally, educational grandfather clauses."[123] Like legacy preferences, grandfather clauses provided a special benefit, in this case exemption from otherwise applicable voting requirements, to certain people based solely upon their ancestry. For example, the Oklahoma grandfather clause invalidated in *Guinn* v. *United States*[124] provided that literacy requirements did not apply to any "person who was, on January 1st, 1866, or any time prior thereto, entitled to vote under any form of government, or who at that time resided in some foreign nation, and no lineal descendant of such person, shall be denied the right to register and vote because of his inability to so read and write sections of such constitution."[125] The Oklahoma Supreme Court had upheld this provision, noting "the virtue and intelligence of the ancestor will be imputed to his descendants, just as the iniquity of the fathers may be visited upon the children unto the third and fourth generation."[126]

The United States Supreme Court in 1915 unanimously struck down this provision as a blatant end-run around the Fifteenth Amendment, which guaranteed that the right to vote could not be restricted on the basis of race. The entire purpose of the law was to "disregard the prohibitions of the Amendment by creating a standard of voting which on its face was in substance but a revitalization of conditions which, when they prevailed in the past, had been destroyed by the self-operative force of the Amendment."[127]

The *Guinn* Court focused on the Fifteenth Amendment because the law was directed at suffrage, but an analysis of grandfather clauses more broadly suggests that they are equally invalid under the Nobility Clauses. Suppose, for example, that a state awarded one hundred extra points on a civil service examination to any person who was a lineal descendant of a state employee, or exempted the children of highway patrol officers from traffic fines, or awarded the majority of hunting licenses to children of state legislators. Such programs would not violate the Fifteenth Amendment, but would run afoul of the Nobility Clauses' prohibition on hereditary privilege. These examples seem strange only because in most areas of life we have thoroughly expunged legal vestiges of such privilege. University admission policies are perhaps the only area in modern life where such practices persist.

Rebutting Objections to Applying the Nobility Clauses to Invalidate Legacy Preferences

Of course, one could make a number of objections to my argument. So let me address what I think are potentially the strongest arguments against my position, and explain why those arguments are ultimately unpersuasive.

First, one might object that legacy preferences are not absolute. After all, they certainly do not guarantee admission; at most, they give one an extra boost in a regime in which large numbers of seats still go to non-legacy applicants. Thus they are different in kind from preferences that guarantee privilege based on ancestry. This objection is unconvincing. The difference between the legacy preferences currently employed and a system that reserved 100 percent or 90 percent of the seats for alumni children is one of degree, not of kind. Suppose a city made one seat on a five-member city council hereditary. Would one argue that this is constitutional because everybody else could still compete for the other four seats? Suppose instead the city said every child of a city council member started with a hundred-vote bonus. Or suppose a state gave fifty extra points on the bar exam to children of bar members. What about five hundred points? Two points? These examples all raise the basic question of how much hereditary privilege is permissible. That question was answered in 1787, and the answer is none whatsoever.

Second, one might object that the Nobility Clauses only forbid hereditary powers with respect to government. The true evil is placing persons in positions of power over others based on heredity. Hereditary distinctions in the selection of university students, who exercise no such power, therefore should not raise any distinctive nobility concerns. Again, this objection is unconvincing. As an initial matter, higher education is almost a prerequisite for exercising positions of power and influence in American society. As the Supreme Court has emphasized, "universities . . . law schools, represent the training ground for a large number of our Nation's leaders."[128] Moreover, although the fear of hereditary governmental power was a paradigmatic concern of the Nobility Clauses, there is no reason to construe the clauses so narrowly. First, ample evidence in contemporary sources indicates a concern about hereditary privilege generally, not just in positions of governmental power. Second, and more importantly, such an argument would permit the government to create a host of hereditary privileges that would fundamentally undermine basic principles of equality. Hereditary exemptions from the income tax or from certain criminal laws, hereditary business licenses, hereditary driver's licenses, and hereditary bar memberships would all be permissible. And if we were concerned only about the exercise of governmental power, there would be little problem with hereditary public university professorships, hereditary poets laureate, hereditary astronauts, hereditary janitors at the state capitol, or hereditary governmental clerical workers of any sort. Finally, there would be no constitutional barrier to creating a public university that limited enrollment solely to children of alumni or children of state legislators. Any argument that the Nobility Clauses are limited to positions of power in government must concede that all of these examples are permissible. The better argument, surely, is that the Nobility Clauses constrain government when it awards benefits just as much as when it decides who will exercise positions of power.

Constitutional law, for understandable reasons, has not been as attentive to the provision of benefits as it has been to the imposition of disabilities. As Abraham Bell of the University of San Diego School of Law and Gideon Parchomovsky of the University of Pennsylvania Law School point out in the property context, "takings—government seizures of property—have been the subject of an elaborate body of scholarship; givings—government distributions of property—have been largely overlooked by the legal academy."[129] The Supreme Court's reluctance to invalidate awards of benefits is readily explained by the lack of clear, discernible standards to evaluate such awards, by problems of party standing to challenge such benefits, and by a fear of opening a Pandora's box of new constitutional challenges. These concerns may be quite relevant in other constitutional contexts, but they have little application to the Nobility Clauses. First, the Nobility Clauses, unlike almost every other constitutional limitation, are explicitly about limiting governmental awards of benefits. That is the whole point; the government cannot single out certain people for special privileges. Second, a prohibition on hereditary privilege poses few of the problems associated with judicial scrutiny of benefits more generally. Judicial application of the Nobility Clauses asks the narrow question of whether a law awards benefits on ancestral lines; it does not entail further inquiry with respect to all other forms of benefits and exemptions.

Third, there is the argument from long-standing practice and tradition. Legacy preferences in public universities ostensibly have a long history; surely, if they were unconstitutional, someone would have noticed before now. At the very least, their long acceptance by the American people suggests that this is an area in which courts should tread lightly, if at all.

Although American universities date to the founding of Harvard College in 1636, truly selective admissions are a creature of the twentieth century. As historian Herbert Wechsler explains, "Throughout the nineteenth century and into the twentieth most American colleges admitted students on the basis of straightforward, published entrance requirements. All students who could demonstrate acceptable mastery of the requirements were admitted."[130] Indeed, prior to the 1920s, even Harvard, Yale, and Princeton had no limits on the size of their entering classes. Any student who passed the qualifying examination was eligible to enroll. In practice, of course, these requirements eliminated the vast majority of the American population from consideration, but, in theory at least, no qualified applicant would be rejected.[131] In such an admissions regime, there was little place for legacy preferences, because admissions was not a zero-sum game.

By the 1920s, these admission rules had led to an unanticipated consequence. Jewish students, often recent emigrants from southern and eastern Europe, consistently performed well on qualifying examinations, and they began to enter the Ivy League in large numbers. The leaders of these universities, displaying the reflexive anti-Semitism so prominent at the time, concluded that something had to be done to curb the number of Jewish students. Their solution was to limit the size of the entering class and to employ a variety of considerations other than academic merit in making admission decisions.[132] As Harvard president A. Lawrence Lowell explained in 1925, the only way "to prevent a dangerous increase in the proportion of Jews" was to "limit the numbers, accepting only those who appear to be the best," based on a "personal estimate of character."[133]

With this change, America's first truly selective admission regimes were in place. For the first time, applicants otherwise qualified for admission under traditional categories might be denied admission due to the limitation of class size. And hand-in-hand with this limitation came a forthright acceptance of legacy preferences—preferences that would clearly benefit the existing elite at the expense of recent Jewish immigrants. At Yale, for example, the new legacy preference increased the percentage of alumni sons from 13 percent in 1920 to 24 percent in 1930.[134] As Jerome Karabel, the leading scholar of these admission policies, explains,

> the preference for alumni sons [dates from] one of the most reactionary moments in American history—a few years in the first half of the 1920s defined by rising xenophobia and anti-Semitism, widespread political repression, the emergence of the Ku Klux Klan as a genuine mass movement, the growing prominence of eugenics and scientific racism, and the imposition by Congress of a racially and ethnically biased regime of immigration restriction.[135]

Although the details are far from clear, it appears that legacy preferences spread to public universities only in the latter half of the twentieth century, as certain universities adopted limitations on class sizes.[136] Accordingly, it is not at all surprising that no one has previously made the connection between legacy preferences and the Nobility Clauses. By the time that public universities began employing legacy preferences in a serious way, equality-based constitutional arguments had come to rest almost exclusively on the Equal Protection Clause, and the role of the Nobility Clauses in limiting hereditary privilege was long forgotten.

Fourth, one might object that invalidating legacy preferences would harm the financial interests of public universities by decreasing alumni contributions and potentially further eroding their position with respect to their private counterparts. There is a tacit agreement that universities will provide special consideration for alumni children in exchange for continued alumni financial support. Eliminating legacy preferences, it is argued, will thus erode the university's financial status, potentially weakening the quality of education for legacy and non-legacy students alike.

As noted elsewhere in this volume, there is ample reason to doubt that the financial consequences would be so dire. The California Institute of Technology, one of America's finest private universities, receives extraordinary funding from donors, yet is fiercely resistant to any hint of legacy preference in its admission policies.[137] Similarly, the two greatest universities in England, Oxford and Cambridge, somehow manage to function without employing legacy preferences.[138]

Even if some diminution in alumni support occurs—that is, even if complying with what I believe the Nobility Clauses command costs money—almost every constitutional provision imposes some costs on government.[139] It would be cheaper for the government to house convicts in dog cages rather than in prison cells, but the Eighth Amendment prohibits that. It would be cheaper to build highways by taking private land without just compensation, but the Fifth Amendment prohibits that. It would be cheaper not to provide jury trials to criminal defendants, but the Fifth Amendment also prohibits that. In short, we rarely recognize monetary costs as sufficient to override important constitutional principles, and the Nobility Clauses should not be treated any differently. Revolutionary Americans were fully aware that granting hereditary privileges might be financially rewarding; the Stuart kings had notoriously raised revenue by selling titles of nobility for large sums of money.[140] But the framers and ratifiers prohibited titles anyway, because no amount of money they might provide would be worth the sacrifice of core principles of equality.

A related objection is that a potential loss in alumni support would affect only public universities, as only they are subject to the Nobility Clauses. Private universities, which include the bulk of the nation's most selective universities, could still employ them.[141] This would put public universities at a significant disadvantage vis-à-vis their private counterparts. This disadvantage, however, is simply inherent in the nature of being bound by the Constitution; public employees, for example, have many costly rights under the First Amendment that private employees lack. More importantly, nothing stands in the way of aggressive efforts to limit the use of legacy preferences by private universities. Most selective private universities receive large amounts of money in the form of research grants from the federal government.[142] It would be quite reasonable for the federal government to distribute its research money only to those institutions that do not offer legacy preferences. Such a policy would solve the current prisoner's dilemma-type problem in which one private selective university would be reluctant to give up legacy preferences without a similar commitment from its competitors.

Legacy preferences, in some sense, will always exist. Inevitably, the children of those persons fortunate enough to have been educated at America's most selective universities will have advantages that other children will lack. The pressing question is whether the state may augment these advantages even further, using those very advantages as the reason for augmentation.

The history of the Nobility Clauses and the long American struggle against entrenched hereditary privilege should tell us that the answer is clearly no. Selective college admissions were unknown in the eighteenth century, but we do know what members of the Revolutionary generation thought about hereditary privilege. They denounced it in every form it might potentially appear. Legacy preferences belong more to the world of eighteenth-century British aristocracy than to the world of twenty-first-century American democracy.[143] It is that British world of inherited privilege that the Revolutionary generation sought to destroy forever. And each day legacy preferences remain in place in public universities is a betrayal not only of America's highest aspirations, but also of the explicit command of the Constitution itself.

8

Heirs of the American Experiment: A Legal Challenge to Preferences as a Violation of the Equal Protection Clause of the Constitution and the Civil Rights Act of 1866

Steve Shadowen and Sozi P. Tulante

Legacy preferences in college admissions grant or withhold an important benefit based on the identity of the applicant's parents or grandparents. In this chapter, we argue that such lineage-based preferences are unlawful in both public and private universities. In public universities, the preferences violate the Equal Protection Clause of the Fourteenth Amendment (which prohibits states from denying "the equal protection of the laws" to any person). In private universities, they violate the Civil Rights Act of 1866, a cornerstone civil rights statute that prohibits ancestry discrimination in the making of contracts, including contracts to attend a private school.[1] In both public and private universities, lineage-based

This chapter is a condensed and modified version of an article that we and Shara Alpern published as S. Shadowen, S. Tulante, and S. Alpern, "No Distinctions Except Those Which Merit Originates: The Unlawfulness of Legacy Preferences In Public and Private Universities," *Santa Clara Law Review* 49 (2009): 51–136.

preferences are unlawful unless they are narrowly tailored to achieve a compelling interest. The universities' stated rationale for granting the preferences—to increase donations from alumni—is neither compelling nor narrowly tailored to achieve the goal of raising money.

Defenders of legacy preferences have asserted that the Equal Protection Clause is essentially unconcerned with discrimination based on family lineage—that such discrimination is not subject to heightened judicial scrutiny and need be supported only by some plausible, even if weak or unconvincing, justification.[2] These claims, always made without reference to the relevant history or cases, are anachronistic: they judge the meaning of the Equal Protection Clause through the false lens of the set of contemporary societal problems—for example, discrimination based on race—that have driven recent equal protection litigation. The clause, they say, is concerned with race, not family lineage.

These legacy-preference defenders have matters exactly backward. Viewed in historical context, discrimination based on ancestry or family lineage emerges as a core concern—if not *the* core concern—of the Equal Protection Clause. Rejecting the lineage-based distinctions that had ossified feudal societies, the Founders intended the self-evident truth that "all men are created equal" specifically to prohibit inherited distinctions among white men, that is, distinctions based on family lineage. The drafters of the Fourteenth Amendment then codified this principle and broadened it to proscribe discrimination based on inherited race. However we see matters today, the drafters of the Equal Protection Clause viewed race discrimination as unlawful precisely because it judged an individual based on the identity of his parents or ancestors rather than on his own merit: family lineage discrimination was unlawful, and race discrimination was lineage discrimination writ large.

This history, and its implications for a proper understanding of the Equal Protection Clause, was succinctly chronicled by Justice Potter Stewart. He wrote that, "the Framers of our Constitution lived at a time when the Old World still operated in the shadow of ancient feudal traditions. As products of the Age of Enlightenment, they set out to establish a society that recognized no distinctions among white men on account of their birth."[3] The original Founders failed to extend this principle to protect African Americans, so that task fell to the Republicans of the 39th Congress—the authors of the Equal Protection Clause—who re-founded the nation after the Civil War. These Founders, concluded Stewart, codified and extended the principle against hereditary distinctions, and the Equal Protection Clause "promised to carry to its necessary conclusion a fundamental principle upon which this Nation had been founded—that the law would honor no preference based on lineage."[4]

This chapter provides the historical detail that underlies Justice Stewart's conclusion. We show that the original Founders' rejection of inherited rank or status among white men was reflected in the Declaration of Independence and in numerous provisions of the 1787 Constitution, including the guarantee of a republican form of government, the prohibition on granting titles of nobility, and the "corruption of blood" clauses. In the wake of the Civil War, the Republicans who used the concept of equality to prohibit race discrimination—legislators like Charles Sumner and John Bingham—expressly invoked the original Founders' principle against inherited distinctions, and they intended the Equal Protection Clause to embody it and make it enforceable by Congress and the courts.

Lineage-based privileges such as legacy preferences are throwbacks to an era and a social organization that this nation rejected long ago; they are "a peculiar practice . . . suited to [a] feudal aristocracy."[5] It is therefore not surprising that we must consult eighteenth- and nineteenth-century law and history in order to make an informed judgment as to their legality. But the Equal Protection Clause's principle against distinctions based on lineage is plainly visible even in contemporary Supreme Court cases. Current equal protection jurisprudence regarding ancestry, race, and parents' marital status is decisively informed by the principle against inherited distinctions. Those types of discrimination—all of which the Supreme Court has subjected to heightened scrutiny—share the same impermissible characteristic of treating children differently based on the identity or status of their parents.

We also argue that legacy preferences are unlawful in private universities. Under current Supreme Court authority, the Equal Protection Clause prohibits discrimination only by government, not by private entities.[6] This limitation does not apply, however, to the Civil Rights Act of 1866, which covers the admission decisions of private as well as public colleges and universities.[7] That statute, which was enacted by the 39th Congress just three months before the Joint Resolution proposing the Fourteenth Amendment, shares with the Equal Protection Clause the goal of eradicating discrimination based on the status or identity of one's parents.

The 1866 act provided that all U.S. citizens shall have the same fundamental rights, including the right to enter and enforce contracts (such as contracts to attend a school). Currently codified as 42 U.S.C. § 1981, the act is a mainstay in contemporary civil rights litigation, supplementing the protections afforded by the more recent, but in some instances more narrow, Civil Rights Act of 1964.[8] In particular, the 1866 act plays a prominent role in contemporary civil rights litigation involving race or ancestry discrimination in the admission and employment decisions of both private and public schools.[9]

In defining the "citizens" who enjoy an equality of rights, the 1866 act expressly and emphatically rejected the view that U.S. citizenship should be based on family lineage. The Supreme Court has construed the act to prohibit discrimination based on "ancestry" and has stated in *dicta* that this includes discrimination based on "the lineage of a family." This Supreme Court precedent, together with the clear legislative history of the act, provides a solid basis for litigation against legacy preferences in private schools.

Given the close relationship between the 1866 Civil Rights Act and the Equal Protection Clause, we consider their history and meaning together below.

The Declaration and Egalitarian Provisions of the 1787 Constitution

The drafters of the 1866 Civil Rights Act intended to codify, for the first time in the young nation's history, the principle of equality that the Founders inscribed in the Declaration and in the egalitarian provisions of the 1787 Constitution. So an understanding of the 1866 act begins with understanding what the Founders were rebelling against. When they asserted that "all [white] men are created equal," what then-extant distinctions among white men were they rejecting?

Historian Gordon Wood has shown that a primary purpose of the American Revolution was to reject a society based on hereditary privilege in favor of one founded on the equality of white men.[10] The Revolution pitted patriots against "courtiers," persons "whose position or rank came artificially from above—from hereditary or personal connections that ultimately flowed from the crown or court."[11] The essence of republicanism was that "a man's merit [would] rest entirely with himself, without any regard to family, blood, or connection."[12] In short, the Revolution was "a vindication of frustrated talent at the expense of birth and blood."[13]

The Declaration's Rejection of Hereditary Privileges

The Declaration's assertion of equality was both intended and widely understood to encompass a rejection of hereditary privileges among white men. Thomas Jefferson wanted to abolish the aristocracy of birth and establish an "aristocracy of virtue and talent, which nature has wisely provided for the direction of the interests of society, & scattered with equal hand through all it's [sic] conditions."[14] When Jefferson inscribed in the Declaration the self-evident truth that "all men are created equal," he understood that this equality included "particularly the denial of a preeminence by birth."[15] For the fiftieth anniversary of the Declaration, he wrote that the Revolution had been founded on the principle that "the mass of mankind has not been born with saddles on their backs, nor a favored few, booted and spurred, ready to ride them legitimately, by the grace of God."[16]

The Declaration echoed the views of Thomas Paine's *Common Sense*,[17] which asserted that, "For all men being originally equals, no one by birth could have a right to set up his own family in perpetual preference to all others for ever, and tho' himself might deserve some decent degree of honours of his cotemporaries, yet his descendants might be far too unworthy to inherit them."[18] By sweeping away the inherited privileges of the feudal world, the new American society would "prepare in time an asylum for mankind."[19]

Jefferson's Declaration was also influenced by George Mason's draft of the Virginia Declaration of Rights,[20] which specifically equated "equality" with, among other things, a prohibition on hereditary privileges in public institutions. It asserted, in its first article, that "all men are created equally free and independent," and its fourth article provided that "emoluments or privileges from the community" are "not . . . descendible."[21]

Jefferson also acknowledged the Declaration's indebtedness to John Locke,[22] whose works were revered by educated Americans in 1776 "as a kind of political gospel."[23] In the First Treatise, Locke rejected the intellectual underpinnings of hereditary succession, as typified in English political theorist Robert Filmer's *Patriarcha*.[24] The Second Treatise elaborated on that rejection, asserting that, in the state of nature, people are in "a state also of equality, wherein all the power and jurisdiction is reciprocal, no one having more than another." Each person is "equal to the greatest and subject to nobody." Accordingly, when people enter into a state of society, legislators "are to govern by promulgated established laws, not to be varied in particular cases, but to have one rule for rich and poor, for the favourite at Court, and the countryman at plough." The rejection of hereditary right is also the foundation for the requirement of government by consent of the governed.[25]

Before submitting his draft to Congress, Jefferson circulated it to John Adams and Benjamin Franklin, both of whom were also fierce opponents of inherited privileges. When Adams wrote in 1766 that "all men are born equal," he intended the phrase specifically to reject "the doctrine that a few nobles or rich commons have a right to inherit the earth."[26]

Franklin's views against hereditary privilege were hardened by his close observation of Britain's House of Lords, whom he mocked as "Hereditary Legislators" who "appeared to have scarce Discretion enough to govern a Herd of Swine"—"there would be more Propriety, because less Hazard of Mischief, in having (as in some University of Germany,) Hereditary Professors of Mathematicks!"[27] Franklin wrote to his daughter that, "descending Honour, to Posterity who could have had no Share in obtaining it, is not only groundless and absurd, but often hurtful to that Posterity, since it is apt to make them proud."[28]

Others who played a leading role in the adoption of the Declaration, such as Samuel Adams, also expressly understood and intended its statement of equality to preclude "the absurd and unnatural claim of hereditary and exclusive privileges."[29]

The 1787 Constitution Advanced the Anti-Hereditary-Privilege Principle

Multiple provisions of the 1787 Constitution memorialize the victory against hereditary privilege.[30] To begin with, Article IV, Section 4 (the "Guaranty Clause") provides that, "the United States shall guarantee to every State in this Union a Republican Form of Government."[31] The essential feature of a republican government is its treatment of citizens without regard to their birth status; to denominate a government "republican" is to distinguish it from an aristocratic one in which public offices are inherited rather than earned.[32]

Next, Article I prohibits the national (Section 9, Clause 8) and state (Section 10, Clause 1) governments from granting any title of nobility.[33] In Chapter 7 of this volume, Carlton Larson amasses a mountain of research establishing that the title-of-nobility clauses were intended to prohibit government from granting lineage-based privileges.[34]

Article III, Section 3, Clause 2 provides that, "no Attainder of Treason shall work Corruption of Blood, or Forfeiture except during the Life of the Person Attainted."[35] The Constitution thus prohibited "corruption of blood" statutes that imposed disabilities on the heirs of persons convicted of certain crimes. Focusing on individual rather than familial merit and conduct, the Founders concluded that "just as no favorite son should be handed his sire's government post, so no child should be punished for the sins of his father."[36]

Similarly, Article I, Sections 9 and 10 prohibit the federal and state governments, respectively, from passing any bills of attainder.[37] These Bills of Attainder Clauses prohibit government from penalizing persons based on their identity or status rather than their conduct.[38] These clauses, together with the ban on titles of nobility, ensure that citizens are "judged on the basis of their behavior, not their birth status."[39]

These and other constitutional provisions, together with the Declaration's assertion of equality, established a strong principle against inherited distinctions among white men. That principle was a cornerstone of the young nation, and it provided a foundation on which others would build.

The Abolitionists and Antebellum Republicans Invoked the Principle

These egalitarian ideas were later recovered and expanded by the abolitionists and radical Republicans to urge an end to chattel slavery.[40] Many abolitionists relied on the Guaranty Clause, asserting that equality is "[t]he very pith and essence of a republican form of government."[41] Others, such as Frederick Douglass, argued that "[t]he Constitution forbids the passing of a bill of attainder: that is, a law entailing upon the child the disabilities and hardships imposed upon the parent. Every slave law in America might be repealed on this very ground. The slave is made a slave because his mother is a slave."[42]

Most importantly, the prewar Republicans asserted that the Declaration's guiding principle of equality was always intended to include African Americans and should be extended to protect them.[43] The Declaration—which Abraham Lincoln called "the white man's charter of freedom"[44] —ensured that "having kicked off the King and Lords of Great Britain, we should not at once be saddled with a King and Lords of our own."[45] For Lincoln and other Republicans, the Founders' principle against inherited privileges should also preclude race slavery:

> It is the same spirit that says, "You work and toil and earn bread, and I'll eat it." No matter in what shape it comes, whether from the mouth of a king who seeks to bestride the people of his own nation and live by the fruit of their labor, or from one race of men as an apology for enslaving another race, it is the same tyrannical principle.[46]

Lincoln asserted that the northern democracy was founded on "the principles of Jefferson," while the southern aristocracy was built on the opposing principles of "classification, caste, and legitimacy."[47] The North fought to "lift artificial weights from all shoulders—to clear the paths of laudable pursuit for all—to afford all, an unfettered start, and a fair chance, in the race of life."[48] The nation had been "dedicated to the proposition that all men are created equal," and in extending the Founders' anti-hereditary-privilege principle to the children of African-American slaves, the war brought to the nation "a new birth of freedom."[49]

Congress Codified and Extended the Declaration's Principle

The debates in Congress over the 1866 Civil Rights Act and the Equal Protection Clause show that Congress intended them to codify the Declaration's no-hereditary-privilege principle and extend it to encompass African Americans. The Declaration had stated an ideal but had two flaws: it failed to encompass African Americans, and it was not enforceable as law by anyone. The 1866 act and then the Equal Protection Clause remedied those defects by codifying and expanding the original Founders' principle against hereditary distinctions. The 1866 act did so by providing for equality of rights among "citizens" and expressly rejecting the contention, notoriously adopted in the *Dred Scott* decision, that citizenship and its concomitant rights were determined by family lineage.[50] Congress then quickly concluded that in equalizing rights only for "citizens," the 1866 act did not go far enough in rejecting rank and status. So the Equal Protection Clause, and then an amended 1866 act, provided that in the reborn republic all "persons" would enjoy equal rights.

The Congressional Debates

Senator Lyman Trumbull of Illinois, the author of the 1866 act, noted that the Declaration and the Constitution's egalitarian provisions had established the principle that all men are created equal.[51] But the mere statement of principle had failed to protect oppressed whites or millions of African Americans, so it was "the intention of this bill to secure those rights."[52] The principle of equality among white men had been the cornerstone of the founding of the republic; the 1866 act would codify and extend that principle, and thus create a new foundation for the reborn nation.[53]

This understanding of the act was widely shared among the leading Republican legislators. For example, Senator Charles Sumner of Massachusetts, the Republicans' intellectual leader on the issue of equality,[54] believed that the greatest victory of the Civil War was that "the Declaration of Independence is made a living letter instead of a promise."[55] He had long preached that distinctions based on birth were precluded by "the emphatic words of the Declaration of Independence, which our country took upon its lips as baptismal vows."[56]

His speech in the Senate on February 5 and 6, 1866,[57] invoked the anti-hereditary-privilege principle of the Founders as the source for the 39th Congress's equal-rights legislation. Proposing that "there shall be no Oligarchy, Aristocracy, Caste, or Monopoly invested with peculiar privileges and powers,"[58] he quoted the Founders:

- *Benjamin Franklin*—"*Every man* of the commonalty, except infants, insane persons, and criminals, is of common right, and by the laws of God, a freeman and entitled to the free enjoyment of liberty."

- *James Madison*—"It is essential for such a government that it be derived from the great body of the society, not from an inconsiderable proportion, OR A FAVORED CLASS OF IT; otherwise a handful of tyrannical nobles, exercising their oppressions by delegation of their powers, might aspire to the rank of republicans, and claim for the government the honorable title of republic."

- *Alexander Hamilton*—"There can be no truer principle than this, that *every individual of the community has an equal right to the protection of government*. . . . we propose a free government. Can it be so, if *partial distinctions* are made?"

- *Roger Sherman*—"What especially denominates it a republic is its dependence on the *public,* or *people at large,* without any hereditary powers."

The nation was founded, "not to create an oligarchy or aristocracy, not to exclude certain persons from the pale of its privileges," but "to establish justice, which is Equality." Sumner defined aristocracy as "the enjoyment of privileges *which are not communicable to other citizens simply by anything they can themselves do to obtain them,*" and he asserted that the 1866 act prohibited it.[59]

The debates overflow with other references to Congress's intention that the 1866 act embody and give effect to the Declaration's principle.[60] The planter aristocracy's domination of blacks and poor whites was impermissible because "we have accepted the sublime truths of the Declaration of Independence. We stand as the champions of human rights for all men, black and white, the wide world over, and we mean that just and equal laws shall pervade every rood of this nation."[61] The act was "one of those measures that are absolutely necessary to carry into effect the decisions of the late war" by "carry[ing] into effect the doctrine of the Declaration."[62]

After the extensive debates on the 1866 act, references to the Declaration as a source for the Equal Protection Clause became routine.[63] In a typical statement, Senator Luke Poland of Vermont asserted that the clause "is essentially declared in the Declaration of Independence and in all the provisions of the Constitution. . . . It certainly seems desirable that no doubt should be left existing as to the power of Congress to enforce principles lying at the very foundation of all republican government."[64]

The Equal Protection Clause was authored by Representative John Bingham of Ohio, who had long asserted that the principle against hereditary distinctions precluded slavery based on inherited race. Melding the Christian and republican visions of a common humanity, Bingham invoked the biblical prescriptions that God "hath made of one blood all nations of men" and is "no respecter of persons," and asserted that the Declaration was "a reiteration of the[se] great truth[s]."[65] The Constitution's inherent principle of equality, he explained, "makes no distinction either on account of complexion or birth."[66] And the Constitution prohibits titles of nobility because "all are equal under the Constitution; and . . . no distinctions should be tolerated, except those which merit originates, and no nobility except that which springs from [talent and merit]."[67] Rather than nobility based on birth, "the ONLY nobility which our free Constitution tolerates" is that based on "patient, humble toil," the "sturdy arm of intelligent industry," and "that imperial exercise of the intellect which enlarges the measure of knowledge and lessens the evils of life."[68]

In the debate on the Equal Protection Clause, Bingham summoned and summarized these principles by asserting that human laws, like those of God, "should be no respecter of persons."[69] Bingham argued that the clause confirmed the protections that the Declaration and the Constitution had secured for whites and extended those protections to African Americans: "the divinest feature of your Constitution is the recognition of the absolute equality before the law of all persons, . . . subject only to the exception made by reason of slavery, now happily abolished."[70] By ratifying the Fourteenth Amendment, the American people would "declare their purpose to stand by the foundation principle of their own institutions."[71]

The Rejection of Family Lineage as the Basis for Citizenship

The debates also show that the Republicans used elegantly simple language to codify and expand the Declaration's principle against hereditary distinctions. The 1866 act extended its substantive rights, including the right to make contracts, to "citizens," and provided that "all persons born" in the United States are citizens. Each of these words is packed with meaning.

The significance of becoming a citizen of a republic rather than the subject of a monarchy is that "none have hereditary rights superior to others."[72] The fundamental premise of the 1866 act was that "a true republic rests upon the absolute equality of rights of the whole people, high and low, rich and poor, black and white."[73]

The means of achieving citizenship also reflect a rejection of hereditary privileges. To obtain citizenship and the equal rights that it ensures, a person need not be born into any designated race, class, or family, but merely be born a human being in the United States.[74] This principle of *jus soli,* or "birthright citizenship," conformed to a strong strain of egalitarianism within the Republican Party that embraced citizenship and civil rights without regard to the accident of birth. Speaking in Faneuil Hall in 1855, Senator Sumner rejected both Know-Nothingism[75] and slavery because they "attaint[ed] men for their religion and also for their birth."[76] A political party that "founds a discrimination on the accident of birth, is not the party for us."[77]

Similarly rejecting Know-Nothingism, Lincoln argued that membership in American society should not be conferred as a hereditary privilege, but should result from voluntary adoption of American ideals that reject such privileges. He noted that half of all American citizens were not descendants of those who were Americans at the Founding. But when immigrants read the Declaration, "they feel that that moral sentiment [of equality] taught in that day evidences their relation to those men, that it is the father of all moral principle in them, and that they have a right to claim it as though they were blood of the blood, and flesh of the flesh, of the men who wrote that Declaration (loud and long continued applause) and so they are."[78]

Legal scholar Garrett Epps shows that the capstone of this line of Republican thought was Carl Schurz's 1859 speech, "True Americanism,"[79] which argued that American nationality "did not spring from one family, one tribe, one country, but incorporates the vigorous elements of all civilized nations on earth." Schurz asserted that the nation must "choose between two social organizations, one of which is founded upon privilege, and the other upon the doctrine of equal rights." While "[t]he dignity of the Roman citizen consisted in his exclusive privileges; the dignity of the American citizen consists in holding the natural rights of his neighbor just as sacred as his own." America is "*the republic of equal rights, where the title of manhood is the title to citizenship.*"[80]

The alternative to birthright citizenship was *jus sanguinis,* or citizenship based on family lineage. These starkly opposing ways of determining citizenship had played a dramatic role in the events leading to the Civil War. In 1820 Congress debated the admission of Missouri in view of its proposed constitution, which excluded from the state "free negroes and mulattoes." Slavery's apologists argued that even free, native-born African Americans had no rights to interstate travel because they inherited their parents' disqualification from U.S. citizenship.[81]

Chief Justice Taney's decision in 1856 in *Dred Scott* v. *Sandford* subsequently used the same reasoning to conclude that African Americans were not citizens of the United States, and that they therefore had "no rights which the white man was bound to respect." Invoking *jus sanguinis,* Taney reasoned that all African Americans were ineligible for naturalization because of their race, and that native-born African Americans "from birth or parentage" inherited their parents' ineligibility. In Taney's view, this denied U.S. citizenship to African Americans who were brought here as slaves as well as "their descendants, whether they had become free or not."[82] Taney's reasoning likewise implied that the American-born children of unnaturalized aliens also were not U.S. citizens.[83]

This fundamental dispute over the means of obtaining citizenship—birthright citizenship versus citizenship-by-lineage—was played out again in the congressional debates over the 1866 act. The Democrats in Congress asserted that the war's outcome had no bearing on this issue—that the law of *jus sanguinis* should continue to apply and native-born African Americans could not be citizens because they "inherited the disqualification of the ancestor."[84] Indeed, the Democrats argued that *Dred Scott* was binding constitutional precedent that precluded a mere statute such as the 1866 act from conferring U.S. citizenship on all persons born in the country.[85]

The Democrats also relied on Justice Curtis's dissent in *Dred Scott,* which concluded that U.S. citizenship (except through naturalization) was determined by one's citizenship in a state.[86] Urging Congress to sustain the president's veto of the 1866 act, Senator Reverdy Johnson of Maryland argued that the former slave states defined citizenship by family lineage: "the constitution and laws of the [slave] States . . . declare . . . that no descendant of a colored mother, whether she was free or not, was to be considered a citizen by virtue of birth."[87] Unstated by Johnson, but nonetheless the fact, those states also determined whether the mother was "colored" for these purposes by examining her family lineage—anyone with one-eighth or more of "negro blood" was deemed to be "black."[88] Johnson complained that, contrary to the southern citizenship-by-lineage statutes, the 1866 act provided that every person born in the United States "is to be considered a citizen by reason of the [mere] fact of his being born."[89]

The Republicans expressly rejected the arguments for determining citizenship by lineage. They rejected Taney's reading of the Constitution,[90] the contention that they lacked constitutional authority to grant birthright citizenship,[91] and the southern citizenship-by-lineage statutes.[92] They instead reaffirmed that, "the bill proposes to make a citizen of every person born in the United States," including "even the infant child of a foreigner born in this land."[93] Adopting birthright citizenship and rejecting citizenship-by-lineage, the Republicans emphasized that the 1866 act secured the equal rights of every person "of whatever caste or lineage they be,"[94] and protected "the children of all parentage whatever."[95]

In rejecting lineage as the basis for citizenship, Congress confirmed the act's prohibition on lineage discrimination in the act's citizenship-based substantive rights (including the right to enter a contract for schooling).[96] The eminent jurist, Representative William Lawrence of Ohio, explained: "it is citizenship . . . that gives the title to these rights to all citizens," and those rights are not "accorded only to citizens of 'some class,' or 'some race,' or 'of the least favored class,' or 'of the most favored class,' or of a particular complexion for these distinctions were never contemplated or recognized as possible in fundamental civil rights, which are alike necessary and important to all citizens, and to make inequities in which is rank injustice."[97]

The Extension of Equal Rights to All "Persons"

The Fourteenth Amendment made birthright citizenship part of the organic law of the land.[98] The Republicans recognized the importance of rejecting hereditary citizenship and wanted to preserve their victory on that issue against any future Democrat-controlled Congress.

The amendment also extended the guarantee of equal protection beyond all "citizens" to all "persons." Bingham successfully argued that the 1866 act's restriction of equal rights to only "citizens" did not go far enough in rejecting the status-based, feudal ideas of the Old World. The 1866 act "commit[ed] the terrible enormity of distinguishing here in the laws in respect to life, liberty, and property between the citizen and the stranger."[99] States should not be permitted to classify on that basis:

> The great men who made [the Fifth Amendment] . . . abolished the narrow and limited phrase of the old Magna Charta of five hundred years ago, which gave the protection of the laws only to "free men" and inserted in its stead the more comprehensive words, "no person," . . . Thus, in respect to life and liberty and property, the people by their Constitution declared the equality of all men.[100]

Congress of course accepted Bingham's proposal, and the Equal Protection Clause extends to all persons. Bingham subsequently sponsored the Enforcement Act of 1870, which, among other things, re-enacted the 1866 act in toto and, in a separate section, reiterated the ban on discrimination in the making or enforcement of contracts but extended the protection to "all persons."[101]

This history shows that the Republicans self-consciously reached back to the Founders' principle against hereditary distinctions and enacted it into positive law in order to reaffirm and extend to African Americans the equality that had been promised by the Declaration. They did so by securing the rights of all citizens (not subjects), defined as all persons born (merely born, not born into a favored race, class, or family) in the United States. And even that protection was too status-based, so the Equal Protection Clause extended its security to all persons regardless of citizenship, and then the 1866 act was modified likewise. Congress thus "put aside the creed of the despot, the monarchist, the aristocrat," and required that "race or color, inferiority or superiority" shall cease to be "terms of exclusion."[102] Inherited privileges had been outlawed:

> All attempts in this country to keep alive the old idea of orders of men, distinctions of class, noble and ignoble, superior and inferior, antagonism of races, are so many efforts at insurrection and anarchy. In a nation of professed freemen whose political axioms are those of universal liberty and human rights, no public tranquility is possible while these rights are denied to portions of the American people.[103]

In the making and enforcement of contracts, and in the states' treatment of all persons within their jurisdictions, discrimination on the basis of lineage or ancestry was prohibited.

Case Law Confirms that Legacy Preferences in Public Universities Are Subject to Strict Scrutiny

The conclusion derived from the legislative history is confirmed by the equal protection case law. The Supreme Court consistently has said that discrimination based on "lineage" or "ancestry" (apart from any additional or concurrent discrimination based on racial group) is inherently suspect.[104] More broadly, the Court has repeatedly held, in a variety of contexts, that heightened scrutiny applies to discrimination based on "the accident of birth."[105]

First, we examine below three sets of such cases: (1) those directly addressing lineage/ancestry discrimination; (2) those establishing that race discrimination is unlawful in significant part because it is lineage discrimination writ large; and (3) those establishing that discrimination against children based on their parents' marital status elicits heightened scrutiny. Then, we look at a fourth instance, a single case that went in a different direction.

Cases on Ancestry/Lineage

In 1943, the Court in *Hirabayashi* v. *United States,* famously held that, "distinctions between citizens solely because of their ancestry are by their very nature odious to a free people whose institutions are founded upon the doctrine of equality."[106] In 1948, in *Oyama* v. *California,* the Court made clear that the prohibited "ancestry" distinctions include those based on individual family lineage—on the identity or status of one's parents—in addition to those based on racial or ethnic group.[107]

The California statute in *Oyama* prohibited aliens who were ineligible for American citizenship from owning agricultural land, and any property that they transferred with the intent to evade the statute escheated to the state. California law generally presumed that a parent conveying property to his child intended a gift, but the statute presumed, in effect, that an ineligible alien conveying to his child intended a trust in which the child held the title, unlawfully, for the benefit of the parent.[108]

Plaintiff Fred Oyama was an American citizen whose father, a Japanese national ineligible for U.S. citizenship, transferred real estate to him. In striking down the statute, the Court in several instances referred to the statute's racial animus, but made clear that the prohibited discrimination was based not on racial group, but "is based solely on [the plaintiff child's] parents' country of origin," that is, on his "different lineage." The statute was unlawful because "the father's deeds were visited on the son."[109]

The Court distinguished, rather than overruled, its prior decision in 1925 in *Cockrill* v. *California,* which had held that the same statute did not unlawfully discriminate against Japanese donors based on their racial or ethnic group.[110] *Oyama* thus made clear that it was the differential treatment of children based on the status of their parents— apart from any concurrent or additional discrimination based on racial or ethnic group or national origin—that made the discrimination unlawful.[111] And the Court subsequently has cited *Oyama* consistently for the proposition that discrimination based on ancestry or lineage is subject to strict scrutiny.[112]

This proscription of discrimination based on lineage was applied and extended in 1982 by the Court in *Plyler* v. *Doe.*[113] The state of

Texas denied a free public education to children who could not prove that they had been lawfully admitted into the United States. Writing for the Court, Justice Brennan held that, "legislation imposing special disabilities upon groups disfavored by virtue of circumstances beyond their control suggests a kind of 'class or caste' treatment that the Fourteenth Amendment was designed to abolish."[114] While undocumented aliens cannot properly be a "suspect class," it was the parents, not the children, who were responsible for having entered the country illegally.[115] Heightened scrutiny applied because "the children who are plaintiffs in these cases 'can affect neither their parents' conduct nor their own status,'"[116] and "no child is responsible for his birth."[117] Denying a public education to the children "poses an affront to one of the goals of the Equal Protection Clause: the abolition of governmental barriers presenting unreasonable obstacles to advancement on the basis of individual merit."[118]

Cases on Race

The case law also recognizes that strict scrutiny applies to race discrimination in part because it is a form of discrimination based on lineage or ancestry.[119] In 2000, in *Rice* v. *Cayetano*,[120] the Court held that the state of Hawaii violated the Fifteenth Amendment's ban on race-based voting qualifications by limiting the franchise to persons with "native Hawaiian" ancestry:

> One of the principal reasons race is treated as a forbidden classification is that it demeans the dignity and worth of a person to be judged by ancestry instead of by his or her own merit and essential qualities. An inquiry into ancestral lines is not consistent with respect based on the unique personality each of us possesses, a respect the Constitution itself secures in its concern for persons and citizens.[121]

As the history detailed above showed, and as the Court has reaffirmed, the Equal Protection Clause protects individuals against discrimination based on their lineage, and race discrimination is one type of such discrimination.

Cases on Parents' Marital Status

The prohibition on hereditary distinctions has likewise animated the Court's jurisprudence applying heightened scrutiny to discrimination against children born out of wedlock. In 1972, in *Weber* v. *Aetna Casualty & Surety Co.*, the Court held that a state could not lawfully prevent such children from recovering statutory death benefits because "legal burdens should bear some relationship to individual responsibility or wrongdoing," and "no child is responsible for his birth." The Equal Protection Clause "enable[s] us to strike down discriminatory laws relating to status of birth."[122] The Court in *Mathews* v. *Lucas*, similarly noted in 1976 that whether a child's parents were married at the time of her birth is a circumstance "determined by causes not within the control of the . . . [child], and it bears no relation to the individual's ability to participate in and contribute to society."[123]

The *Kotch* Decision

Against all of these consistent cases stands a single authority, the five-to-four decision in 1947, in *Kotch* v. *Board of Riverport Pilot Commissioners for Port of New Orleans*, upholding a Louisiana statute that gave incumbent state riverboat pilots discretion to select only their friends and relatives as apprentices. Writing for four dissenters, Justice Wiley B. Rutledge asserted that discrimination based on lineage is unlawful under the Equal Protection Clause:

> [The statute as applied] makes admission to the ranks of pilots turn finally on consanguinity. Blood is, in effect, made the crux of selection. That, in my opinion, is forbidden by the Fourteenth Amendment's guarantee against denial of the equal protection of the laws. The door is thereby closed to all not having blood relationship to presently licensed pilots. . . . [I]t is beyond legislative power to make entrance to [employment as a pilot] turn upon such a criterion.[124]

In upholding the statute, the majority noted that it was sui generis, affecting the "unique institution of pilotage in the light of its history in Louisiana."[125] The majority concluded, moreover, that open competition for the apprentice positions would "adversely affect . . . the public interest."[126]

James Torke at the Indiana University School of Law has demonstrated that the majority decision is best understood as a reaction against the then-recently passed era of substantive due process attacks on economic regulation.[127] During that era, an activist, reactionary

Supreme Court had invoked the Due Process Clause of the Fourteenth Amendment to strike down minimum-wage, child-labor, and other ameliorative New Deal-era legislation. Throughout the *Kotch* litigation, the plaintiffs had foolishly cast their arguments in the discredited language of substantive due process, with "only a sideways glance" at the discrimination based on lineage.[128]

These litigation dynamics, together with the majority's own acknowledgment of the unique facts of the case, prevent the *Kotch* majority opinion from supporting legacy preferences in college admissions. While the public interest in *Kotch* required the absence of rivalry for the pilotage jobs, the public interest in college admissions demands open, fair competition: "all members of our heterogeneous society must have confidence in the openness and integrity of the educational institutions that provide this elite training."[129] The *Kotch* dissent, not the majority, provides the relevant rationale for analyzing lineage-restricted admissions to public universities.

The Supreme Court has consistently cited *Oyama*, decided the year after *Kotch*, for the proposition that ancestry discrimination is subject to strict scrutiny. The *Oyama* decision, the strong legislative history, and the other case law addressed above provide solid grounds for courts to apply strict scrutiny to legacy preferences in public universities. As Justice Stewart concluded, the history of the Equal Protection Clause makes clear that "the law would honor no preference based on lineage."[130]

Case Law Confirms the Unlawfulness of Legacy Preferences in Private Universities under the 1866 Act

The 1866 Civil Rights Act has generated fewer relevant cases than has the Equal Protection Clause, but the rejection of discrimination based on lineage is equally clear. In 1976, in *Runyon* v. *McCrary,* the Supreme Court held that the 1866 act's proscriptions apply to the admission decisions of private schools.[131] In 1987, in *St. Francis College* v. *Al-Khazraji,* the Court indicated that the act prohibits discrimination based on "ancestry," including "the lineage of a family."[132]

In *Al-Khazraji*, the Court held that an American born in Iraq could state a claim of unlawful discrimination to the extent that he alleged that he was "subjected to intentional discrimination based on the fact that he was born an Arab, rather than solely on the place or nation of his origin, or his religion."[133] Holding that the act bars "race" discrimination, the Court observed that dictionaries in the mid-nineteenth century defined race very broadly to include, for example:

> a "continued series of descendants from a parent who is called the stock," . . . "the lineage of a family," . . . or "descendants of a common ancestor," . . . . The 1887 edition of Webster's expanded the definition somewhat: "The descendants of a common ancestor; a family, tribe, people or nation, believed or presumed to belong to the same stock."[134]

The Court noted that it was "not until the 20th century that dictionaries began referring . . . to race as involving divisions of mankind based upon different physical characteristics." Even today, dictionaries still define race as including "a family, tribe, people, or nation belonging to the same stock."[135]

The Court accordingly held that "Congress intended to protect from discrimination identifiable classes of persons who are subjected to intentional discrimination solely because of their ancestry or ethnic characteristics. Such discrimination is racial discrimination that Congress intended [the act] to forbid whether or not it would be classified as racial in terms of modern scientific or social theory." "Ancestry" being an improper classification, *Al-Khazraji* was required to show only that he was discriminated against because he "was born an Arab," not because he had "a distinctive physiognomy."[136]

Discrimination based on family lineage fits comfortably within *Al-Khazraji's* broad definition of "race" or "ancestry" discrimination. In the Court's language, legacy preferences discriminate on the basis of ancestry, and they do so against "identifiable classes of persons"—classes consisting of the children of non-alumni.

This reading is confirmed by multiple aspects of *Al-Khazraji*. The Court repeatedly referred to "race" as including "the lineage of a family," and similarly equated race with "stock," that is, lineal descent. And the Court held that race included "ancestry,"[137] which in both common usage and Supreme Court usage includes family lineage within only two generations.[138] Indeed, *Al-Khazraji* cites *Oyama* as an example of discrimination based on "ancestry."[139]

The Court explicitly separated race and ancestry from any connection to group physiognomy or ethnicity.[140] The requirement that Al-Khazraji show that he was discriminated against because he was "born an Arab" thus meant no more than that he was born to a parent who had some measure of "Arab blood," without any requirement that his parents have "Arab" physiognomy, characteristics, or culture. The touchstone is discrimination based on birth, that is, descent, or family lineage. Indeed, the act also protects "whites,"[141] so Al-Khazraji could have also satisfied the requirement by showing, if it was true, that he was discriminated against because he "was born a white"—that is, born to a parent who had some "white blood."[142]

Lastly, in defining the scope of the prohibited discrimination, *Al-Khazraji* looked to the 1866 debates as well as dictionaries. As we showed in detail above, those debates reveal that Congress expressly incorporated into the act the Declaration's proscription on hereditary distinctions among white men and confirmed the prohibition on lineage classifications by rejecting them as a basis for obtaining the citizenship that conferred the act's substantive rights. Congress proscribed discrimination based on inherited race by codifying and expanding the more fundamental prohibition on inherited distinctions. The legislative history thus compels a literal reading of *Al-Khazraji's* statement that the prohibited "race" discrimination includes discrimination based on "the lineage of a family."[143]

Legacy Preferences Do Not Narrowly Serve a Compelling Interest

Legacy preferences are subject to strict scrutiny, and the universities therefore must prove that their use is narrowly tailored to serve a compelling interest.[144] The universities cannot rely on the interest that overcame strict scrutiny of affirmative action for racial minorities in college admissions—an interest in a diverse student body.[145] Legacy preferences undermine student-body diversity, whether measured by class or race.[146] Considering legacy status in the admissions process could help achieve diversity only if universities gave it negative rather than positive weight.

The schools are therefore left with trying to justify the preferences on the ground that they cause alumni to increase donations. We hope that, when push comes to shove, no university will actually rely on this justification. As American political philosopher Michael Sandel has argued, using admission decisions as a tool to raise money "is a kind of corruption."[147] A university's proper purpose is to teach and conduct research, to which ends raising money is only a means. Thus, "when the goal of money-making predominates to the point of governing admission, the university has strayed far from the scholarly and civic goods that are its primary reason for being."[148]

If any university nevertheless offers this "corrupt" justification for legacy preferences, the law will reject it. Raising money from discrimination's beneficiaries is not a *legitimate* interest. Consider, for example, the *Brown* v. *Board of Education* decision in 1954.[149] Topeka's Board of Education could not have justified its racially segregated schools by asserting that the white parents would have been willing to pay more taxes if the schools remained all white. To contend that the recipients of a preference are willing to pay for it is simply to restate that they have obtained something of value. Thus, in *Plyler* v. *Doe,* the Court rejected fiscal concerns as a basis for denying a public education to the children of undocumented workers. To assert that discrimination will help save or raise money, said the Court, is simply to "justify . . . classification with a concise expression of an intention to discriminate."[150] If granting legacy preferences caused alumni to increase their donations, those increases would not be a legitimate, cognizable justification.

In any event, Chad Coffman and his colleagues in Chapter 5 in this volume lucidly show that granting legacy preferences does not in fact cause alumni to increase their giving.[151] Instead, preferring alumni children is simply a way for schools to over-select from the pool of their own wealthy alumni.[152] Rather than prompting alumni to increase donations, the preferences cause schools to admit more wealthy children and thereby exacerbate the already scandalous class divide on elite campuses.[153]

These children from wealthy families already enjoy enormous advantages in the admissions competition, including the best secondary schooling, SAT preparation courses, superior guidance counseling, and other cultural capital.[154] Legacy policies add to these resources an expressly inherited advantage—one that, in Senator Sumner's words, is "not communicable to other citizens simply by anything they can themselves do to obtain [it]."[155] Simply put, legacy preferences magnify the wealth and cultural advantages that alumni children already have over their wrong-birth peers.

Finally, even if legacy preferences caused alumni to donate more (they do not) and even if such a justification were cognizable (it is not), the schools could not show that using legacy preferences is a narrowly tailored means of raising funds. Again the data are dispositive. Coffman and his colleagues in Chapter 5 show that alumni donations typically account for only 3.5 percent to 5.1 percent of elite schools' budgets.[156] Moreover, among alumni contributions, the top 1 percent of gifts account for approximately 70 percent of the total dollar value.[157] Given that the children of the largest donors get special consideration regardless of any alumni connection, the alumni donations that are potentially positively affected by legacy preferences typically account for only about 1 percent to 1.5 percent of a school's annual budget.[158]

Not surprisingly, elite schools without legacy preferences can and do easily make up for any funding losses caused by the absence of legacy policies. For example, data show that any such shortfalls are more than offset by schools' heightened efforts to obtain grants and contracts.[159]

If schools insist on using the admissions process to raise money, they could simply sell a small number of admission slots on the open market. We agree with Sandel that selling admissions, whether directly or through legacy preferences, is corrupt. But selling them directly has advantages over granting legacy preferences. The former, unlike the latter, both provides refreshing candor and avoids lineage discrimination. And outright sales would stop the current intolerable policy that forces the victims of legacy preferences to pay for them. Under the current policy, the alumni/donors take tax deductions in the full amount of their "donations" to the university, without reducing their tax write-offs to account for the value of the legacy preferences that they receive. Thus, the non-legacy applicants, who are also taxpayers, are forced to subsidize the preferences that they are denied. Candidly selling the admission slots on the open market would allow the universities to continue using the admissions process to raise money, but would avoid ancestry discrimination and the insult and injury of requiring wrong-birth students to subsidize their own undoing.

Conclusion

Legacy preferences offend an American egalitarian tradition that stretches back to the founding. They are unlawful, rather than merely shameful, because the Republicans of the 39th Congress who were re-founding the nation consciously reached back to the Declaration's principle against hereditary distinctions, broadened it to encompass a ban on discrimination based on inherited race, and enacted it into positive law.

Affirmative action in favor of racial minorities in college admissions, designed (depending on one's view) to help compensate for four hundred years of oppression, help build and sustain an African-American and Hispanic middle class, and expose college students to a diversity of cultures and views, is subject to strict scrutiny under the Equal Protection Clause. It would be absurd if legacy preferences in college admissions—affirmative action in favor of the nation's elites—were not subject to strict scrutiny as well. Unlike preferences in favor of racial minorities, however, legacy preferences cannot survive the strict scrutiny to which they are subject.

9

Privilege Paving the Way for Privilege: How Judges Will Confront the Legal Ramifications of Legacy Admissions to Public and Private Universities

Boyce F. Martin, Jr., with Donya Khalili

> "Fathers send their sons to college either because they went to college or because they didn't."
>
> —Linville L. Hendren, former University of Georgia physics professor

In 2002, I authored the majority opinion in the Sixth Circuit in the landmark affirmative action case, *Grutter* v. *Bollinger*, finding that the University of Michigan law school's admissions policy, which sought to admit and enroll a diverse student body through a complex algorithm, gave a bonus for minority students but did not include a quota.[1] The Supreme Court affirmed the opinion, finding, as I had, that our education institutions have a compelling interest in promoting diversity in their student bodies.[2]

Thus, I enter the debate on college admission policies firmly on the side of even more diversity. However, while diversity is an important goal, an admissions policy based primarily on academic skills and benefits to the community is, in my view, the appropriate standard. Unfortunately, the ideal standard of focusing on academic skills, benefits to the community, and a commitment to diversity is undermined by the substantial weight that legacy status carries in the admissions process of many elite public and private universities and graduate schools. At elite public and private schools around the country, students who have a parent or close relative who graduated from that school have a substantially higher rate of acceptance, sometimes as much as twice as high. In 2008, Dartmouth's admission rate of legacy students was twice that of those who did not have a relative who had previously attended, a rate that had remained consistent over the previous five years.[3] At Villanova University, approximately 25 percent of students have a family member who has graduated from the school, and the Villanova website proudly announces that special preferences are applied to legacy applicants.[4] At the University of Virginia, half of the 1,400 legacy applicants every year are accepted, a substantially higher admittance rate than for non-legacy applicants to this prestigious public school.[5]

This is all in spite of studies—such as one done at Duke University, where the admittance rate for children of alumni is double that of the overall admittance rate—revealing that legacy students typically underperform compared to their peers once they matriculate.[6] Another recent study of Princeton students announced the not-surprising result that legacy admits had lower SAT scores and grades than those admitted without such a preference.[7] This can undermine the perceived value of a degree and could create rancor among students who are not accepted because a less-qualified legacy applicant was admitted or a perception that legacy admits are less qualified than their non-legacy peers.

But legacy admissions are problematic legally as well, especially for elite public schools such as the University of Virginia and the University of Michigan.[8] Because many, if not most, institutes of higher education have long discriminated on the basis of race, religion, and/or gender, admissions preference given to the children of those who used to be the only people who could be admitted perpetuates the effects of class and race discrimination from generations ago. Most of the beneficiaries of legacy admissions are white Protestant students.[9] These preferences operate like "educational grandfather clauses," continuing the disenfranchisement of minority students—much like the literacy tests required for new voters, but not for voters whose ancestors had voted (all white), that were used in the post-Civil War South to prevent former slaves from voting.[10] If our universities have a commitment and, indeed, a compelling interest in fostering a diverse campus community, legacy preferences fight their attempts to achieve a "critical mass" of diverse students. While this will change, slowly, as the diversity of student bodies increases,[11] the overwhelming percentage of alumni still will be white for a long time.[12] For example, at the University of Virginia, as Daniel Golden notes, "91% of legacy applicants accepted on an early-decision basis for next fall are white; 1.6% are black, 0.5% are Hispanic, and 1.6% are Asian. Among applicants with no alumni parents, the pool of those accepted is more diverse: 73% white, 5.6% black, 9.3% Asian and 3.5% Hispanic."[13]

Because of the effects of legacy preferences on diversity in education,[14] new focus has been placed on their role in admissions. In 2003, Senator Edward Kennedy introduced legislation to compel colleges to make their data on legacy admissions public, but ultimately the bill was not passed.[15] The Georgia and California public university systems have stopped considering whether a student is a legacy of one of their schools in admission decisions after being forced, by the courts and by a voter initiative, respectively, to end racial preferences.[16] Later, after the discovery in 2002 that, based on legacy preferences, Texas A&M University had admitted 321 whites and 3 blacks who otherwise would not have been acepted, the university abolished the preferences.[17] I expect legal challenges to the practice of legacy preferences, especially at public universities such as the University of Virginia, to begin in the near future.

What Is a Judge to Do?

After the Civil War, pervasive discrimination against former slaves led to the passage of the Fourteenth Amendment to the U.S. Constitution, which provides in relevant part: "No state shall . . . deny to any person within its jurisdiction the equal protection of the laws."[18] Later, the Supreme Court expressly declared that "equal protection analysis in the Fifth Amendment area [which applies to the federal government] is the same as that under the Fourteenth Amendment."[19] Thus, public universities and schools are not permitted to discriminate in their admissions unless that distinction is justified by a sufficient purpose. Additionally, private universities and schools that operate as nonprofit organizations are not permitted to discriminate on the basis of race and maintain their tax-exempt status.[20]

Until recently, most commentators have considered legacy preferences to be indefensible and destructive, but legal. In his dissent in the *Grutter* case, Justice Clarence Thomas stated *in dicta* that "while legacy preferences can stand under the Constitution, racial discrimination cannot."[21] However, as this opinion is certainly not binding, the first judge to confront this issue after the Supreme Court's decision in *Grutter* will face a nearly clean slate. While there has been a recent uptick in academic writing on the appropriateness and legality of legacy admissions, there has been only one decision addressing the constitutionality of legacy preferences. In 1976, Judge Hiram Ward of the United States District Court for the District of North Carolina ruled that the University of North Carolina at Chapel Hill was free to favor the children of alumni because the school had shown a rational reason for the legacy preference: "monetary support for the university."[22] However, as this case was decided before the Supreme Court had described all of our current standards of review and determines the question of whether legacy preferences are constitutional in a scant five sentences, it is neither binding nor persuasive to future courts.

Thus, the first judge to examine this issue post-*Grutter* will need to determine again under what legal standard to examine the potential constitutional violation. This could be the most important decision in the case because the level of protection given to various possible classifications vary widely. Under the Equal Protection Clause of the Fourteenth Amendment, there are three legal standards under which our courts have analyzed questions of discrimination: strict scrutiny, heightened scrutiny, and the rational basis test. Different levels of scrutiny, or deference to the law, are applied based on the type of discrimination. Discrimination that we as a society are particularly concerned about, such as that based on race, is subject to a high test to determine if it is permissible. However, we are more deferential when examining cases of discrimination that we are less concerned about, such as that based on age. Because a law that discriminates on the basis of a particular classification could be constitutional under the rational basis test but, if defined under heightened or strict scrutiny, it might not be constitutional, the judge likely will spend a substantial amount of time determining what test is appropriate to apply to this classification.

The strict scrutiny test is applied to cases of potential discrimination on the basis of suspect classifications such as race[23] and national origin,[24] or discrimination that impairs a fundamental right such as the right to vote[25] or travel.[26] Under strict scrutiny, a law or policy that (1) uses a suspect classification will be sustained only if it involves (2) a compelling objective, and (3) the classification is necessary for that objective.[27] As the Supreme Court has previously found that the right to an education is not a fundamental right,[28] legacy admissions would be analyzed under this test only if the Supreme Court revisited this issue or found that legacy admissions are a suspect classification. Chapter 8 of this volume eloquently argues for the application of strict scrutiny to legacy admissions.[29] In it, the authors define the classification as one based on bloodline, which they contend is a suspect classification extremely similar to one based on race.[30]

Heightened, or intermediate, scrutiny is applied to alleged discrimination on the basis of gender[31] or illegitimacy.[32] Under this standard, a law or policy that (1) uses a quasi-suspect classification will be sustained if it involves (2) an important objective, and (3) the classification is substantially related to that objective. Only objective reasoning actually adopted by the legislature is considered; hypothesizing is not allowed. It is possible that a judge could find that legacy admissions are a quasi-suspect classification because, as is the case with children born to unmarried-parents, "no child is responsible for his birth."[33] Thus, to penalize a child's ability to get into a school based on whether his parent was able to get in, especially if that parent was unable to get in because of previous discrimination on the basis of race or religion, would be unjust to the child because he has no control over this status. However, to be a quasi-suspect classification, the judge would have to find that there was a history of discrimination against persons of that legal status, however the judge defines it, though a "badge of identification" is not required, like that which makes obvious a person's race or gender.[34]

The rational basis test is applied to all other forms of potential discrimination, including discrimination on the basis of sexual orientation,[35] age,[36] and disability.[37] Under the rational basis test, a law or policy that does *not* (1) divide its objects using a suspect classification (that is, race or national origin), (2) use a quasi-suspect classification (that is, gender or illegitimacy), or (3) impair a fundamental right (that is, to vote, run for office, access courts, or travel interstate) will be sustained if it involves (4) a legitimate objective and (5) the classification is reasonably related to that objective.[38] Most laws to which this is applied, such as those affecting the economy and social welfare, are upheld, and the "rational basis" can be the one actually used in setting the policy or law or a hypothetical, reasonable rationale.[39] Only classifications that are purely arbitrary and without a rational basis are invalidated under the rational basis test.[40] This is the most commonly applied test under the Equal Protection Clause and could be applied to legacy preferences should the judge not find either strict or heightened scrutiny appropriate, as is most often the case.[41]

There are, thus, rational arguments for applying each of the potential standards when evaluating the constitutionality of legacy preferences in admissions. As I do not know the specifics of the case that will come before the first judge to evaluate this issue after *Grutter*, I will not hazard a guess as to what test that judge will apply nor can I know what test I would apply were the case before me. However, after the judge defines the classification and determines what test to apply, the judge will proceed to look to the reasons that the school has used to justify its legacy admissions policy.

What a Judge Will Hear

After identifying the proper standard, the judge will move on to determining whether the school's reasons for giving preferences to legacy applicants satisfy the test. The judge will decide whether the reasons offered by the school are sufficient for the test, whether compelling, important, or legitimate, and whether the preference as applied at that school as part of its admissions system is narrowly tailored, or substantially or reasonably related to the objective, as required by the appropriate test. The first tests of the constitutionality of legacy admissions will likely vary based on the weight of the preference in the context of admissions at that school and by the explanations that the school offers for their inclusion, which will likely include financial benefits, attachment to the school, and ranking benefits.

In *Grutter*, both I and the Supreme Court agreed with the law school that schools have a compelling state interest in maintaining a diverse student body.[42] To do so, many amicus briefs argued, along with the law school, that schools require a "critical mass" of minority students to yield educational benefits for the entire student body and to "assembl[e] a class that is both exceptionally academically qualified and broadly diverse."[43] In finding a compelling interest, the Supreme Court recognized that:

> given the important purpose of public education and the expansive freedoms of speech and thought associated with the university environment, universities occupy a special niche in our constitutional tradition. . . . In announcing the principle of student body diversity as a compelling state interest, Justice Powell invoked our cases recognizing a constitutional dimension, grounded in the First Amendment, of educational autonomy: "The freedom of a university to make its own judgments as to education includes the selection of its student body." Bakke, supra, at 312, 98 S.Ct. 2733. From this premise, Justice Powell reasoned that by claiming "the right to select those students who will contribute the most to the 'robust exchange of ideas,'" a university "seek[s] to achieve a goal that is of paramount importance in the fulfillment of its mission." 438 U.S., at 313, 98 S.Ct. 2733 (quoting *Keyishian* v. *Board of Regents of Univ. of State of N. Y.*, supra, at 603, 87 S.Ct. 675). Our conclusion that the Law School has a compelling interest in a diverse student body is informed by our view that attaining a diverse student body is at the heart of the Law School's proper institutional mission, and that "good faith" on the part of a university is "presumed" absent "a showing to the contrary." 438 U.S., at 318-319, 98 S.Ct. 2733.[44]

Additionally, the courts recognized that a diverse student body "better prepares students for an increasingly diverse workforce and society, and better prepares them as professionals," which benefits our nation's business world, military, and leaders.[45]

> In order to cultivate a set of leaders with legitimacy in the eyes of the citizenry, it is necessary that the path to leadership be visibly open to talented and qualified individuals of every race and ethnicity. All members of our heterogeneous society must have confidence in the openness and integrity of the educational institutions that provide this training. As we have recognized, law schools "cannot be effective in isolation from the individuals and institutions with which the law interacts." See *Sweatt* v. *Painter*, *supra*, at 634, 70 S.Ct. 848. Access to legal education (and thus the legal profession) must be inclusive of talented and qualified individuals of every race and ethnicity, so that all members of our heterogeneous society may participate in the educational institutions that provide the training and education necessary to succeed in America.[46]

However, these arguments, based on the strict scrutiny test for race-based discrimination, do not apply to legacy admissions. It cannot be argued that these admissions of students whose parents and/or grandparents attended universities are adding to the diversity of the student body; indeed, as previously noted, legacy admits to universities and professional schools are overwhelmingly white. Instead, schools argue that legacy preferences help build cross-generational relationships with institutions and cement relationships with alumni donors. Whether colleges have admission policies that benefit minority applicants, athletes, cello players, or residents of Kansas, the theory is that those receiving the benefit either have valuable perspectives or faced disadvantage—and that they will add something to the campus community because of that. This argument is more difficult to make when what sets apart the applicant is likely a form of advantage and socioeconomic status that matches the historically dominant groups on campus.

There are a number of policy arguments that lean against permitting legacy admissions. Universities, especially public universities, are engines of class and societal improvement, and making it easier for people of privilege to attain an education than those who are attempting to improve their station fights this governmental interest. We have an interest in not perpetuating the effects of class and race discrimination from previous generations. Additionally, society has a strong interest in ensuring that all young people view the gates of educational and cultural institutions as being open to them and in respecting each person as an individual.

Over the years, schools have argued various positions in support of their legacy admission policies. I will discuss each below but, as I previously noted, it would be impossible for me to make a decision as to whether legacy admission policies are likely to be held as constitutional as the fact pattern is not before me. While it is not possible to foretell what standard our hypothetical judge will apply to the issue of legacy admissions, previous arguments used by schools to justify legacy preferences are known. The school (or schools) involved in the first legal challenges will, no doubt, offer additional reasons supporting their use of legacy preferences, but I have investigated several used often in articles about the issue. Additionally, whether any of the following arguments could ultimately be successful will depend on the standard of review that is applied by the judge: the compelling interest required by strict scrutiny, an important objective required by heightened scrutiny, or a reasonable belief, as required by the rational basis test.

Justification 1: Legacy Admissions Increase Endowments Because Alumni with Children Applying to School Are Bigger Donors

The most obvious argument in favor of admitting legacy students is that of money: families of children applying to schools with legacy admissions are more likely to give generously to improve their child's chances of admission than schools without similar policies. Specifically, colleges say that legacy preferences help build cross-generational relationships with institutions and cement relationships with alumni donors.[47] At Duke University, the admissions director recently noted that his office works alongside the Office of Alumni Affairs to "evaluate the level of commitment a family has made to the University . . . [taking into account] financial contributions [and] all of the different ways that a family can maintain its ties to Duke."[48] In an article, journalist Jacques Steinberg tells the story of the alumni father of an applicant pausing in the middle of negotiating a six-figure donation to the school to see if his child will be accepted.[49] When he was not, the father withdrew the donation, stating "our philanthropy follows our children and our children aren't going to Middlebury."[50] And this makes intuitive sense: parents are trying to buy admission to prestigious colleges that they attended for their children. If parents with means will pay substantial sums for SAT tutoring and consultants to help their children prepare their college applications,[51] why would parents not make substantial donations to ensure admission? A 2007 study by Texas A&M economics professor Jonathan Meer and Princeton economics professor Harvey S. Rosen demonstrates that alumni with children gave more than alumni without children and that the giving increased as those children who applied to the university neared eighteen.[52] The study also showed that alumni giving dropped off after the admissions decision and, in fact, dropped off substantially if the child was not accepted to the university.[53] However, as argued in Chapter 5 and elsewhere in this volume, the evidence may not support this intuition.[54] It appears that, after adjusting for the relative wealth of the alumni communities at institutions that do and do not have legacy admission policies, alumni donations are essentially the same over time.[55] In short, a policy of legacy preferences may not actually prove a financial boon to a university so much as the age of an applicant child multiplied by the alumni giving that would have occurred regardless. Thus, it is possible that, in the long run, legacy preferences do not actually benefit a school that applies them.

However, even if legacy preferences do yield higher donations, a judge might find that the preferences were not sufficiently tailored, as required by the test being applied, to permit the discrimination, as schools could increase donations by alumni by other means that do not require discrimination. Thus, this rationale, while likely the stronger of the schools' available arguments, is still vulnerable under any of the tests.

Justification 2: Legacy Admissions Foster a Number of Students on Campus with a History and Connection with the School

A school may argue that legacy preferences help colleges maintain a sense of tradition and community. The dean of undergraduate

Admissions at Duke, Christoph Guttentag, states that "the Duke community extends for generations, and one of the ways that bond is maintained is by paying attention when children of alumni apply to Duke."[56] However, while it may be difficult to judge an applicant's merits, it seems unfair to value a student based on the activities of their relatives in the community. Additionally, giving preferences to legacy students because they are assumed to have a better understanding of the college seems a poor justification of favored status as an applicant's essay and letters of recommendation can easily demonstrate an appreciation and connection with a school. Thus, this justification alone is a fairly weak argument for legacy preferences in admission as an even better result in terms of admitting students who feel strongly about and connect with the school is available through the standard application process. As there is a way to reach the same result without classifying the students based on whether their parents attended the school, it is possible that this argument alone could not survive even rational basis scrutiny. However, it may have more power when combined with the funding argument above.[57]

Conclusion

I do not know what test will be applied to determine whether legacy preferences in admission policies violate the Equal Protection Clause nor whether preference will survive the tests applied. But it is clear to me that legacy preferences are destructive to the diversity of our campuses and the perception of merit in admissions and that they perpetuate the class and race discrimination that the rest of our laws are fighting to stop. I look forward to reading the first cases to examine this issue in light of the Supreme Court's decision in *Grutter* and hope that more universities join California, Georgia, and Texas A&M in ending their legacy admission policies voluntarily in the years to come.

10

The Political Economy of Legacy Admissions, Taxpayer Subsidies, and Excess "Profits" in American Higher Education: Strategies for Reform

Peter Sacks

American universities and colleges have claimed for years that they need to provide legacy preferences in order to generate good will among alumni so that they will donate more generously. Other chapters in this volume raise serious questions about the empirical basis for that claim, suggesting that higher education could survive just fine financially without providing preferences based on ancestry. Assume for the moment, however, that legacy preferences are an essential lure to producing alumni donations. If so, that would raise a separate and important question of law and public policy: if alumni *are* receiving a benefit (increased chances for admissions for their offspring), why are those donations tax-deductible?

This chapter explores this issue in depth, beginning with an examination of the conventional paradigm of not-for-profit educational institutions as charitable organizations whose donors make tax-deductible gifts without any expectation of private economic gain. It then explores why the conventional view grossly mischaracterizes the actual relationships that elite universities maintain with donors and other stakeholders to the organization, including the alumni parents of children who apply for admission to the university. In the transaction's economic essence, these donors may sometimes be motivated by the belief that parent donors are investing in shares of the enterprise on the expectation of some future economic benefit: an admissions ticket for their legacy children to enter the freshman class.

The chapter then goes on to examine the justifications for legacy preferences, including the claim by universities of a First Amendment right to select students as they see fit, including offering legacy applicants a substantial admissions preference. Then it explores the vast tax subsidies provided by the federal government to private universities, which make them quasi-public institutions. It then lays out an argument that the admissions preference for legacies violates a basic principle of tax deductions for charitable contributions: that donors should receive nothing of value in return. Finally, it outlines strategies for reform to make universities accountable to the public in exchange for the generous taxpayer subsidies provided these institutions.

To Profit or Not to Profit?

Harvard University and the University of Phoenix would seem to have virtually nothing in common. Harvard, of course, is among the richest and most powerful institutions in America, a self-styled educator to the nation's future leaders. The oldest university in America, Harvard's tradition as a molder of presidents, chief executives, and Supreme Court justices is undisputed. Indeed, this tradition underscores the very essence of *legacy,* the inherited gift of a Harvard education that is passed through one's ancestors from one generation of graduates to the next.

By contrast, the University of Phoenix's educational mission is more modest, focused on making college accessible to nurses, firefighters, police officers, and other working adults. While Harvard's enterprise is centered on the reproduction and maintenance of American elites—employing legacy admissions and other methods for ensuring this reproduction of class privilege—the notion of legacies at the University of Phoenix is nonsensical. For many of its working-class students who return to school in order to advance their careers, a University of Phoenix degree is a portal *into* the American middle class, not a credential for maintaining or reproducing class status.

Both universities are private institutions: they receive no direct budgetary support from state taxpayers, like, for example, the University of Michigan or the University of California. But the word "private" is actually a relative term in higher education; some colleges and universities are more "private" than others. In a regulatory sense, the University of Phoenix falls on what would seem to be the less-private, more-public side of the spectrum. It is a private, "for-profit" institution, meaning that, like other publicly held corporations in the United States, the company has a board of directors, a management team, student customers who pay tuition, and shareholders to whom the company is ultimately accountable.

But in one important respect the University of Phoenix is actually more private, or at least more independent, than Harvard. Except for students who receive federally backed student loans, and except for Phoenix's legal responsibility to keep shareholders informed of operations that materially affect company profits, the University of Phoenix operates with few ties to the federal government and American taxpayers.

Harvard, by contrast, is so dependent upon federal largesse that Harvard would not be Harvard were its financial ties to the federal government to be severed. First, Harvard receives hundreds of millions of dollars per year from the government to do research in medicine, science, and other fields. Harvard's second tether to the federal government is related to the university's "nonprofit" status. As a nonprofit educational institution, Harvard receives tax-free gifts from private donors who use the "charitable deduction" rules of the federal tax code to reduce the amount of income taxes they owe the government.

These connections to the federal government are vital to Harvard's particular business model. Unlike Phoenix, whose revenues primarily come from charging students tuition, Harvard depends on non-tuition sources of revenue to build its "nonprofit" profits. Harvard's accumulated net earnings are not considered profits per se; rather, in the tax-exempt world, Harvard's profit is known as an endowment.

While the University of Phoenix pays corporate income taxes on its profits, Harvard generally pays no income tax on contributions to the endowment; nor does the university pay tax on the income to the endowment as a result of Harvard's investing its endowment in income-producing assets such as stocks and bonds.

In short, not only are individual and corporate donations to Harvard's endowment tax-free—for both Harvard and its donors—but also the income that Harvard earns from investing its endowment.

Why, then, should the University of Phoenix, a private institution that serves many working adults, including many first-generation college students, have to pay federal income taxes, while Harvard—also a private university that caters to American elites—does not?

The simplistic, legalistic answer, as I have already suggested, is that the University of Phoenix is a for-profit corporation and Harvard is a 501 (c) (3) tax-exempt institution as defined by the Internal Revenue Code. Phoenix is a profit-seeking corporation, thus required to pay taxes; Harvard is a "charitable" organization, and therefore tax-exempt. As a "for-profit" corporation, the University of Phoenix is owned by its shareholders. These shareholders buy and sell stocks of the company on a public stock exchange. Harvard, by contrast, allegedly has no shareholders who invest in the enterprise on the expectation of future returns.

Daniel Halperin, a Harvard law professor who writes frequently about higher education and taxes, explains that the existence of shareholders is the critical feature that separates a for-profit corporation from a tax-exempt organization. "A for-profit organization will clearly have taxable income if it sets aside profits for current or future distribution to shareholders or owners," writes Halperin. He continues, "However, a charitable organization is distinguished from a for-profit entity by what has been referred to as the 'non-distribution constraint,' which precludes remittance of profits to shareholders or members. Further, since a charitable organization, unlike a business corporation, will not have shareholders or owners who demand a return on their investment, it need not operate at a profit over the long term."[1]

Thus, the "non-distribution" feature of Harvard's retained earnings, its endowment, and the absence of any investors or shareholders in the Harvard enterprise, would seem to make for an open-and-shut case that Harvard is indeed a nonprofit organization, allowing all contributions and any income to Harvard's endowment to be exempt from federal taxation.

This conventional paradigm's underlying premise is that Harvard has no shareholders who receive returns on their Harvard investment. In the following pages, I will argue that this conventional view grossly mischaracterizes the actual relationships Harvard and similar universities maintain with donors and other stakeholders to the organization. These include the alumni parents of children who apply for admission to the university. If we are to believe Harvard's claim—that it needs to provide legacy preferences in order to create good will and to entice donations—then alumni donors are essentially investing in shares of the Harvard enterprise on the expectation of some future economic benefit.

Elite universities such as Harvard have long viewed these arrangements, giving preferential treatment to the children, siblings, and grandchildren of alumni, as an entitlement, a fundamental right as a private institution. But the practice is fundamentally improper on a number of counts. The preferential treatment of the children of alumni donors is wholly incompatible with the social compact between the American government and nonprofit organizations that are exempted from federal taxation. In particular, the private, unstated arrangements between alumni donors and universities are at odds with the essential premise of the government's creation of the charitable deduction for individual gifts to charities dating back to 1917. The ensuing public-private compact was this: because individuals gave to charities, such as schools and colleges, with no expectation of self-enrichment, then the government should encourage such an act of altruism and, at the very least, not tax it.[2]

If we are to believe universities—that alumni preferences are necessary to facilitate fundraising—then the arrangement shatters the first principle underlying the charitable deduction, that donations to nonprofit organizations not "enrich the giver."

Nowadays, the popular perceptions of the quality of colleges and universities are shaped by *U.S. News & World Report*'s annual ranking of "America's Best Colleges." In large measure, these rankings are determined by factors that reward wealth and prestige above all else, creating a brand-name mentality in higher education that has led parents, students, and institutions to value prestige and rankings above all other good things that colleges can do for students and families.

In this hypercompetitive environment for admission to a prestigious university, the market value of a Harvard or a Princeton or a Yale admission slot has increased dramatically in recent decades. What is more, the increasing scarcity and value of an admission to a brand-name college or university has reaped sizable economic rewards for such institutions. Institutional endowment wealth produces academic prestige, which in turn attracts more wealth and more academic prestige.

The competition for admission has become so intense that even being a legacy applicant is not a sure bet for admission. But, it is a good bet. In fact, the universities *must* make it a good bet, paying out with admission offers to legacies more often than not, in order to entice potential alumni donors. Indeed, at a university like Harvard or Princeton, a legacy applicant has a 30 percent or 40 percent chance of admission, compared to a 10 percent to 15 percent chance for the ordinary applicant.[3] Those are pretty good odds for the alumni parents who may believe they must make a tax-deductible donation—or remain on the sidelines and risk being among the six or seven in ten legacy applicants who do not get in.

How Private Universities Justify Legacy Admissions

The prevailing view among elite institutions is that they are entitled to give an admissions boost to legacies for two inter-related reasons. One is a property claim, which holds that, as a private institution, the university has the right to conduct its business affairs as it deems fit, including complete discretion over the composition of its student body, restricted only by federal laws against racial, religious, and gender discrimination.

In a 2003 commentary in the *Chronicle of Higher Education*, Debra Thomas and Terry Shepard, both Rice University officials, summed up the property rights rationale for legacy preferences. Since public universities, subsidized by taxpayers, had the right to limit enrollments to state residents, so too should private institutions have the right to grant admissions preference to alumni and other families who donate money to the institutions, they argued. Merit, they asserted, has really nothing to do with the process by which colleges pick and choose the students who might best serve the interests of the institution. "Colleges and universities have done themselves a disservice by trying to portray their admissions decisions as 'fair,'" the Rice officials said. "Those decisions, like most other conclusions about the potential of human beings, involve experience, judgment, perception, and intuition." They went on, suggesting that admission decisions are less about merit than artistic judgments. "In other words," the authors concluded, "they are an art. And 'fair' has no meaning in art. We should strive to describe our admissions processes as what they are: not fair, but rational."[4]

Indeed, in the era of "enrollment management" and similar highly sophisticated techniques, colleges and universities have borrowed from the corporate world to identify, recruit, admit, and enroll the most profitable students; admissions has become less about merit—or art for that matter—and more about the cold rationality of business.

In other words, not-for-profit universities see the legacy preference as a potential profit center: in 2006, for example, alumni donors gave colleges and universities $8.4 billion in charitable contributions, which accounted for about 33 percent of the total voluntary support to higher education.[5]

Closely related to the claim of a private property right that universities exercise when deciding on the composition of their student bodies is a First Amendment claim. According to this argument, private universities have a right to create and maintain the college culture, particularly the kinds of students who contribute to this culture.

Consider what the late William F. Buckley, Jr., had to say about the impending challenges to legacy admissions. He was commenting in 2003 on the revelation, first reported by the *Wall Street Journal,* that William Fitzsimmons, Harvard's dean of undergraduate admissions, personally read all applications from legacies. Legacies, Fitzsimmons said, contributed to Harvard's culture in a myriad of ways, and "make Harvard a happier place."[6] Buckley argued that Harvard's or any other private university's admission policies were off limits from federal intrusion because the practice was a harmless exhibition of the everyday tribalism that was "part of life."

"Harvard's business should be its own," Buckley wrote in the *New York Times*. "There are tribal instincts in life, colleges and universities are part of life, and nobody has proved that any harm whatever has been done by private colleges writing their own admissions policies, as long as they don't illegally discriminate against anyone, black or white."[7]

Indeed, this same tribalism has been in play at Harvard, Yale, and a number of highly selective universities and professional schools for generations. With the rise of selective admissions at America's elite universities, these institutions continued to tailor and modify their admission systems over the years in ways that provided built-in admission advantages to children of the chosen tribe, including the descendants of alumni. In order to exclude the undesirables who were not members of the chosen tribe (such as Jews), universities such as Harvard and Yale created extraordinary barriers to admission.

My point is that the tribal instinct at America's elite universities is not a relic of history, but, as Buckley observed, is very much in play when these universities continue to assert a First Amendment right to decide which students will sustain into the future the culture of their "tribe."

Buoyed by U.S. courts, private institutions have created as much or as little "diversity" as they deemed fit, under the shield of the First Amendment. Courts have deferred to the discretion of the universities and their right to decide what was educationally best for the university. This definition of "academic freedom" was precisely the right that Justice Lewis Powell supported when the U.S. Supreme Court upheld the University of California's diversity argument in the 1978 *Bakke* case. The "attainment of a diverse student body. . . clearly is a constitutionally permissible [438 U.S. 265, 312] goal for an institution of higher education," Justice Powell wrote. "Academic freedom, though not a specifically enumerated constitutional right, long has been viewed as a special concern of the First Amendment. The freedom of a university to make its own judgments as to education includes the selection of its student body."[8]

In this, Powell was reiterating Justice Felix Frankfurter's earlier conception of academic freedom: "It is the business of a university to provide that atmosphere which is most conductive to speculation, experiment and creation," Frankfurter wrote. "It is an atmosphere in which there prevail 'the four essential freedoms' of a university—to determine for itself on academic grounds who may teach, what may be taught, how it shall be taught, and who may be admitted to study."[9] In the Supreme Court's review of two University of Michigan affirmative action cases, Justice Clarence Thomas suggested that universities have hidden behind the First Amendment to create "selective" admission systems that were, in effect, tools for racial and religious discrimination. Still, Justice Sandra Day O'Connor's majority opinion reiterated the academic freedom rationale in upholding the Michigan law school's wide discretion when selecting its students. "The Law School's educational judgment that such diversity is essential to its educational mission is one to which we defer," O'Connor wrote. "Our holding today is in keeping with our tradition of giving a degree of deference to a university's academic decisions, within constitutionally prescribed limits."[10]

Of course, this latitude is not unlimited. The Supreme Court made this clear when applying civil rights laws to private schools in the 1976 *Runyon* case; in striking down racial quotas at the University of California–Davis Medical School in the 1978 *Bakke* case; and in striking down the University of Michigan's race-based point system in *Gratz* v. *Bollinger*.[11]

The Gift: Federal Taxpayers and Private Colleges and Universities

The irony is that endowment-maximizing universities, particularly private nonprofit institutions, assert First Amendment rights of unfettered control over their admission decisions and methods, including the right to reserve scarce enrollment space for legacies, while also receiving significant budgetary support from federal taxpayers. As I have previously suggested, the federal government supports institutions through the following channels: providing grants to universities for conducting research in science, medicine, and dozens of other fields; exempting charitable donations to universities from federal taxation; and exempting endowment income from federal income taxes.

With respect to the first channel, again consider Harvard. In the five-year period between fiscal 2004 and fiscal 2008, Harvard received more than $2.5 billion from federal agencies for research, which was about four times the amount Harvard received from non-federal sources. In fact, federal research support to Harvard in fiscal 2008 alone, about $529 million, nearly equaled the total of non-federal payments for the entire five-year period.[12] In fiscal 2008, the federal government accounted for fully 15 percent of Harvard's $3.5 billion in total income.[13]

But Harvard's dependence on federal research support is actually relatively small compared to other universities, not even ranking among the top ten in 2004–05. During that year, the government provided colleges and universities with $55.6 billion. Seven of the ten largest recipients of federal support were private institutions, most of which provide significant admission preferences to legacies. Specifically, the top ten recipients of federal funds are:

- California Institute of Technology: $1.9 billion
- Johns Hopkins University: $1.5 billion
- Massachusetts Institute of Technology: $1.1 billion
- Columbia University: $940 million
- Stanford University: $836 million
- University of Chicago: $822 million

- University of Washington: $810 million
- University of Michigan, Ann Arbor: $660 million
- University of Pennsylvania: $648 million
- University of California, Los Angeles: $586 million[14]

As indicated in Table 10.1, the federal government accounted for an average of almost 15 percent of the revenue for private, nonprofit colleges and universities between 1996 and 2005. The federal contribution was about half the percentage of revenues that such institutions received from student tuition and fees, and was about equal to the percentage of revenues from private gifts, including those from alumni and other donors. In terms of revenue per full-time student, the federal government's support of these private not-for-profit institutions averaged $6,458 from 1996 through 2005, almost equal to the revenue per student from private donations to endowments. Tuition and fees provided revenues of $14,433 per full-time student.[15]

In addition to these direct federal payments, charitable donations to private universities, including gifts from parents and alumni who have children intending to apply for scarce admission slots, are exempt from federal taxation. As seen in Table 10.2, the government's revenue loss from the charitable deduction to educational institutions, at $5.9 billion in fiscal 2007, was the single largest "tax expenditure" for education in the federal budget, according to the Joint Committee on Taxation.[16] For fiscal years 2007 through 2011, as shown in Table 10.3, the revenue loss from the charitable deduction for corporations and individuals is expected to total almost $37 billion, with tax benefits accruing to individuals accounting for the lion's share of the government's revenue loss for this deduction.[17]

Though significant, the value of the charitable contribution deduction pales in comparison to what colleges and universities save from the income-tax exemption. "We Americans have decided that the work of nonprofit colleges and universities is so invaluable that they should be exempt from taxes," then-Senate Finance Committee chairman Charles Grassley wrote in a *Chronicle of Higher Education*

Table 10.1 Total Revenue of Private, Not-for-Profit, Degree-Granting Institutions, by Source of Funds and Type of Institution, 1996-97 through 2004-05

Total Revenue by Source of Funds						
Type of Institution and Year	**Total**	**Student Tuition and Fees**	**Federal**	**State**	**Local**	**Private Gifts**
Percentage Distribution						
Four-year						
1996-97	100.00	27.64	NA	1.00	0.56	12.28
1997-98	100.00	27.67	11.75	0.99	0.55	13.88
1998-99	100.00	29.21	12.21	1.08	0.57	14.81
1999-2000	100.00	24.44	10.14	0.92	0.48	13.66
2000-01	100.00	38.00	16.33	1.42	0.62	19.36
2001-02	100.00	39.59	17.56	1.53	0.59	18.30
2002-03	100.00	33.96	15.72	1.42	0.45	13.63
2003-04	100.00	28.58	13.65	1.07	0.36	11.82
2004-05	100.00	29.42	14.06	1.04	0.35	11.95
Average		**30.95**	**13.93**	**1.16**	**0.50**	**14.41**
Revenue per Full-Time-Equivalent Student in Constant 2006-07 dollars						
Four-year						
1996-97	49,385	13,649	NA	496	278	6,066
1997-98	49,927	13,816	5,868	495	274	6,930
1998-99	48,284	14,104	5,893	523	277	7,152
1999-2000	58,073	14,193	5,886	533	279	7,930
2000-01	37,302	14,175	6,091	529	230	7,220
2001-02	36,807	14,574	6,463	563	216	6,736
2002-03	43,650	14,822	6,862	618	195	5,949
2003-04	52,983	15,143	7,232	564	190	6,262
2004-05	52,411	15,418	7,371	543	182	6,262
Average	**47,647**	**14,433**	**6,458**	**541**	**236**	**6,723**

Source: National Center for Education Statistics, Digest of Education Statistics 2007, March 2008, Table 341, http://nces.ed.gov/pubs2009/2009020_0.pdf.

Table 10.2. Estimates of Individual Federal Tax Expenditures for Education (FY2007)

Tax credits for tuition for post-secondary education	3.1
Deduction for interest of student loans	0.9
Deduction for higher education expenses	2.2
Exclusion of earnings of Coverdell education savings accounts	0.1
Exclusion of tax on earnings of qualified tuition programs	0.6
Exclusion of scholarship and fellowship income	1.6
Exclusion of employer-provided education assistance benefits	0.8
Exclusion of employer-provided tuition reduction benefits	0.2
Parental personal exemption for students age 19 to 23	0.4
Exclusion of interest on state and local government qualified private activity bonds for student loans	0.3
Exclusion of interest on state and local government qualified private activity bonds for private nonprofit and qualified public educational facilities	1.1
Deduction for charitable contributions to educational institutions	5.9
TOTAL	17.2

Source: Joint Committee on Taxation, "Estimates of Federal Tax Expenditures for Fiscal Years 2007–2011," JCS-3-07 (Washington, D.C.: Government Printing Office, 2007).

commentary in 2008. "So John Doe pays taxes. John Deere pays taxes. But Johns Hopkins does not."[18] In her August 20, 2007, memorandum to the Senate Finance Committee, Jane G. Gravelle, an economist at the Congressional Research Service, estimated the forgone corporate income tax revenue for some 765 nonprofit colleges and universities, which had accumulated endowments totaling $340 billion in 2006. An average rate of return of 15.3 percent on the value of those endowments yielded income of $52 billion. A corporate income tax rate of 35 percent "would have resulted in $18 billion in taxes, a benefit four and a half times the benefit of charitable deductions tax expenditures," according to Gravelle.[19]

Table 10.3. Deduction for Charitable Contributions for Educational Institutions (Billions of Dollars)

Corporations					Individuals					Total
2007	2008	2009	2010	2011	2007	2008	2009	2010	2011	
0.7	0.8	0.8	0.8	0.8	5.9	6.2	6.5	6.9	7.3	**36.8**

Source: Joint Committee on Taxation, "Estimates of Federal Tax Expenditures for Fiscal Years 2007–2011," JCS-3-07 (Washington, D.C.: Government Printing Office, 2007).

Admissions Preferences for Legacies Violate the Principle of Tax Deductions for Charitable Contributions

In the early 1970s, private, nonprofit higher education was in a very different state than it enjoys nowadays. Owing to concerns about a looming "crisis" of the nonprofit "voluntary" sector, including the future of charitable giving to private colleges and universities, the Commission on Private Philanthropy and Public Needs, known as the Filer Commission, came into being.

Named in honor of its chairman, John H. Filer, former chairman of Aetna, Yale Law School graduate, and Republican state senator from New Haven, the privately initiated effort involved dozens of studies and several hundred pages of analysis and policy recommendations. The Filer Commission's work was published in 1975 under the main title, *Giving in America*; it stands as a decent history of the unusually central role played by charitable giving in the United States. The report is also a seminal defense of the nonprofit sector generally, offering a number of reforms to ensure its continued economic vitality. Amid the growing egalitarian forces in American culture of the post–World War II era and the increasing importance of state colleges and universities, policymakers, economists, and other scholars were voicing concerns about the equity of the taxpayer subsidy for private education and whether the charitable deduction in particular ought to be modified in the public interest. The Filer Commission's report, in a sense, represented the establishment's counterrevolution against this growing criticism.

The charitable deduction, which the government created to immunize gifts to charity from taxes after the U.S. government instituted the income tax in 1913, would become a fixture of American life. According to the Filer report, the charitable deduction was necessary to counter the steep tax rates of the new income tax system. The underlying rationale for the deduction was one of fairness to the giver: a person who gave to charity should not have to pay income taxes on the amount that he or she gave away.

Why? Because the system depended upon one fundamental proposition: that the donation to charity did not *enrich the giver*. "So deeply rooted is (the charitable deduction) in American ways, in fact, that it would appear to enjoy almost constitutional status in many Americans' eyes," the report observed.[20]

But equity concerns about unjustified tax exemptions and immunities, including those granted certain charitable organizations such as colleges and universities, came to a head in the late 1960s and early 1970s, a result of the Vietnam-era's growing skepticism of entrenched wealth and power. Even the quasi-constitutional entitlement, the charitable deduction, was up for debate. Some economists, for example, were growing skeptical of the theoretical basis of the charitable deduction, suggesting that individual gifts to charity were often a form of private consumption under the cloak of altruism.

The Filer Commission, however, would have none of that, and argued that not only should the charitable deduction be maintained but also should be expanded significantly, so that even the masses of tax filers who did not itemize deductions, but used the standard deduction, could also use the charitable deduction for gifts to charitable organizations, such as colleges and universities.

> We recognize that in some eyes giving money away can be and is considered a form of consumption. . . . In return for a contribution, a donor in some circumstances may acquire enhanced status in the community, or even power and influence, and will often derive some measure of ego satisfaction.
>
> For countless numbers of donors, however, the Commission believes that private giving is primarily altruistic, that most people do not enhance their wealth or their power when they give and are not providing for their personal needs, and that they should not therefore be taxed on the amount of money they give away. We think it entirely appropriate, in other words, for the person who earns $55,000 and gives $5,000 to charitable organizations to be taxed in exactly the same way as the person who earns $50,000 and gives away nothing. . . .
>
> In light of these criteria, the Commission believes that the charitable deduction should be retained and added onto rather than replaced by another form of governmental encouragement to giving. The Commission affirms the basic philosophical rationale of the deduction, that giving should not be taxed because, unlike other uses of income, it does not enrich the disburser.[21]

That bedrock principle of the charitable deduction—that gifts to charity must not enrich the giver—remains to this day an integral part of the Internal Revenue Code. Internal Revenue Service Publication 526, "Charitable Contributions," states that taxpayers who donate to charity, including, for example, donors to universities, must subtract out the value of any benefits accruing from the contribution.

"If you receive or expect to receive a financial or economic benefit as a result of making a contribution to a qualified organization, you cannot deduct the part of the contribution that represents the value of the benefit you receive," Publication 526 states.[22]

What's more, the IRS has developed specific guidelines for gifts to private schools that may be directly applicable to private colleges and universities. In a 1983 ruling, the IRS confronted the thorny problem of parents of students or parents of prospective students making gifts to private schools that were, in fact and deed, nondeductible tuition expenses disguised as charitable donations.

The ruling noted various schemes that schools had created to entice parents to "donate" money while conveying the impression that a failure to donate could jeopardize a student's standing at the school, including the chance of admission. When donations are perceived as a general cost of doing business with the school, resulting in an expectation of private gain conditional upon the gift, then the transaction violates the principle of the charitable deduction.

The IRS ruling states:

> Whether a transfer of money by a parent to an organization that operates a school is a voluntary transfer that is made with no expectation of obtaining a commensurate benefit depends upon whether a reasonable person, taking all the facts and circumstances of the case into account, would conclude that enrollment in the school was in no manner contingent upon making the payment, that the payment was not made pursuant to a plan (whether express or implied) to convert nondeductible tuition into charitable contributions, and that receipt of the benefit was not otherwise dependent upon the making of the payment.[23]

For countless individuals who give to charity and claim a deduction for the full amount of the gift, the non-enrichment principle is undoubtedly honored. Thus, I would not presume to argue that, as a general notion, the charitable deduction ought to be repealed for individuals who give to educational institutions. But the Filer Commission's belief that individuals give to charity without any expectation of personal gain may be a relic of more innocent times, especially in the modern higher education industry. I do not have individual accounts, admissions, or smoking guns to prove, on a case by case basis, that Harvard, Yale, Princeton, or any number of wealthy universities have participated in implicit quid-pro-quo deals, in which the universities promised an acceptance of admission to a legacy in exchange for generous donations from the applicant's family. (Daniel Golden's 2006 book, *The Price of Admission,* presents some convincing evidence that such quid-pro-quo exchanges are by no means unusual at many of America's endowment maximizing, prestige-driven universities, including "development admits" whose parents are not alumni.)[24] At a minimum, however, there is ample circumstantial evidence that alumni parents who donate tax-deductible gifts to their alma maters stand to reap substantial economic gains upon a child's admission to the university.

What is an offer of admission worth? Because elite colleges and universities are most selective in their admissions—which is to say, they maintain relatively high average SAT scores for incoming freshmen—the graduates of such institutions enjoy a competitive advantage in the job market or in other postgraduate endeavors, such as admission to graduate and professional schools. With greater access to the most highly paid professions and the most desirable employers, graduates of elite universities enjoy greater lifetime earnings than graduates of less prestigious schools.[25]

Although I do not intend to rigorously quantify the economic benefits to alumni families that accrue from their donations to top universities, a rough estimate may be illuminating. The brief analysis that follows indicates that legacy families can—and do—contribute substantial sums to elite institutions, not based upon selfless acts of charity, but because their children stand to reap substantial economic returns in the labor market.

Parents who consider giving money to universities, to which their children also apply for admission, would perhaps consider whether the expected value of the market returns of the donation justifies the cost. Unless an alumnus is seeking an incalculable sense of immortality by purchasing naming rights to the university stadium or the undergraduate arts and sciences building, it is possible to determine the maximum donation that would make economic sense.

Economists who have researched this question have demonstrated the significant economic advantages to students who matriculate at highly selective private universities compared to less selective public institutions. Estimates of the annual wage premium from attending an elite university range from approximately 10 percent to 20 percent, according to one literature review by Anthony P. Carnevale and Stephen J. Rose, professors at the Georgetown University Center on Education and the Workforce.[26]

According to the Census Bureau's Current Population Surveys, people who have earned bachelor's degrees from any U.S. college or university can expect lifetime earnings of about $2.1 million, in 1999 dollars.[27] Applying the wage premium estimates summarized by Carnevale and Rose to the Census Bureau's earnings estimate of $2.1 million suggests that one's lifetime income boost from matriculating at a highly selective university ranges from $210,000 to $420,000 (depending on whether the wage premium is 10 percent or 20 percent).

Let us look at the mid-range estimate, yielding an income gain of $315,000, on average, if one matriculates at an elite college. That advantage also happens to be the average income premium of earning a master's degree versus a bachelor's degree, based on national census data. This suggests that earning a bachelor's degree from an elite university provides one with an earnings boost equivalent to obtaining a master's degree at an "average" U.S. institution, a not unreasonable proposition.

For alumni parents considering a donation to the university, their child's expected lifetime income premium of $315,000 must be discounted by the uncertain probability of the child's admission. We know from the work of researchers William G. Bowen, Martin A. Kurzweil, and Eugene M. Tobin, who have studied the admissions behavior of highly selective colleges, that such institutions do offer a significant admissions advantage to alumni children.[28] The authors have calculated that the probability of admission for a legacy applicant is boosted by about twenty percentile points, for a given SAT profile. This means, for instance, that if a student has a 60 percent chance of admission under regular admission channels, given her SAT scores, then her real chance of admission would rise to 80 percent as a legacy applicant.

Let us assume, for instance, that an alumni family faces just this circumstance for one of its children. The parents are considering a donation to the university, which they believe may enhance their child's college application. This family must discount the potential earnings of $315,000 by the 80 percent chance of admission, yielding an expected lifetime income premium of some $252,000. On that basis, then, a four- or five-figure gift would seem to be a prudent and reasonable expenditure for an alumni parent whose child is being considered for admission.

Indeed, one cannot overstate the importance of alumni donations at elite private universities—and the relationship of those donations to legacy preferences. In testimony before the Senate Finance

Committee, Daniel Golden, a former reporter at the *Wall Street Journal*, described for the Senate Finance Committee how one university president, in an unguarded moment, connected the dots between alumni donations, the economic health of the university, and legacy preferences.

According to Golden, Princeton president Shirley Tilghman "responded with admirable candor" to the question of why Princeton continued to give an admissions advantage for legacies. "We are deeply dependent on the generosity of our alumni each and every year," she told the *Journal*. "They are extremely important to the financial well-being of this university."[29]

Tilghman did not offer any empirical evidence that legacy preferences are necessary to fundraising, and evidence in other chapters of this book questions the link. But there is no doubt that alumni donations—perhaps as part of a quid-pro-quo exchange between universities and alumni for maintaining the legacy admissions advantage—are financially important to universities.

Table 10.4 below illustrates this importance. In the 1991–92 academic year, alumni gave Princeton about $21.5 million. By 2007–08, even during a severe economic recession, alumni participation rates increased slightly, to more than 59 percent, while their donations surged to more than $54 million, a record.[30]

In order to maximize donations from alumni parents, universities must maintain a relatively complex gaming strategy. In order to entice potential alumni donors to enter the admissions lottery for their children, the university would do well to offer a somewhat ambiguous promise: legacy applicants are given special consideration, but no guarantees. Clearly, the chance of a legacy being admitted must not be certain, because that promise would undermine alumni participation rates in annual campaigns and the dollar amount of their gifts. Why would alumni parents try to improve the odds of admission for their children if admission already was certain?

At the same time, if legacy admission rates were too low, that also would undermine donor participation rates: parents might calculate that the potential payoff, an offer of admission, is not worth the cost.

The contention that alumni parents give back to their alma maters without any expectation of a benefit of admission is therefore

Table 10.4. Princeton University Annual Giving Dollar and Participation Totals by Campaign Year

Year	Amount ($)	Participation %
1991-92	21,500,713	54.8
1992-93	19,010,021	55.3
1993-94	20,221,289	56.1
1994-95	21,170,663	56.1
1995-96	25,229,298	58.8
1996-97	29,602,821	61.0
1997-98	31,417,263	60.2
1998-99	32,675,084	61.0
1999-00	35,717,687	60.8
2000-01	36,698,032	59.4
2001-02	36,379,117	58.3
2002-03	34,562,041	59.0
2003-04	36,488,569	59.2
2004-05	36,976,959	58.6
2005-06	40,408,142	58.2
2006-07	49,040,759	58.5
2007-08	54,109,304	59.2

Source: Princeton University Office of Development, 2007–2008 AG Campaign Reports, http://giving.princeton.edu/ag/progress/08reports.xml.

false on its face. Owing to economic imperatives, as Princeton's president suggested, universities want to maintain legacy admissions. Further, to entice alumni donations, universities want parents to believe there is a significant admission preference for legacies. The quid pro quo is real and quantifiable. Without the promise of quid pro quo, the business model of the elite private universities, which depends upon a tight nexus between admissions and fundraising, simply does not work.

In a compelling empirical study of the relationship between alumni donations to their alma maters and their children's admission prospects, Jonathan Meer of Stanford and Harvey S. Rosen of Princeton obtained proprietary and highly sensitive donation records for an unnamed private, nonprofit university. The data, spanning the years 1983 through 2006, showed unequivocally that donors' contributions were profoundly influenced by the "perception that the institution might confer a reciprocal benefit."[31]

For instance, prior to the child of an alumnus reaching about sixteen years of age, the probability of the alumni parent donating to the university remained at a relatively constant 15 percent. After the child applied for admission to the university, the probability of the parent making a gift surged to about 25 percent. If the child did not apply for admission, the odds of the parents making a donation to the university dropped to less than 15 percent and declined steadily through the child's early twenties. But if the child's application was accepted, the parents' donation odds immediately surged to about 35 percent, then fell off to a steady 15 percent by the time the child reached age twenty-five.

In sharp contrast, if the child's application was rejected, then the odds of the parents donating to the university fell off a cliff, approaching zero and even slightly negative probability during the child's early twenties.[32]

In other words, alumni are extremely important to the financial well-being of Princeton and similar institutions, as Tilghman put it, but that importance depends significantly on whether their children are admitted to the university. A rejected legacy applicant actually harms the university's financial well-being, prompting parents to donate less to their alma maters than they normally would. This latter finding flags an important tradeoff in the fundraising value of legacy preferences: disappointed alumni may give even less than they would have had their expectations not been raised by the existence of the legacy preference.

"In short, alumni giving varies systematically with the age and admissions status of their children," Meer and Rosen tell us. "This child-cycle of alumni giving is consistent with the hypothesis that some donations are made in the hope of a reciprocal benefit."[33]

Strategies for Reform

In October 2004 when the Higher Education Act was being considered for re-authorization in Congress, the national debate over affirmative action in college admissions was escalating following the

July 2003 U.S. Supreme Court decisions involving the University of Michigan's use of race in admissions. Perhaps as a means of gaining political leverage, some liberal defenders of affirmative action saw an opening: exposing the extent to which many universities granted a similar kind of affirmative action to the children of wealthy legacies could diffuse efforts to force colleges to ban race preferences. In this vein, the late Massachusetts senator Ted Kennedy proposed legislation aimed at attacking legacy preferences in college admissions by simply requiring colleges to publicly report details of their legacy admission programs. But even that relatively modest initiative ignited a full-bore counterattack from the big guns in the higher education lobby, and in the end, Kennedy's bill received little support.

Indeed, there is a certain tilting-at-windmills sense about past efforts to openly attack legacy preferences by trying to persuade Congress to ban them or punish them because they are wrong or unfair. Wrong and unfair are fine motives for passing laws, but noble and idealistic motives are often not sufficient to get much traction in the public policy arena. That may be particularly true in the case of legacy preferences: a powerful lobby representing the higher education industry sees a bread-and-butter issue and is willing to battle for it ferociously in the halls of Congress; at the same time, many members of Congress are sympathetic to the industry because they and their families are often beneficiaries of legacy preferences. What is more, there is a stealthy quality to the issue. Unlike health care reform, fixing the banking system, or creating jobs, it is fair to say that addressing the legacy preference problem is not among the top priorities of the administration, Congress, or the public. And there is one more reason that reform is intractable. While the private institutional and personal gains of legacy preferences are concentrated among universities and donors, the social costs are diffused widely among taxpayers and the public, an externality that diminishes the incentive for politicians and other policymakers to create new laws or enact new regulations, regardless of concerns about equity or justice.

Nevertheless, legacy preferences in college admissions may be an issue of a different order of magnitude than has been treated in the past in Congress, or judging by the somewhat passé reaction of the press to the indignant statements of past presidential contenders on the subject. The issue of legacy preferences should be a far more pressing issue for policymakers and the public because it has become increasingly clear that the high-stakes higher education industry, in its pursuit of wealth and prestige, has abdicated the privilege of its nonprofit status through the systematic abuse of a fundamental feature of the American tax system: the charitable deduction and its bedrock premise that donations to charity must not enrich the giver.

In a December 2006 hearing, Iowa senator Charles Grassley linked the issues of excessive endowments, taxpayer subsidies, and the admission practices of elite universities, including their preferential treatment of legacies and "the children of multimillionaires whom the university hopes might give money down the road." He went on, "We need to think whether these reserved spaces at our top colleges is a public policy that should be subsidized by the tax code—as is currently the case—and also whether it is in keeping with the requirement that as charities, colleges and universities operate in the public interest."[34]

In other words, U.S. tax policy is subsidizing the excessive accumulation of wealth at the wealthiest American colleges and universities, whose admissions systems cater primarily to wealthy families and their children. In recent years, many scholars, writers, journalists, policymakers, educational leaders, and others have been drawing attention to the dangerously widening gap between rich and poor in America. Particularly, critics of the status quo have exposed how vastly unequal access to educational opportunities threatens not just our sense of moral dignity but also our future economic vitality. Should we persist on the present course, the United States will increasingly resemble a third-world nation, with a thin layer of marvelously well-educated elites at the top, served by a broad swath of the uneducated working poor at the bottom—and the disappearing middle in between.

Legacy preferences are but the most egregious example of how the U.S. government—by permitting massive tax benefits to universities and donors who benefit from these preferences—is not just a passive party, but an active participant in creating and perpetuating the growing inequalities between America's rich and not rich.

The question of legacy preferences raises fundamental questions about the government and its relationship to the private, not-for-profit sector. The issue begs one to question just how private or public the not-for-profit educational institutions that employ the preference really are, and whether they are fulfilling their public obligations as tax-exempt enterprises.

Thus, the first major area for reform is the government's treatment of excessive endowment accumulation in the tax-exempt higher education industry. The legacy issue begs one to ask what is the real nature and purpose of the endowment. Has the government, through the tax code, encouraged universities to accumulate excessive endowments for private, not charitable, purposes, in contradiction to IRS rules that the endowments of tax-exempt charities must not "inure" to the benefit of private interests? That tax-exempt universities allocate immensely valuable admissions space for a group of insiders—the children, grandchildren, and siblings of alumni—assisted by the very endowments that American taxpayers subsidize, may violate on its face the IRS's rule that "none of the earnings of the organization may inure to any private shareholder or individual."[35]

The second major area of reform is to address the abuse of the charitable deduction by alumni and other parents who donate money to universities with the expectation of a future reciprocal benefit in the form of a "fat envelope" from the admissions office. Perhaps the most efficient vehicle for reducing the risk of these abuses is the income tax return, which could be revised to solicit information from individuals claiming a charitable deduction for gifts to tax-exempt colleges and universities. The revised form could include following questions: (1) Are you a graduate of the university to which you made the donation? (2) Do you have or have you had a child or grandchild under consideration for admission to the institution within three years of the donation? (3) Was the child admitted to the university within three years of the first donation? Depending on the tax filer's answers to these questions, the claim of a charitable deduction for gifts to the university may not be valid. These relatively simple changes could help restore confidence that insiders' gifts to universities are, in fact, genuine acts of charity.

Of course, legacy preferences—based as they are on ancestry and not merit—are objectionable whether or not they are connected to tax-deductible donations. But by removing the tax benefit for alumni giving, the entire enterprise may come crashing down, universities having lost their economic rationale for providing the legacy preference.

This brings me to the final arena for reform, and that resides at the institutional level. Colleges and universities may find that it is in their best interest to change their behavior voluntarily now in order to avoid far more aggressive and punitive sanctions from the federal government down the road.

For example one option would be for universities to simply stop giving admission preferences to legacies in the spirit of maintaining the integrity of their charitable enterprises. If legacy preferences were stopped, donations from alumni parents would, without dispute, be charitable contributions, and therefore, deductible on their face. Indeed, there may be scenarios in which universities calculate that financially it would be more prudent to quit providing legacy preferences in order not to endanger future donations that may be deemed to violate possible new laws on the deductibility of gifts from alumni parents.

Short of a voluntary ban on legacy preferences, universities could modify their admission systems in ways that mitigate the self-dealing aspects of legacy admissions. For example, universities could chose to give an admissions advantage to legacies but also provide an equivalent admissions advantage to students of modest economic backgrounds. One suspects that, if elite universities were to improve substantially their records of access to students from all social classes, that would go a long way to proving to Congress that the public is actually getting something worthwhile in return for its generous subsidies of this industry.

Notes

Chapter 1

1. See Chapter 6, 123–24.

2. See Chapter 5.

3. See Chapter 3, 34, 39–43.

4. See Chapter 5, 119–21 (research universities) and n.11 (liberal arts colleges).

5. Thomas J. Espenshade, Chang Y. Chung, and Joan L. Walling, "Admission Preferences for Minority Students, Athletes, and Legacies at Elite Universities," *Social Science Quarterly* 85, no. 5 (December 2004): 1431.

6. In his book, *The Price of Admission: How America's Ruling Class Buys Its Way into Elite College—and Who Gets Left Outside the Gates* (New York: Crown, 2006), Daniel Golden does provide an excellent overview of a number of preferences for the rich in college admissions—a leg up for wealthy "development" admits, for the children of celebrities, for athletes in elite sports such as fencing and crew, and legacy preferences—but the volume you hold in your hands is the first ful-length book to comprehensively examine legacy preferences. We are fortunate to have a chapter by Golden that updates and expands upon his previous work.

7. Scott Jaschik, "Looking to the Past to Ban Legacy Admissions," *Inside Higher Education*, November 20, 2008.

8. "Public Views on Higher Education: A Sampling," *Chronicle of Higher Education*, May 7, 2004.

9. See Chapter 3, 63 (Dole), 65 (Edwards), 65 and 67 (Kennedy), and 68 (Bush); Chapter 4, 89 (Grassly); Daniel Golden, "Admissions Preferences Given to Alumni Children Draw Fire," *Wall Street Journal,* January 15, 2003 (Miller).

10. See Richard D. Kahlenberg, "Toward A New Affirmative Action," *Chronicle of Higher Education,* May 30, 2010; and Richard D. Kahlenberg, "Affirmative Action after the Seattle and Louisville Decisions: Re-examining the Socioeconomic Alternative," Paper presented at a conference of the American Association for the Advancement of Science and National Action Council for Minorities in Education, January 15, 2008, Washington, D.C., http://php.aaas.org/programs/centers/capacity/documents/Kahlenburg_Post-Seattle.doc.

11. See Chapter 3, 64.

12. See Chapter 6, 142. ("universities should be placed on notice that in the event affirmative action policies fall by the wayside—either because of judicial rulings or voter initiatives—the civil rights community is unlikely to let stand the hypocrisy of continued legacy preferences.")

13. Anthony P. Carnevale and Jeff Strohl, "How Increasing College Access Is Increasing Inequality, And What to Do About It," in *Rewarding Strivers: Helping Low-Income Students Succeed in College,* ed. Richard D. Kahlenberg (New York: The Century Foundation Press, 2010), 112.

14. Carnevale and Strohl, "How Increasing College Access," 79.

15. Carnevale and Strohl, "How Increasing College Access," 151.

16. Kahlenberg, "Five Myths About College Admissions," *Washington Post,* May 23, 2010; and Carnevale and Strohl, "How Increasing College Access," 145

17. Thomas R. Dye, *Who's Running America? The Bush Restoration,* (Upper Saddle River, N.J.: Prentice Hall, 2002), p. 148.

18. See Chapter 2, 23.

19. See Chapter 2, 28.

20. See Chapter 3, 34, 39–43.

21. See Chapter 3, 43.

22. See Chapter 3, 50–53.

23. See Chapter 3, 55.

24. See Chapter 3, 56.

25. See Chapter 3, 65.

26. See Chapter 3, 64, 66–67.

27. See Chapter 4, 71, 83.
28. See Chapter 4, 73.
29. William G. Bowen, Martin A. Kurzweil and Eugene M. Tobin, *Equity and Excellence in American Higher Education* (Charlottesville, Va.: University of Virginia Press, 2005), 105–06.
30. See Chapter 4, 83.
31. See Chapter 6, 125.
32. See Chapter 4, 73.
33. See Chapter 4, 76. See also Chapter 6, 125.
34. See Chapter 4, 78.
35. See Chapter 5, 113.
36. See Chapter 4, 92–93.
37. See Chapter 4, 80.
38. See Chapter 4, 96–97.
39. See Chapter 4, 97.
40. Ben Wildavsky, *The Great Brain Race: How Global Universities Are Reshaping the World* (Princeton, N.J.: Princeton University Press, 2010), 114. Oxford and Cambridge eliminated legacy preferences in the early 1960s as part of an effort to eliminate hereditary preferences and grant admission based on merit. See Steve P. Shadowen, "Personal Dignity, Equal Opportunity, and the Elimination of Legacy Preferences" (forthcoming).
41. See Chapter 10, 232.
42. See Chapter 5, 104.
43. See Chapter 10, 232.
44. See Chapter 5, 104.
45. See Chapter 5, 119–21.
46. See Chapter 5, 113.
47. See Chapter 5, 113.
48. See Chapter 5, 101–2.
49. Vanderbilt dropped legacy preferences during the study period but subsequently reinstated them.
50. See Chapter 5, 116. See also Chapter 3, 53 (at the University of Georgia and Texas A&M, alumni contributions have remained strong following elimination of legacy preferences) and Chapter 4, 92 (that the six University of California campuses, and the University of Georgia did not see declines in overall giving following the elimination of legacy preferences—indeed they saw increases).

51. See Chapter 4, 93.
52. See Chapter 4, 99.
53. Bowen, et al., *Equity and Excellence* 168.
54. See Chapter 6, 127.
55. See Chapter 6, 127.
56. See Chapter 6, 129, and Figure 2, 131.
57. See Chapter 6, 132.
58. See Chapter 6, 140.
59. See Chapter 6, 136.
60. Shadowen, "Personal Dignity."
61. See Chapter 3, 60.
62. Correspondence with Steve Shadowen.
63. *Rosenstock* v. *Board of Governors of the University of North Carolina,* 423 F. Supp. 1321 (M.D.N.C. 1976).
64. See Chapter 3, 61.
65. For a third legal theory, challenging legacy preferences for having a negative disparate impact on racial minorities, see Kathryn Ladewski, "Note: Preserving a Racial Hierarchy: A Legal Analysis of the Disparate Racial Impact of Legacy Preferences in University Admissions," *Michigan Law Review* 108 (2010): 577–601.
66. See Chapter 7, 145.
67. See Chapter 7, 145.
68. See Chapter 7, 146.
69. See Chapter 7, 149.
70. See Chapter 7, 154–59.
71. See Chapter 7, 148 and 172.
72. See Chapter 7, 161.
73. See Chapter 7, 166.
74. See Chapter 7, 170–71.
75. See Chapter 8, 175.
76. See Chapter 8, 190, quoting *Rice* v. *Cayetano,* 528 U.S. 495 (2000).
77. See Chapter 8, 189–91.
78. See Chapter 8, 195.
79. See Chapter 8, 196.
80. See Chapter 9, 200.

81. See Chapter 9, 202.
82. See Chapter 9, 203–4.
83. See Chapter 9, 206.
84. See Chapter 9, 208–9.
85. See Chapter 3, 63.
86. See Chapter 3, 65–68.
87. See Chapter 3, 58.
88. See Chapter 10, 223.
89. See Chapter 10, 224.
90. See Chapter 10, 226.
91. See Chapter 10, 226.
92. See Chapter 10, 228.
93. See Chapter 10, 215.
94. See Chapter 10, 234.
95. See Chapter 8, 196–97.
96. See Chapter 10, 235–36.
97. Shadowen, "Personal Dignity."

Chapter 2

1. James Bryant Conant, *Education for a Classless Society,* Occasional Pamphlets of the Graduate School of Education, Harvard University, no. 4, June 1940.

2. Thomas Jefferson to Roger C. Weightman, June 24, 1826, in *The Portable Thomas Jefferson,* ed. Merrill D. Peterson (New York: Penguin Books, 1975), 585.

3. *Memoirs, Correspondence and Private Papers of Thomas Jefferson,* vol. 1, ed. Thomas Jefferson Randolph (London: Henry Colburn and Richard Bentley Colburn, 1829), 31.

4. Thomas Jefferson to John Adams, October 28, 1813, in *The Adams-Jefferson Letters: The Complete Correspondence between Thomas Jefferson and Abigail and John Adams,* ed. Lester J. Cappon (Chapel Hill: University of North Carolina Press, 1988), 388.

5. Ibid., 388–89.

6. Ibid., 389.

7. Alexis de Tocqueville, *Democracy in America,* trans. Henry Reeve (New York: The Colonial Press, 1900), 50–51.

8. *The Adams-Jefferson Letters,* 390.

9. Daniel Golden, "For Five Supreme Court Justices, Affirmative Action Isn't Academic," *Wall Street Journal,* May 14, 2003.

10. Register of Debates in Congress, 19th Cong., 1st sess., May 16, 1826, 727–28, quoted in Alan F. Zundel, *Declarations of Dependency: The Civic Republican Tradition in U.S. Poverty Policy* (Albany: State University of New York, 2000), 33.

11. "Speech at Kalamazoo, Michigan, August 27, 1856," in *Collected Works of Abraham Lincoln,* vol. 2, ed. Roy P. Basler (New Brunswick, N.J.: Rutgers University Press, 1953), 361–66.

12. Will Hutton, "The American Prosperity Myth," *The Nation,* September 1–8, 2003.

13. *The Adams-Jefferson Letters,* 388.

14. For critiques of class bias in U.S. higher education, see Daniel Golden, *The Price of Admission: How America's Ruling Class Buys Its Way into Elite Colleges—and Who Gets Left Outside the Gates* (New York: Crown, 2006), and Peter Schmidt, *Color and Money: How Rich White Kids Are Winning the War Over College Affirmative Action* (New York: Palgrave Macmillan, 2007). See also Richard D. Kahlenberg, *The Remedy: Class, Race, and Affirmative Action* (New York: Basic Books, 1997).

Chapter 3

1. Rainer Christoph Schwinges, "Student Education, Student Life," in *A History of the University in Europe:* Vol. 1, *Universities in the Middle Ages,* ed. Hilde de Ridder-Symoens (Cambridge, England: Cambridge University Press, 1992), 202–11. Maria Rosa di Simone, "Admission," in *A History of the University in Europe:* Vol. 2, *Universities in Early Modern Europe,* ed. Hilde de Ridder-Symoens (Cambridge, England: Cambridge University Press, 1996), 285–325.

2. Schwinges, "Student Education, Student Life." di Simone, "Admission."

3. di Simone, "Admission."

4. Ibid.

5. Ibid.

6. Harold S. Wechsler, *The Qualified Student: A History of Selective College Admission in America* (New York: John Wiley, 1977), 3–15.

7. W. Bruce Leslie, *Gentlemen and Scholars: College and Community in the "Age of the University," 1865–1917* (University Park, Penn.: Pennsylvania State University Press, 1992), 214–15.

8. Wechsler, *The Qualified Student;* Leslie, *Gentlemen and Scholars.*

9. Scott Gelber, "Pathways in the Past: Historical Perspectives on Access to Higher Education," Manuscript prepared as part of the Social Science Research Council's Transition to College project, 2007.

10. Wechsler, *The Qualified Student.*

11. Henry Adams, *The Education of Henry Adams,* ed. Jean Gooder (New York: Penguin Books, 1995), 56.

12. Jerome Karabel, *The Chosen: The Hidden History of Admission and Exclusion at Harvard, Yale, and Princeton* (New York: Houghton Mifflin, 2005), 44.

13. Richard Farnum, "Patterns of Upper-Class Education in Four American Cities, 1875–1975," in *The High Status Track: Studies of Elite Schools and Stratification,* ed. Paul W. Kingston and Lionel S. Lewis (Albany: State University of New York Press, 1990), 53–73.

14. Wechsler, *The Qualified Student.*

15. Karabel, *The Chosen,* 13–38.

16. Leslie, *Gentlemen and Scholars,* 218.

17. Karabel, *The Chosen,* 13–38.

18. Richard M. Freeland, *Academia's Golden Age: Universities in Massachusetts, 1945–1970* (New York: Oxford University Press, 1992), 43–44

19. Cameron Howell and Sarah E. Turner, "Legacies in Black and White: The Racial Composition of the Legacy Pool," NBER Working Paper 9448 (Cambridge, Mass.: National Bureau of Economic Research, 2004).

20. Karabel, *The Chosen,* 23, 39–76.

21. John D. Lamb, "The Real Affirmative Action Babies: Legacy Preferences at Harvard and Yale," *Columbia Journal of Law and Social Problems* 26, no. 3 (1993): 491–521.

22. Karabel, *The Chosen,* 55.

23. Ibid., 75.

24. Richard Farnum, "Prestige in the Ivy League: Democratization and Discrimination at Penn and Columbia, 1890–1970," in *The High Status Track: Studies of Elite Schools and Stratification,* ed. Paul W. Kingston and Lionel S. Lewis (Albany: State University of New York Press, 1990), 53–73.

25. David O. Levine, *The American College and the Culture of Aspiration, 1915–1940* (Ithaca, N.Y.: Cornell University Press, 1986), 138, 139.

26. Karabel, *The Chosen,* 573. Levine, *The American College and the Culture of Aspiration, 1915–1940,* 141–45, 150–57.

27. Levine, *The American College and the Culture of Aspiration, 1915–1940,* 141–45, 150–57.

28. Ibid.

29. Karabel, *The Chosen,* 48, 76, 114–15,123–26.

30. Marcia Graham Synnott, *The Half-Opened Door: Discrimination and Admissions at Harvard, Yale, and Princeton, 1900–1970* (Westport, Conn.: Greenwood Press, 1979), 152–54. Joseph A. Soares, *The Power of Privilege: Yale and America's Elite Colleges* (Stanford, Calif.: Stanford University Press, 2007), 91.

31. Karabel, *The Chosen,* 116.

32. Ibid., 108.

33. Richard M. Freeland, *Academia's Golden Age: Universities in Massachusetts, 1945-1970* (New York: Oxford University Press, 1992), 41–45.

34. Alan M. Dershowitz and Laura Hanft, "Affirmative Action and the Harvard College Diversity-Discretion Model: Paradigm or Pretext?" *Cardozo Law Review* 1, no. 2 (1979): 379–424. Synnott, *The Half-Opened Door,* 206.

35. Hugh Hawkins, "The Making of the Liberal Arts College Identity," *Daedalus* 128, no. 1 (Winter 1999): 1–25.

36. Freeland, *Academia's Golden Age,* 44.

37. Michael Greenberg and Seymour Zenchelsky, "Private Bias and Public Responsibility: Anti-Semitism at Rutgers in the 1920s and 1930s," *History of Education Quarterly* 33, no. 3 (Autumn 1993): 295–319.

38. Scott Gelber, "Pathways in the Past."

39. Karabel, *The Chosen,* 2.

40. Lamb, "The Real Affirmative Action Babies," 491–521.

41. Synnott, *The Half-Opened Door,* 156.

42. Benjamin Fine, *Admission to American Colleges: A Study of Current Policy and Practice* (New York: Harper and Brothers, 1946), 68–73, 121–24.

43. Nicholas Lemann, *The Big Test: The Secret History of the American Meritocracy* (New York: Farrar, Straus & Giroux, 1999), 5–9, 42–52. Karabel, *The Chosen,* 139–65.

44. Merrill D. Peterson, *The Portable Thomas Jefferson* (New York: Penguin, 1975), 533–39.

45. Lemann, *The Big Test,* 39–41.

46. Karabel, *The Chosen,* 159, 174, 189.

47. Hawkins, "The Making of the Liberal Arts College Identity." Freeland, *Academia's Golden Age,* 73–77.

48. Karabel, *The Chosen,* 239.

49. Ibid., 214–15.

50. Ibid., 4, 262–93. William G. Bowen and Sarah A. Levin, *Reclaiming the Game: College Sports and Educational Values* (Princeton, N.J.: Princeton University Press, 2003), 59–60.

51. Synnott, *The Half-Opened Door,* 202.

52. Karabel, *The Chosen,* 4, 262–93. Bowen and Levin, *Reclaiming the Game,* 59–60.

53. Richard Farnum, "Patterns of Upper-Class Education in Four American Cities, 1875–1975," 53–73.

54. Freeland, *Academia's Golden Age,* 100–101.

55. Gelber, "Pathways in the Past."

56. Karabel, *The Chosen,* 539–40.

57. John H. Langbein, "The Twentieth-Century Revolution in Family Wealth Transmission," *Michigan Law Review* 86 (February 1988): 722–51.

58. Paul K. Conkin, Henry Lee Swint, and Patricia S. Miletich, *Gone with the Ivy: A Biography of Vanderbilt University* (Knoxville: Tenn: The University of Tennessee Press, 1985), 469–70.

59. John Greene and Robert Minton, *Scaling the Ivy Wall: Getting into the Selective Colleges* (New York: Abelard-Schuman, 1975), 176.

60. Bowen and Levin, *Reclaiming the Game,* 43–56.

61. Peter Schmidt, *Color and Money: How Rich White Kids Are Winning the War Over College Affirmative Action* (New York: Palgrave Macmillan, 2007), 69–72.

62. *Sweezy* v. *New Hampshire,* 354 U.S. 234 (1957).

63. *Keyishian* v. *Board of Regents* 385 US 589 (1967).

64. Karabel, *The Chosen,* 295–96.

65. Ibid., 316–17, 399, 478.

66. Ibid., 475.
67. Ibid., 315.
68. Ibid., 485.
69. Jerome Karabel, "The Legacy of Legacies," *New York Times,* September 13, 2004.
70. Lemann, *The Big Test,* 148–54.
71. Soares, *The Power of Privilege,* 88–101.
72. Karabel, *The Chosen,* 359–63.
73. Ibid., 359–63. Soares, *The Power of Privilege,* 88–101.
74. Karabel, *The Chosen,* 450–78.
75. Ibid., 450–78.
76. Ibid., 359–63.
77. Ibid., 450–78.
78. Ibid., 359–63.
79. Ibid., 467.
80. David Karen, "The Politics of Class, Race, and Gender: Access to Higher Education in the United States, 1960–1986," *American Journal of Education* 99, no. 2 (February 1991): 208–37.
81. Karabel, *The Chosen,* 448.
82. Freeland, *Academia's Golden Age,* 402.
83. Greene and Minton, *Scaling the Ivy Wall,* 177.
84. Karabel, *The Chosen,* 297, 666.
85. David Karen, "'Achievement' and 'Ascription' in Admission to an Elite College: A Political-Organizational Analysis," *Sociological Forum* 6, no. 2 (1991): 349–80.
86. Hunter M. Breland, James Maxey, Gall T. McLure, Michael J. Valiga, Michael A. Boatwright, Veronica L. Ganley, and Laura M. Jenkins, *Challenges in College Admissions: A Report of a Survey of Undergraduate Admissions Policies, Practices, and Procedures* (Washington, D.C.: American Association of Collegiate Registrars and Admissions Officers, 1995).
87. Schmidt, *Color and Money,* 26–27.
88. Brendan M. Cunningham and Carlena K. Cochi-Ficaono, "The Determinants of Donative Revenue Flows from Alumni of Higher Education: An Empirical Inquiry," *Journal of Human Resources* 37, no. 3 (Summer 2002), 540–69.
89. Ben Gose, "The Fall of the Flagships," *Chronicle of Higher Education,* July 5, 2002.

90. Daniel Golden, "Admissions Preferences Given to Alumni Children Draws Fire," *Wall Street Journal,* January 15, 2003.

91. Kimberly Miller, "UF, 2 Others Use 'Dirty Little Secret' for Alumn' Kids," *Palm Beach Post,* August 10, 2008.

92. Schmidt, *Color and Money,* 244–45.

93. Robert Lerner and Althea K. Nagai, *Preferences at the University of Virginia* (Washington, D.C.: Center for Equal Opportunity, 1999).

94. Breland et al., *Challenges in College Admissions.*

95. Data compiled by Steve D. Shadowen, Sozi P. Tulante, and Shara L. Alpern in researching the article "No Distinctions Except Those Which Merit Originates: The Unlawfulness of Legacy Preferences in Public and Private Universities," *Santa Clara Law Review* 49 (2009): 51–136.

96. Bill Paul, *Getting In: Inside the College Admissions Process* (Reading, Mass.: Addison-Wesley, 1995), 193–95, 237–38.

97. Ibid.

98. Saul Levmore, "Surprising Admissions," *University of Toledo Law Review* 34, no. 1 (Fall 2002): 113–19.

99. Elizabeth Farrell, "When Legacies Are a College's Lifeblood," *Chronicle of Higher Education,* January 19, 2007.

100. University of Pennsylvania admissions statistics and background on its legacy programs available at http://www.alumni.upenn.edu/aca/.

101. Diane Sheldon, "DAA Puts Special Emphasis on Legacy Students," *Duke Chronicle,* December 3, 2007.

102. Ann E. Kaplan, *Voluntary Support of Education, 2008* (New York: Council for Aid to Education, 2009).

103. *Rosenstock* v. *Board of Governors of University of North Carolina et al.* 423 F. Supp. 1321 (1976).

104. Lamb, "The Real Affirmative Action Babies."

105. *Regents of the University of California* v. *Bakke,* 438 U.S. 265 (1978).

106. Karabel, *The Chosen,* 502–13.

107. Lamb, "The Real Affirmative Action Babies." Karabel, *The Chosen,* 502–13.

108. Golden, "Admissions Preferences Given to Alumni Children Draws Fire." Schmidt, *Color and Money,* 184–85.

109. Schmidt, *Color and Money.*

110. Telephone interview with Ward Connerly, a former University of California regent who spearheaded the regents' efforts to eliminate legacy preference. See also Schmidt, *Color and Money,* 144–46.

111. Peter Schmidt, "New Pressure Put on Colleges to End Legacies in Admissions," *Chronicle of Higher Education,* January 30, 2004.

112. Schmidt, *Color and Money,* 131–40.

113. Ibid., 158–59.

114. Debra Thomas and Terry Shepard, "Legacy Preferences Are Defensible, Because the Process Can't Be 'Fair,'" *Chronicle of Higher Education,* March 14, 2003.

115. Jeffrey Selingo, "U.S. Public's Confidence in Colleges Remains High," *Chronicle of Higher Education,* May 7, 2004.

116. Schmidt, *Color and Money,* 203–10.

117. *Grutter* v. *Bollinger,* 539 U.S. 306 (2003).

118. Todd Ackerman, "Legislators Slam A&M over Legacy Admissions," *Houston Chronicle,* January 3, 2004.

119. Howell and Turner, "Legacies in Black and White."

120. Schmidt, "New Pressure Put on Colleges to End Legacies in Admissions."

121. Schmidt, *Color and Money,* 211–21.

122. Ibid.

123. Interview with Senator Rodney Tom, May 2009.

Chapter 4

1. Based on college responses in the Common Data Set as reported in the 2009 *U.S. News & World Report* rankings. Of the top thirty national universities in the rankings, three—the University of California at Berkeley, the University of California at Los Angeles, and Vanderbilt University—reported that they do not consider alumni/alumnae relations in admission decisions. Vanderbilt officials subsequently told the author that they do consider legacy status. Princeton and Notre Dame characterized legacy status as "important," and the University of Virginia as "very important." Of the top thirty liberal arts colleges, only Davidson reported not considering alumni/alumnae status. A Davidson official told the author in 2009 that it does in fact take legacy

status into account. Scripps College said alumni/alumnae relations were "very important," and six other top colleges said they were important.

2. http://www.princeton.edu/profile/admission/undergraduate-admission/.

3. Richard D. Kahlenberg and Steve Shadowen, "Obama: Stay Away from Notre Dame's Commencement," *American Prospect* Online, May 12, 2009, http://www.prospect.org/cs/articles?article=obama_skip_notre_dames_commencement.

4. The numbers for Brown were available at the Brown Alumni Association website, http://alumni.brown.edu/services/advise/list-brown.html#B, but are no longer; the numbers for the University of Pennsylvania are available at the Penn Alumni website, http://www.alumni.upenn.edu/aca/overview.html; the numbers for Dartmouth are from an e-mail communication to the author from Roland Adams, director of media relations, Dartmouth University, April 23, 2009. Also see Anya Perret, "College Is Twice as Likely to Admit Legacy Applicants," *The Dartmouth,* April 17, 2008, http://thedartmouth.com/2008/04/17/news/admissions/.

5. Daniel Golden, "Admisisons Preference Given to Alumni Children in College Draws Fire," *Wall Street Journal,* January 15, 2003.

6. Compliance Review No. 01-88-6009, Office for Civil Rights, United States Department of Education, October 4, 1990, 27–28.

7. Thomas J. Espenshade, Chang Y. Chung, and Joan L. Walling, "Admission Preferences for Minority Students, Athletes, and Legacies at Elite Universities," *Social Science Quarterly* 85, no. 5 (December 2004): 1426, 1431.

8. William G. Bowen, Martin A. Kurzweil, and Eugene M. Tobin, *Equity and Excellence in American Higher Education* (Charlottesville: University of Virginia Press, 2005), 105.

9. "Admissions Overview," University of Pennsylvania, Penn Alumni website, www.alumni.upenn.edu/aca/overview.html.

10. I prefer not to identify the college because I learned this information as a parent during a campus tour for prospective applicants.

11. Daniel Golden, *The Price of Admission: How America's Ruling Class Buys Its Way into Elite Colleges—and Who Gets Left Outside the Gates* (New York: Crown, 2006), 37–38.

12. The numbers for Stanford are from an e-mail communication to the author from Shawn Abbott, director of admission, May 2, 2009. The numbers for Cornell are from "Profile of the Class of 2012," Cornell

University Undergraduate Admissions Office, available at http://dpb.cornell.edu/documents/1000001.pdf. The numbers for Yale are from "Yale College Freshmen with Alumni Parents, Class of 1980 to Class of 2012," Yale University Undergraduate Admissions Office. The information for Vanderbilt is from a 2009 telephone interview by the author with Douglas Christiansen.

13. "Alumni Association Legacy Scholarships," Calvin College Alumni Association, http://www.calvin.edu/alumni/informed/association/scholarships/#legacy.

14. Golden, *The Price of Admission,* 131, 138.

15. Ibid., 118–20.

16. Douglas S. Massey and Margarita Mooney, "The Effects of America's Three Affirmative Action Programs on Academic Performance," *Social Problems* 54, no. 1 (February 2007): 114.

17. "Duke's Class of 2011 Will Be Its Most Selective, Diverse—And Larger Than Expected," Duke Office of News and Communications, June 11, 2007, http://news.duke.edu/2007/06/admissions_print.ht.

18. Nathan Martin and Kenneth Spenner, "A Social Portrait of Legacies at an Elite University," Paper presented at the annual meeting of the American Sociological Association, Sheraton Boston and the Boston Marriott Copley Place, Boston, Massachusetts, July 31, 2008, p. 12.

19. Office of the Registrar, response to a letter in the *Princeton Alumni Weekly,* April 9, 2001, http://www.princeton.edu/paw/web_exclusives/more/more_letters/letters_legacies.html.

20. Thomas J. Espenshade and Chang Y. Chung, "The Opportunity Cost of Admission Preferences at Elite Universities," *Social Science Quarterly* 86, no. 2 (June 2005): 301.

21. Bowen et al., *Equity and Excellence in American Higher Education,* 167–68.

22. "Student Scholarships," Calvin College Alumni Association, http://www.calvin.edu/alumni/informed/association/scholarships/.

23. E-mail communications to the author from Tysen Kendig, March/April 2009.

24. Seema Mehta, "Legacy Enrollments Offered in Two Top L.A.-area School Districts," *Los Angeles Times,* May 16, 2009.

25. "Undergraduate Admission and Enrollment," Princeton University, http://www.princeton.edu/profile/admission/undergraduate-admission/.

26. Golden, *The Price of Admission,* 131.

27. "Contributions to Colleges and Universities Up 6.2 Percent To $31.60 Billion," Press release on the Voluntary Support of Education Survey 2008, Council for Aid to Education, http://www.cae.org/content/pdf/VSE_2008_Survey_Press_Release_with_Tables.pdf.

28. John Hechinger, "The Tiger Roars," *Wall Street Journal*, July 17, 2006.

29. All endowment figures in this article are from the National Association of College and University Business Officers Endowment Study 2009, http://www.nacubo.org/Research/NACUBO_Endowment_Study.html. The $600 million figure for Cooper Union's endowment comes from the 2008 NACUBO study.

30. Golden, *The Price of Admission*, 132.

31. Generations Fundraising Campaign, University of Notre Dame.

32. Jonathan Meer and Harvey S. Rosen, "Altruism and the Child-Cycle of Alumni Donations," Working Paper no. 150 (Princeton, N.J.: Center for Economic Policy Studies, Princeton University, May 2007), 15–16, 24, 29.

33. David Karen, "'Achievement' and 'Ascription' in Admission to an Elite College: A Politico-Organizational Analysis," *Sociological Forum* 6, no. 2 (June 1991).

34. Telephone interview by the author, not for attribution, 2009.

35. Telephone interview by the author with Mary Sapp, assistant vice president for planning and institutional research, University of Miami, 2009.

36. Telephone interview by the author with Jim Sullivan, University of Miami Legacy Admission Counselor, 2009. The succeeding quotes from Sullivan derive from this interview.

37. E-mail communication to the author from Robin Matross Helms.

38. In-person interview by the author with Philip Altbach, director, Center for International Higher Education, Boston College, 2009.

39. E-mail communication from David Shepherd, United World College, to Krista Slade, executive director, Asia-Pacific, Council for Advancement and Support of Education, May 13, 2009. Provided to the author by Krista Slade.

40. Akiyoshi Yonezawa and Masateru Baba, "The Market Structure for Private Universities in Japan," *Tertiary Education and Management* 4, no. 2 (1998): 145.

41. Howard Newby, Thomas Weko, David Breneman, Thomas Johaneson, and Peter Maasen, *OECD Reviews of Tertiary Education: Japan*

(Paris: Organisation for Economic Co-operation and Development, 2009), 47, http://www.oecd.org/dataoecd/44/12/42280329.pdf.

42. E-mail communication to the author from Akiyoshi Yonezawa, March 24, 2009.

43. Ibid.

44. Telephone interview by the author with Joanna Motion, vice president for international operations, Council for Advancement and Support of Education. 2009.

45. Altbach interview.

46. Telephone interview with Joanna Motion.

47. "Our Benefactors," Saïd Business School, University of Oxford, http://www.sbs.ox.ac.uk/about/Pages/benefactors.aspx.

48. Polly Curtis, "Oxford's £1.25bn Fundraising Bid to Rival Ivy League," *The Guardian,* May 28, 2008.

49. John Gill, "Oxford Says Goodbye to Man With the Midas Touch," *The Times Higher Education Supplement,* August 14, 2008, 8.

50. Martha Ann Overland, "In Asia, American-Style Fundraising Takes Off," *The Chronicle of Higher Education*, 12/5/08.

51. E-mail communication to the author from Krista Slade, 5/11/09

52. Stanley Ho Alumni Challenge, http://www.hku.hk/alumnichallenge/.

53. James Doran, "Wild Card," Conde Nast Portfolio, May 2008, pp. 144, 148

54. Altbach interview.

55. "Fulfilling America's Promise of a Great Education," Website for Senator Sheldon Whitehouse, http://whitehouse.senate.gov/issues/issue/?id=94727e26-9c91-44fd-bda4-43f3ef0aae20.

56. E-mail communication to the author from Rebecca Hatcher, archivist, manuscripts and archives, Sterling Memorial Library, Yale, May 26, 2009. Also, for the senator's grandfather's Yale connection, see "Mary C. Alexander Weds S. Whitehouse," *New York Times,* October 15, 1920. For his father, see the obituary for Charles Whitehouse, *New York Times,* July 1, 2001.

57. E-mail communication from Rebecca Hatcher. Also, see Tim McCarten, "Sheldon Whitehouse '82 Takes Office As Rhode Island's Junior Senator," *Virginia Law Weekly,* January 26, 2007.

58. Golden, *The Price of Admission,* 225.

59. "Public Views on Higher Education: A Sampling," *Chronicle of Higher Education,* May 7, 2004.

60. Golden, *The Price of Admission,* 253–55.

61. Connie Bruck, "McCain's Party," *New Yorker,* May 30, 2005.

62. John McCain, *Faith of My Fathers* (New York: HarperCollins, 2000), 53.

63. Telephone interview with Guido Calabrese by the author, 2009.

64. Yale Law School receives about 200 applicants for transfer each year, and typically accepts about 10 to 15 of them, which is an acceptance rate of about 5 percent to 7.5 percent. That is about as competitive as first-year application, which has an acceptance rate of 6.9 percent. Yale Law School website, http://www.law.yale.edu/about/fastfacts.htm.

65. For Cardin's father and son, see Steny Hoyer, "In Honor of the Memory of Michael Cardin," 105th. Cong., 1st. sess., *Congressional Record—House* 144 (March 31, 1998): H1791. For his nephew, Jon S. Cardin, see the Wikipedia entry, http://en.wikipedia.org/wiki/Ben_Cardin.

66. Claire McCaskill, Commencement Address, University of Missouri, May 2008, http://coas.missouri.edu/news/commencement508.html.

67. Sahil K. Mahtani, "Exercising Harvard Pride: The Mogul Who Revamped the MAC," *Harvard Crimson,* June 6, 2005.

68. See information on the Malkin Athletic Center, Harvard University Athletics website, www.gocrimson.com/information/facilities/malkin. See also the biographical statement on the Malkin Securities website, https://malkinsecurities.com/about-us/bios/peter-l-malkin.

69. Class of 1955, 50th Reunion Report, Harvard University Archives.

70. Harvard alumni and student directories; "Facebook" pages for Elizabeth and George Malkin.

71. Telephone interview by the author with not-for-attribution source, 2009.

72. Steve D. Shadowen, Sozi P. Tulante and Shara L. Alpern, "No Distinctions Except Those Which Merit Originates: The Unlawfulness of Legacy Preferences in Public and Private Universities," *Santa Clara Law Review* 49, no. 1 (2009): 131–32.

73. Golden, *The Price of Admission,* 126–27.

74. Todd Ackerman and Clay Robison, "End 'Legacy' Program, A&M Urged," *Houston Chronicle,* January 8, 2004, 21.

75. *Texas A&M Foundation Annual 2008 Report,* Texas A&M Foundation Trust Company, 2008, http://giving.tamu.edu/PDFs/AR08_Final.pdf.

76. Telephone interviews by the author with Alice Reinarz and Kathy McCoy, 2009.

77. Telephone interview by the author with Kathryn Greenwade, 2009.

78. Telephone interview by the author with Keith Marshall.

79. Ibid.

80. "Message from Richard Herman, Chancellor of the Urbana-Champaign Campus," Brilliant Futures: The Campaign for the University of Illinois at Urbana-Champaign, June 1, 2007, http://brilliantfutures.illinois.edu/storydetail.aspx?id=669.

81. Jodi S. Cohen, Stacy St. Clair, Tara Malone, "Clout Goes to College," *Chicago Tribune,* May 29, 2009, 1.

82. Golden, *The Price of Admission,* 263–64.

83. Telephone interview by the author with Richard Bischoff, 2009.

84. Shadowen, Tulante, and Alpern, "No Distinctions Except Those Which Merit Originates," 132.

85. Golden, *The Price of Admission,* 267–68.

86. "Berea College Financial Eligibility Guidelines," Berea College, Office of Admissions, http://www.berea.edu/prospectivestudents/documents/BereaCollegeFinancialEligibilityGuidelines.pdf.

87. Golden, *The Price of Admission,* 276–77.

88. Ibid., 270.

89. See ibid., Chapters 2 and 3, for an in-depth examination of development preference.

90. Robert Morse, "Methodology: Undergraduate Ranking Criteria and Weights," *U.S. News & World Report,* August 19, 2009, http://www.usnews.com/articles/education/best-colleges/2008/08/21/undergraduate-ranking-criteria-and-weights.html.

91. Shadowen, Tulante, and Alpern, "No Distinctions Except Those Which Merit Originates," 128.

92. Laura Fitzpatrick, "Colleges Face a Financial-Aid Crunch," *Time,* March 26, 2009.

Chapter 5

1. For example, see Steve D. Shadowen, Sozi P. Tulante, and Shara L. Alpern, "No Distinctions Except Those Which Merit Originates: The

Unlawfulness of Legacy Preferences in Public and Private Universities," *Santa Clara Law Review* 49, no. 1 (2008): 125, and Katherine Lassila, "Q&A: Rick Levin, Why Yale Favors Its Own," *Yale Alumni Magazine*, November/December 2004, 28–29.

2. Shadowen et al., "No Distinctions Except Those Which Merit Originates."

3. In Shadowen et al., "No Distinctions Except Those Which Merit Originates," the variables include Real Gifts measured in Dollars and Real Gifts per Undergrad as reported by the U.S. Department of Education, and Alumni Giving Rate as reported by *U.S. News & World Report*. Their control variables include proxies for school size, acceptance rate, public versus private institution, and Pell Grants per Undergrad.

4. Shadowen et al., "No Distinctions Except Those Which Merit Originates," 129–30.

5. Charles T. Clotfelter, "Alumni Giving to Elite Private Colleges and Universities," *Economics of Education Review* 22, no. 2 (2003): 109–20.

6. Jonathan Meer and Harvey S. Rosen, "Altruism and the Child Cycle of Alum Donations," *American Economic Journal: Economic Policy* 1, no. 1 (2009): 258–86. Jonathan Meer and Harvey S. Rosen, "Family Bonding with Universities," CEPS Working Paper no. 187 (Princeton, N.J.: Princeton University, Center for Economic and Policy Studies, 2009).

7. Meer and Rosen state that "the top one per-cent of gifts in 2007 in their sample accounted for 81.6 percent of the total in 2007."

8. They do not find a significant effect on giving based on whether parents attended the school.

9. James Monk, "Patterns of Giving to One's Alma Mater among Young Graduates from Selective Institutions," *Economics of Education Review* 22, no. 2 (2003): 121–30.

10. Phanindra V. Wunnava and Michael A. Lauze. "Alumni Giving at a Small Liberal Arts College: Evidence from Consistent and Occasional Donors," *Economics of Education Review* 20, no. 6 (2001): 533–43.

11. Because 11 schools tied at number 96, the "top 100 schools" actually include 106 institutions. We also collected and analyzed data from the top 100 liberal arts colleges; however, we were able to confirm definitively only that one liberal arts college lacks any preference policy

(Berea). We also found that the coefficients on the independent variables in our models were significantly different for liberal arts institutions when compared to national universities. Because there is a structural difference in the determinants of alumni giving and insufficient variance in legacy preference policies, we exclude liberal arts institutions from our data.

12. Council for Aid to Education, Data & Trends on Private Giving to Education, FAQs, http://www.cae.org/content/pro_data_faq.htm.

13. Ibid.

14. "Federal Student Aid FAFSA," U.S. Department of Education, http://www.fafsa.ed.gov. Also, the Pell Grant Information Site (www.thepellgrant.com) suggests that, "students with a total family income up to $50,000 may be eligible for Pell Grants, though most Pell funding goes to students with a total family income below $20,000."

15. See, for example, "Top Colleges for Getting Rich," Forbes.com, July 30, 2008, http://www.forbes.com/2008/07/30/college-salary-graduates-lead-cz_kb_0730topcolleges.html.

16. "PayScale College Salary Report: Methodology Overview," PayScale.com, 2008, http://www.payscale.com/best-colleges/salary-report.asp.

17. In the e-mail each school was asked, "Does your institution have a legacy preference, either formal or informal? In other words, does an applicant having a relative who is an alumnus impact the acceptance process in any way?"

Example responses affirming legacy preference:

"While being a legacy is something we take into consideration, it is only one of many factors that we use in making admission decisions."

"When reviewing applications for admissions, [the institution] does consider and take into account if a student happens to be a sibling/legacy. That being said, simply being a sibling/legacy does not guarantee admission but it is something we like to be aware of."

"To answer your question regarding legacy applicants, it is something we take into consideration, however the most important components of an application are the strength and performance within your high school curriculum."

Example responses denying legacy preference:

"We do not have a legacy preference and we do not require that you provide this information on our application."

"Legacy status in no way influences a student's chances of admission."

18. "Newsworthy Items," Common Data Set Initiative, www.commondataset.org.

19. Ibid. The data we used can be found in chart C7 [Relative importance of each of the academic and nonacademic factors in first-time, first year, degree-seeking (freshman) admissions] of the CDS, which is located in section C. First time, First-Year (Freshman) Admission. The factor we collected our data from was entitled "alumni/ae relations."

20. The form instructs institutions to record deferred giving in present value terms.

21. ALUMREC also comes from the VSE dataset.

22. ($399.73–$124.62) /$ 124.62

23. Marie Thibault, "Billionaire University," Forbes.com, August 5, 2009, http://www.forbes.com/2009/08/02/billionaire-study-harvard-stanford-business-billionaires-colleges-09-wealth.html.

24. SAT is the "old" SAT, or prior to the addition of a writing test, thus a perfect score would be 1600.

25. Using the log of the dependant variables is consistent with the methodology employed in the previous literature and allows us to interpret the coefficients in percentage terms.

26. Shadowen et al., "No Distinctions Except Those Which Merit Originates," 131.

27. Georgia Institute of Technology (dropped legacy preference in 2004), Texas A&M (2004), University of Georgia (2002), University of Iowa (2006), University of Massachusetts, Amherst (2006), University of Nebraska at Lincoln (2006), Vanderbilt (2006). Because the model contains fixed effects for school and the California public university system dropped legacy preferences prior to the beginning of our data, they do not contribute to the measured coefficient.

28. We also explored whether years since dropping legacy preference had any explanatory power and found it did not.

29. Chapter 4 in this volume reports that alumni giving accounts for 27.5 percent of private giving. Our data is generally consistent with that figure. In our view, however, when evaluating the potential financial impact on the school as a whole, it is important to focus on expenditures, not just giving (that is, include spending from all sources). Expenditures represent a more complete measure of the output of the organization.

30. We also tested whether legacy preferences had an impact on other (non-alumni) sources of financing or on expenditures as a whole and found no statistically significant relationship.

Chapter 6

1. "Lexington: The Curse of Nepotism," *Economist*, January 8, 2004, 70.

2. "Naked Hypocrisy: The Nationwide System of Affirmative Action for Whites," *Journal of Blacks in Higher Education* 18 (Winter 1997–98): 40–43.

3. John D. Lamb, "The Real Affirmative Action Babies: Legacy Preferences at Harvard and Yale," *Columbia Journal of Law and Social Problems* 26 (1993): 504 (citing Jerome Karabel and David Karen, "Go to Harvard, Give Your Kid a Break," *New York Times*, December 8, 1990, A25).

4. Michael Dannenberg, "Prepared Remarks for the Secretary of Education's Commission on the Future of Higher Education," New America Foundation, February 24, 2006.

5. Steve D. Shadowen, Sozi P. Tulante, and Shara L. Alpern, "No Distinctions Except Those Which Merit Originates: The Unlawfulness of Legacy Preferences in Public and Private Universities," *Santa Clara Law Review* 49 (2009): 56 (citing Jerome Karabel, *The Chosen: The Hidden History of Admission and Exclusion at Harvard, Yale, and Princeton* [New York: Houghton Mifflin, 2005], 549).

6. Melissa E. Clinedinst and David A. Hawkins, *2009 State of College Admission* (Arlington, Va.: National Association for College Admission Counseling, 2009), 14. The National Association for College Admission Counseling (NACAC) estimates that the number of high school graduates, steadily increasing since the mid-1990s, reached a peak of 3.33 million in 2008–09. The NACAC estimates that, though the number of graduates will decline in 2010, it will again rise to 3.31 million by 2017–18. Ibid., 11.

7. John H. Pryor et al., *The American Freshman: National Norms for Fall 2008* (Los Angeles, Calif.: Higher Education Research Institute, January 2009), 2. This percentage was fairly stable from 1989 to 2005, hovering around 70 percent. The percentage of incoming first-year students who were accepted by their first-choice college also declined from 2007 (80.6 percent)

to 2008 (77.8 percent). The most selective colleges—those that accept fewer than 50 percent of applicants—received far more applications per institution, on average, than other colleges and universities and these institutions were more likely to offer an early decision option and to maintain a wait list, in part to manage this application volume. They also placed relatively more weight on the student essay, counselor and teacher recommendations, class rank, extracurricular activities and work, and portfolios. Clinedinst and Hawkins, *2009 State of College Admission*, 20, 27.

8. Shadowen, Tulante, and Alpern, "No Distinctions Except Those Which Merit Originates," 57.

9. "Naked Hypocrisy," 40–43.

10. Jane Mayer and Alexandra Robbins, "Dept. of Aptitude—How George W. Made the Grade," *New Yorker*, November 8, 1999, 30. See also Jack Greenberg, "Affirmative Action in Higher Education: Confronting the Condition and Theory," *Boston College Law Review* 43, no. 3 (2002): 536–37. "So if his father and grandfather had not been stars at Yale, and his grandfather had not been a Yale trustee, George almost certainly would have ended up at Texas." Ibid., 536, n91 (quoting Nicholas D. Kristof, "The Campaign 2000: The Cheerleader; Earning A's in People Skills at Andover," *New York Times*, June 10, 2000, A1).

11. Nathan D. Martin and Kenneth I. Spenner, "Capital Conversion and Accumulation: A Social Portrait of Legacies at an Elite University," *Research in Higher Education* 50, no. 7 (2009): 644.

12. Daniel Golden, "Family Ties: Preference for Alumni Children in College Admissions Draws Fire," *Wall Street Journal*, January 15, 2003, A1; see also, generally, William G. Bowen and Derek Bok, *The Shape of the River: Long-term Consequences of Considering Race in College and University Admissions* (Princeton: Princeton University Press 1998), p. 28 (finding that "[t]he overall admission rate for legacies was almost twice that for all other candidates").

13. Shadowen, Tulante, and Alpern, "No Distinctions Except Those Which Merit Originates," 51, 56.

14. Dave Newbart, "Wealthy Squeeze Out Low-Income Students at Many Top Colleges," *Chicago Sun Times*, June 13, 2004, 8.

15. Ibid.

16. "Lexington: The Curse of Nepotism."

17. Alice Gomstyn, "Top Colleges Mum on Legacy Admissions," ABC NEWS/Money online, April 11, 2008, http://abcnews.go.com/Business/IndustryInfo/story?id=4626882&page=1.

18. Ibid.

19. Cameron Howell and Sarah E. Turner, "Legacies in Black and White: The Racial Composition of the Legacy Pool," *Research in Higher Education* 45, no. 4 (2004): 329.

20. Ibid.

21. Ibid. The school also recognizes as legacies the children of Mary Washington College alumnae from the years before 1972.

22. Anna Haigh, "Legacy Admissions: A Heated Debate," *Daily Pennsylvanian* (University of Pennsylvania), October 29, 2004, http://www.dailypennsylvanian.com/node/43651.

23. Martin and Spenner, "Capital Conversion and Accumulation," 624, n1.

24. Todd Ackerman, "A&M Abolishes Legacy Program," *Houston Chronicle*, January 10, 2004, A1.

25. Golden, "Family Ties."

26. Alan Gordon and Bryan Chang, "Privileging the Privileged," *College Hill Independent* (Brown University/Rhode Island School of Design), April 8, 2004. "According to Andrea van Niekerk, an Assistant Dean of Admissions at Brown, legacy status here is not reduced to a number; rather, it's something admissions officers keep in the back of their minds as they read applications."

27. Howell and Turner, "Legacies in Black and White," 325, 329 (quoting Lani Guinier, "Colleges Should Take 'Confirmative Action' in Admissions," *Chronicle of Higher Education*, December 14, 2001, B12).

28. Ibid. (quoting Mark Megalli, "So Your Dad Went to Harvard: Now What About the Lower Board Scores of White Legacies?" *Journal of Blacks in Higher Education* 7 [Spring 1995], 72). Eligibility "for a legacy preference at most universities 'is a near-perfect proxy for being white,' said Michael A. Olivas, a law professor and authority on higher education at the University of Houston." Adam Liptak, "A Hereditary Perk the Founding Fathers Failed to Anticipate," *New York Times*, January 15, 2008, A12. Parenthetically, elite, historically black colleges and universities such as Spelman, Morehouse, Howard, Hampton, Dillard, Xavier, and Fisk extend legacy preferences.

29. In fact, blacks were not allowed to gain admission to Texas A&M University until 1963. Michael King, "Naked City: Texas A&M's Racial Legacy," *Austin Chronicle*, January 16, 2004, http://www.austinchronicle.com/gyrobase/Issue/print?oid=oid%3A193354.

30. Howell and Turner, "Legacies in Black and White," 329 (citing Theodore Cross, "Suppose There Was No Affirmative Action at the Most Prestigious Colleges and Graduate Schools," *Journal of Blacks in Higher Education* 18 [Winter 1998]: 44–51).

31. Martin and Spenner, "Capital Conversion and Accumulation," 644. "The annual pre-college household income of legacies (about $240,000/year) is nearly triple that of students with no degree parents and is about 44% higher than students with college degree parents." Ibid., 633.

32. Golden, "Family Ties," A1. "Naked Hypocrisy," 40–43. In the fall of 1997, 148 legacy admits enrolled at Princeton, which was twice the number of all black students who enrolled that year.

33. "Naked Hypocrisy," 40. In 1997, Harvard admitted twice as many legacies (264) as minorities (132); Yale (290/104), University of Virginia (1,059/309), and Columbia (399/116), about three times as many; MIT (325/64) about five times as many; University of Pennsylvania (948/154) about six times as many; and Cornell (1,150/143) about eight times as many.

34. Todd Ackerman, "Legislators Slam A&M Over Legacy Admissions," *Houston Chronicle*, January 4, 2004, A1.

35. Golden, "Family Ties," A1. Among applicants with no alumni parents, the pool of those accepted was more diverse: 73 percent white, 5.6 percent black, 9.3 percent Asian, and 3.5 percent Hispanic.

36. "Generational Gains in Postsecondary Education Appear to Have Stalled, New ACE Report Finds," Press Release, The American Council on Education, October 9, 2008, http://www.acenet.edu/AM/Template.cfm?Section=Search&template=/CM/HTMLDisplay.cfm&ContentID=34225. The report found that the percentage of young adults aged twenty-five to twenty-nine and older adults aged thirty and above with at least an associate degree in 2006 was about the same, approximately 35 percent. For Hispanics and American Indians, however, young adults have even less education than previous generations. In 2006, among older Hispanics, 18 percent had at least an associate degree, but just 16 percent of young Hispanics had reached that same educational threshold. The postsecondary educational attainment rates of African Americans remained relatively the same for both age groups, at approximately 24 percent. The percentages for whites were 41 percent for young adults and 37 percent for older adults.

37. Clinedinst and Hawkins, *2009 State of College Admission*, 14.

38. Ibid. Presumably, this number would be even lower without the influence of the nation's historically black colleges and universities. U.S.

Department of Education, National Center for Education Statistics, *The Condition of Education 2005: Appendix 1 Supplemental Tables*, NCES 2005-094 (Washington, D.C.: U.S. Government Printing Office, 2005), Table 31-1, p. 181. "Compared with students in other racial/ethnic groups, a relatively high percentage of Black students (13 percent) attended colleges where they constituted 75 percent or more of the enrollment." U.S. Department of Education, National Center for Education Statistics, *The Condition of Education 2009*, NCES 2009-081 (Washington, D.C.: U.S. Government Printing Office, 2005), p. 94. For example, in 2000, the *Tampa Tribune* noted that at the University of Florida, "Of the 220,000 total students in the system, 32 percent are minorities, records show. But the numbers are skewed by Florida A&M University, the historically black university that in 1998 claimed a 99 percent minority student body. In contrast, the state's oldest and most selective college, the University of Florida, is only 5.5 percent black and 9 percent Hispanic." Grace Frank, "Regents Likely to OK One Florida," *Tampa Tribune*, February 2, 2000, p. 1.

39. Clinedinst and Hawkins, *2009 State of College Admission*, 14.

40. Nearly 20 percent of the enrolled students counted among the 2008 Integrated Postsecondary Education Data System (IPEDS) data for the top fifty colleges were listed as "Unknown" or "Non-resident Aliens." U.S. Department of Education, National Center for Education Statistics, IPEDS Peer Analysis System, 2008, Four-year, Not-for-profit and Public, Degree-granting, Title-IV Participating Institutions; "Best Colleges 2008," *U.S. News & World Report,* Aug. 17, 2007; Thomas D. Snyder, Sally A. Dillow, Charlene M. Hoffman, *Digest of Education Statistics, 2008* (Washington, D.C.: U.S. Department of Education, National Center for Education Statistics, March 2009), Table 227.

41. Kati Haycock, Mary Lynch, and Jennifer Engle, *Opportunity Adrift: Our Flagship Universities Are Straying from Their Public Mission* (Washington, D.C.: The Education Trust, January 2010), 3.

42. Danette Gerald and Kati Haycock, *Engines of Inequality: Diminishing Equity in the Nation's Premier Public Universities* (Washington, D.C.: The Education Trust, January 2006), 3. And the table is already tilted significantly in favor of the rich, even at state flagship universities. According to The Education Trust, from 1995 to 2003, while the percentage of students from families earning less than $20,000 per year declined from 14 percent to 9 percent, and the percentage of students from

families earning between $20,000 and $39,999 declined from 19 percent to 15 percent, the representation of students from families earning more than $100,000 increased by 12 percentage points.

43. Gerald and Haycock, *Engines of Inequality,* 3.

44. Richard Kahlenberg, "Economic Affirmative Action in College Admissions: A Progressive Alternative to Racial Preferences and Class Rank Admissions," The Century Foundation, New York, April 2003, 2 and n. 4. "The exceptions include California and Washington (public initiative), Texas and Georgia (court decision), and Florida (executive order)."

45. *Grutter* v. *Bollinger,* 539 U.S. 306, 367–68 (2003) (Ginsburg, J., concurring).

46. 347 U.S. 483 (1954), 494.

47. *Roberts* v. *United States Jaycees*, 468 U.S. 609, 625 (1984).

48. *Regents of University of California* v. *Bakke*, 438 U.S. 265, 298 (1978) ("preferential programs may only reinforce common stereotypes holding that certain groups are unable to achieve success without special protection based on a factor having no relation to individual worth"); *Fullilove* v. *Klutznick*, 448 U.S. 448, 545 (1980) (Stevens, J., dissenting) ("a statute of this kind inevitably is perceived by many as resting on an assumption that those who are granted this special preference are less qualified in some respect that is identified purely by their race can only exacerbate rather than reduce racial prejudice"); *United Jewish Organizations* v. *Carey*, 430 U.S. 144, 173–74 (1977) (Brennan, J., concurring in part) ("preferential treatment may act to stigmatize its recipient groups, for although intended to correct systemic or institutional inequities, such a policy may imply to some the recipients' inferiority and especial need for protection"); *Richmond* v. *J. A. Croson Co.*, 488 U.S. 469, 493 (1989) (stating that racial classifications used for something other than remedying identified past discrimination "may in fact promote notions of racial inferiority and lead to a politics of racial hostility").

49. *DeFunis* v. *Odegaard*, 416 U.S. 312, 343 (1974) (Douglas, J., dissenting).

50. Daniel Ibsen Morales, "A Matter of Rhetoric: The Diversity Rationale in Political Context," *Chapman Law Review* 10 (2006): 187.

51. "Naked Hypocrisy," 40.

52. Greenberg, "Affirmative Action in Higher Education," 536.

53. The University of Florida, the University of Michigan, and the University of Washington continue to grant legacy preferences even though

they do not give preferences to racial minorities. See Shadowen, Tulante, and Alpern, "No Distinctions Except Those Which Merit Originates," 135.

54. *Ex parte Virginia*, 100 U.S. 339, 344-45 (1879).

55. U.S. Constitution, amend. 14, sec. 1. In considering whether a state has violated the Equal Protection Clause, courts apply different levels of scrutiny to different types of classifications. A classification based on race, based on national origin, or affecting fundamental rights is given the most exacting scrutiny. *Clark* v. *Jeter*, 486 U.S. 456, 461 (1988) (citations omitted); *Adarand Constructors* v. *Pena*, 515 U.S. 200, 227 (1995) ("all racial classifications, imposed by whatever federal, state, or local governmental actor, must be analyzed by a reviewing court under strict scrutiny"). Any attempt by the government to apportion burdens or benefits on the basis of individual racial classifications, therefore, is reviewed under strict scrutiny. Such a classification "can be justified only if it furthers a compelling government purpose and, even then, only if no less restrictive alternative is available." *Regents of University of California* v. *Bakke*, 438 U.S. 265, 357 (1978).

56. *Parents Involved in Community Schools* v. *Seattle School District No. 1*, 551 U.S. 701 (2007) Brief of Historians as Amici Curiae in Support of Respondents at 3 (citing *Plessy v. Ferguson*, 163 U.S. 537, 559 (1896) (Harlan, J., dissenting)). See, for example, Act of July 28, 1866, ch. 308, 14 Stat. 310, 343 (donating federally owned land in the District of Columbia "for the sole use of schools for colored children").

57. Ibid.

58. Ibid. (citing *Plessy v. Ferguson*, 163 U.S. 537, 559 (1896) (Harlan, J., dissenting)). Congress also enacted race conscious legislation authorizing the expenditure of $500,000 "for the immediate subsistence and clothing of destitute Indians." Resolution of Dec. 21, 1865, No. 1, 14 Stat. 347, 347.

59. *San Antonio Independent School District* v. *Rodriguez*, 411 U.S. 1, 34 (1973).

60. *Regents of University of California* v. *Bakke,* 438 U.S. 369–74 (1978).

61. Ibid., 311–12.

62. *Bakke,* 438 U.S. at 312 (quoting *Sweezy* v. *New Hampshire*, 354 U.S. 234, 263 (1957) (Frankfurter, J., concurring in result)).

63. Ibid., 311–12.

64. Ibid., 315.

65. Harvard University's admissions committee reported, "The effectiveness of our students' educational experience has seemed to the

Committee to be affected as importantly by a wide variety of interests, talents, backgrounds and career goals as it is by a fine faculty and our libraries, laboratories and housing arrangements." Ibid., 322 n55 (quoting Fred L. Glimp, "Final Report to the Faculty of Arts and Science," *Official Register of Harvard University* 65, no. 25 [1968]: 93, 104–05). For years, Harvard purported to meet that goal by seeking to admit students from different regions with diverse personal interests and parental backgrounds; however, that admissions approach resulted in "very few ethnic or racial minorities attend[ing] Harvard College." Ibid. Harvard modified the admissions criteria to allow an applicant's race to "tip the balance in his favor" because "[a] farm boy from Idaho can bring something to Harvard College that a Bostonian cannot offer. Similarly, a black student can usually bring something that a white person cannot offer." Ibid., 323. The school, however, did not want the committee to set a precise number of minority applicants it had to admit. Ibid., 323–24.The committee reported that the revised admissions plan admitted enough minorities to avoid "a sense of isolation among the black students themselves" and to achieve the "benefits to be derived from a diverse student body. . ." Ibid., 323.

66. Ibid., 316; see also 317 and n51 (describing Princeton's admission policies).

67. Ibid., 317.

68. Ibid., 317–18.

69. 539 U.S. 306 (2003).

70. 539 U.S. 244 (2003).

71. Ibid., 325.

72. Ibid., 328.

73. Ibid., 332–33.

74. Ibid., 334 (quoting *Bakke*, 438 U.S. at 317).

75. Ibid., 334 (citations omitted).

76. Ibid., 334 (quoting *Bakke*, 438 U.S., at 317).

77. Ibid., 343. *Accord id.,*351 (Thomas, J. dissenting) ("I agree with the Court's holding that racial discrimination in higher education admissions will be illegal in 25 years."). But see ibid., 386–87 (Rehnquist, C.J., dissenting) (criticizing the majority's "possible 25-year limitation").

78. 539 U.S. 244 (2003).

79. *Gratz,* 539 U.S. at 254. Furthermore, starting in 1999, the university established an Admissions Review Committee (ARC), to provide an additional level of consideration for applicants who (1) are academically

prepared to succeed at the University, (2) achieved a minimum selection index score, and (3) possessed a quality or characteristic important to the university's composition of its freshman class, such as high class rank, unique life experiences, challenges, circumstances, interests or talents, socioeconomic disadvantage, and underrepresented race, ethnicity, or geography. After reviewing "flagged" applications, the ARC determines whether to admit, defer, or deny each applicant. Ibid., 256–57.

80. The Sixth Circuit Court of Appeals heard the *Gratz* case on the same day as it heard *Grutter*. The Sixth Circuit later issued an opinion in *Grutter*, upholding the admissions program used by the University of Michigan Law School, which the school appealed to the Supreme Court. The parties in *Gratz* asked the Court to hear that case as well, despite the fact that the Court of Appeals had not yet rendered a judgment, so that the Supreme Court could address the constitutionality of the consideration of race in university admissions in a wider range of circumstances. The Court did so.

81. Judith Lichtenberg, "How the Academically Rich Get Richer," *Philosophy and Public Policy Quarterly* 24, no. 4 (Fall 2004): 22.

82. Shadowen, Tulante, and Alpern, "No Distinctions Except Those Which Merit Originates," 56.

83. Malcolm Gladwell, "Getting In: The Social Logic of Ivy League Admissions," *New Yorker*, Oct. 10, 2005, p. 80 (citing Karabel, *The Chosen*).

84. Gail Heriot, "Thoughts on *Grutter* v. *Bollinger* and *Gratz* v. *Bollinger* as Law and as Practical Politics," *Loyola University of Chicago Law Journal* 36 (Fall 2004): 154 and n95 (quoting Marcia Graham Synnott, *The Half-Opened Door: Discrimination and Admissions at Harvard, Yale, and Princeton, 1900–1970* [Westport, Conn.: Greenwood Press, 1979]).

85. Ibid.

86. Martin and Spenner, "Capital Conversion and Accumulation," 624.

87. Shadowen, Tulante, and Alpern, "No Distinctions Except Those Which Merit Originates," 125–26.

88. Cross, "Suppose There Was No Affirmative Action at the Most Prestigious Colleges and Graduate Schools," 50.

89. 78 F.3d 932 (5th Cir. 1996), *reh'g en banc denied*, 84 F.3d 720 (5th Cir. 1996), *cert. denied*, 116 S. Ct. 2581 (1996). In *Hopwood*, a panel of the Fifth Circuit ruled that the defendants had shown no compelling state interest for an affirmative action program at the University of Texas School

of Law that granted preferences to African-American and Mexican-American applicants. Specifically, the Hopwood panel held that: (1) diversity was not a compelling state interest; and (2) the defendants had not presented sufficient evidence of a remedial need for the affirmative action program. See ibid, 944, 955.

90. Ross Ramsey, "Ruling in UT Suit Stirs Fears of 'Resegregation,'" *Houston Chronicle*, March 20, 1996, A1.

91. Todd Ackerman, "A&M Puts All Admissions Decisions on Hold," *Houston Chronicle*, March 22, 1996, A25.

92. Office of Attorney General, State of Texas, Letter Opinion no. 97-001 (February 5, 1997). The attorney general specifically advised: "*Hopwood* proscribes the use of race or ethnicity, in the absence of a factual showing by an institution or the legislature which establishes: (1) either that the institution has discriminated in the not too distant past against the racial group benefited by the preference or that the institution has been a passive participant in acts of private discrimination by specific private actors against the benefited racial group; (2) that there exist present effects of the past discrimination that are not due to general societal discrimination; and, (3) that the scholarship is narrowly tailored to remedy those present effects. Unless or until these facts can be established, the consideration of race or ethnicity is expressly prohibited." Ibid., 24.

93. Brian T. Fitzpatrick, "Strict Scrutiny of Facially Race-Neutral State Action and the Texas Ten Percent Plan," *Baylor Law Review* 53 (2001): 289, 294, n16. See also, generally, Danielle Holley and Delia Spencer, "The Texas Ten Percent Plan," *Harvard Civil Rights-Civil Liberties Law Review* 34 (1999): 245.

94. Thurston Domina, "Higher Education Policy as Secondary School Reform: Texas Public High Schools after Hopwood," *Education Evaluation and Policy Analysis* 200 (September 1, 2007).

95. Texas Education Code Annotated, sec. 51.803 (2007).

96. Holly K. Hacker, "Class Rank Is Low on Many Colleges' Lists: UT Admitting More to Make Up for Law Some Say Ignores Other Factors," *Dallas Morning News*, December 2, 2007, 1A. As of late 2007, nearly three quarters of the freshmen at University of Texas were in the top 10 percent of their high school class; whereas, fewer than half of the freshmen at Texas A&M were from the top tenth.

97. Carlos Guerra, "Universities Seeing the Wisdom of State's Top-10-percent Rule," *San Antonio Express-News*, March 27, 2007, 1B; see also

Fitzpatrick, "Strict Scrutiny of Facially Race-Neutral State Action and the Texas Ten Percent Plan," 295.

98. Adam Cohen, "Coloring the Campus," *Time,* September 17, 2001, 48. University administrators and lawmakers continued to tweak the law. Fearing a legal challenge, officials at Texas A&M in 2002 withdrew a proposal to offer automatic enrollment to the top 20 percent at selected low-income, predominantly minority high schools. Jim Yardley, "Desperately Seeking Diversity: The 10 Percent Solution," *New York Times*, April 14, 2002, A4.

99. Lydia Lum, "Texas A&M to Leave Race Out of Admissions Decisions," *Black Issues in Higher Education,* January 1, 2004, 10.

100. Ibid.

101. Ibid. The University of Texas, Rice University, and other state schools contemporaneously announced they would institute race preferences. Ron Nissimov, "Black Lawmakers Rip A&M Decision," *Houston Chronicle*, December 5, 2003, A37.

102. Ibid. See also Danna Harman, "Family Ties: An Unfair Advantage?" *The Christian Science Monitor*, February 6, 2004, http://www.csmonitor.com/2004/0206/p13s01-legn.html.

103. Todd Ackerman and Clay Robinson, "End 'Legacy' Program, A&M Urged," *Houston Chronicle*, January 8, 2004, A21.

104. Ibid.

105. *Bakke*, 438 U.S. at 404 (Blackmun, J., concurring).

106. "Bonus Points/Legacy Policy Points Out A&M Hypocrisy on 'Merit,'" *Houston Chronicle*, January 9, 2004, A24.

107. Greg Winter, "Texas A&M Ban on 'Legacies' Fuels Debate on Admissions," *New York Times*, January 13, 2004, A16.

108. Paul Burka, "Agent of Change," *Texas Monthly*, November 1, 2006, http://www.texasmonthly.com/preview/2006-11-01/feature.

109. "Bonus Points/Legacy Policy Points Out A&M Hypocrisy on 'Merit,'" A24.

110. Winter, "Texas A&M Ban on 'Legacies' Fuels Debate on Admissions," A16.

111. Nissimov, "Black Lawmakers Rip A&M Decision," A37; see also Ackerman and Robinson, "End 'Legacy' Program, A&M Urged," A21.

112. Ackerman, "A&M Abolishes Legacy Program," A1.

113. Winter, "Texas A&M Ban on 'Legacies' Fuels Debate on Admissions," A–16.

114. Robert M. Gates, President, Texas A&M University, "Statement on Legacy," December 13, 2003.

115. Burka, "Agent of Change," 154. Gates explained that admitting minority students was not the problem, the problem was convincing them to enroll. He said only 44 percent of black students who are accepted choose to enroll. The figures are 48 percent for Hispanic students and 33 percent of Asian-Americans. This sharply contrasts with the 62 percent of admitted white students who choose to enroll. He said his proposed Regent's Scholarships of $5,000 per year and intensive outreach efforts should entice more minority students to enroll.

116. Burka, "Agent of Change."

117. Shikha Dalmia, "Legacies of Injustice," *Reason,* February 2008, http://reason.com/archives/2008/02/19/legacies-of-injustice.

118. Golden, "Family Ties," A1.

Chapter 7

1. U.S. Constitution, art. 1, sec. 9, cl. 8.

2. U.S. Constitution, art. 1, sec. 10, cl. 1.

3. William Blackstone, *Commentaries on the Laws of England,* vol. 1 (Oxford: Clarendon Press, 1765–1769; Chicago: University of Chicago Press, 1979), 396.

4. Ibid., 403–06 (discussing the titles of knight, baronet, esquire, and gentleman as titles of commoners).

5. George Washington, letter to Jean de Heintz, January 21, 1784, in *The Papers of George Washington: Confederation Series,* vol. 1, ed. W. W. Abbot and Dorothy Twohig (Charlottesville: University Press of Virginia, 1992), 67.

6. John Taylor, *An Enquiry into the Principles and Tendency of Certain Public Measures* (Philadelphia: Thomas Dobson, 1794), 29.

7. Gordon S. Wood, *The Radicalism of the American Revolution* (New York: A. A. Knopf, 1992), 181.

8. J. V. Beckett, *The Aristocracy in England: 1660–1914* (New York: Blackwell, 1986), 40–42.

9. Thomas Paine, *Common Sense,* ed. Isaac Kramnick (New York: Penguin Books, 1986), 72–79.

10. Virginia Declaration of Rights of 1776, art. 4.

11. Maryland Declaration of Rights of 1776, art. 40.

12. New Hampshire Constitution of 1784, art. 1, sec. 9.

13. North Carolina Declaration of Rights of 1776, art. 22.

14. Massachusetts Constitution, art. 6.

15. Benjamin Rush, *Observations upon the Present Government of Pennsylvania* (Philadelphia: Styner and Cist, 1777), 8.

16. Articles of Confederation, art. 6, cl. 1.

17. Akhil Reed Amar, *America's Constitution: A Biography* (New York: Random House, 2005), 125.

18. For overviews of the controversy, see Minor Myers, Jr., *Liberty without Anarchy: A History of the Society of the Cincinnati* (Charlottesville: University Press of Virginia, 1983), 48–69; Edgar Erskine Hume, "Early Opposition to the Cincinnati," *Americana* 30 (1936): 597.

19. Myers, *Liberty without Anarchy,* 261–62.

20. Ibid., 260–61.

21. Ibid., 32.

22. Aedanus Burke, *Considerations on the Society or Order of the Cincinnati* (Charleston: A. Timothy, 1783), 4 (writing under the pseudonym Cassius) (noting that the medal was "to be worn by each member, as the French and British Nobility wear their Stars and Ribbons, the insignia of their peerage").

23. John C. Meleney, *The Public Life of Aedanus Burke: Revolutionary Republican in Post-Revolutionary South Carolina* (Columbia: University of South Carolina Press, 1989), 17–24.

24. Burke, *Considerations on the Society or Order of the Cincinnati,* 1, 7, 8.

25. Ibid., 7, 8, 13.

26. Ibid., 30.

27. Jack M. Balkin, "*Bush* v. *Gore* and the Boundary Between Law and Politics," *Yale Law Journal* 110 (2001): 1444–45.

28. Myers, *Liberty without Anarchy,* 49.

29. *Connecticut Courant,* December 23, 1783, 2.

30. "To the Good People of the State of Connecticut," *Connecticut Journal,* April 7, 1784, 1.

31. Henry Knox, letter to George Washington, February 21, 1784, in *The Papers of George Washington,* ed. Abbot and Twohig, 143.

32. *Independent Gazetteer,* April 17, 1784, 2.

33. Ibid.

34. Ibid.

35. Henry Knox, letter to George Washington, February 21, 1784.

36. "Extracts from the Speech of the Governor of South Carolina to the General Assembly," *Salem Gazette,* April 8, 1784, 3.

37. Ibid.

38. *Boston Gazette,* April 19, 1784, 3.

39. *Newport Mercury,* May 22, 1784, 2.

40. Samuel Adams, letter to Elbridge Gerry, April 23, 1784, in James T. Austin, *The Life of Elbridge Gerry,* vol. 1 (Boston: Wells and Lilly, 1828), 424, 425.

41. Samuel Adams, letter to Elbridge Gerry, April 19, 1784, in Austin, *The Life of Elbridge Gerry,* 422.

42. Quoted in Hume "Early Opposition to the Cincinnati" 615.

43. Ibid.

44. Isaac Backus, *A Church History of New England,* vol. 2 (Providence: John Carter, 1784), 366.

45. *Norwich Packet,* April 1, 1784, 2.

46. Ibid.

47. Myers, *Liberty without Anarchy,* 154.

48. The Count de Mirabeau, *Considerations on the Order of Cincinnatus* (Philadelphia: T. Seddon, 1786), 5, 15, 19, 25, 30, and 50 ("neither do the laws of any of the states, nor of the articles of the confederation, authorize individuals to create titles, and confer them upon themselves, by their own private authority").

49. John Adams, letter to the Marquis de Lafayette, March 28, 1784, in *The Works of John Adams,* vol. 8, ed. Charles Francis Adams (Boston: Little, Brown and Co., 1853), 192.

50. Ibid.; see also John Adams, letter to Elbridge Gerry, April 25, 1785, in Austin, *The Life of Elbridge Gerry,* 427, 429 ("Is not this institution against our confederation? Is it not against the declarations of rights in several of the states?").

51. John Adams, letter to Elbridge Gerry, April 25, 1785.

52. Quoted in Hume, "Early Opposition to the Cincinnati," 608; see also John Jay, letter to Gouverneur Morris, February 10, 1784, in *The Correspondence and Public Papers of John Jay,* vol. 3, ed. Henry P. Johnston (1890; New York: B. Franklin, 1970), 109, 111–12 ("The institution of the Order of Cincinnatus does not, in the opinion of the wisest men whom I have heard speak on the subject, either do credit to those who formed and patronized or to those who suffered it.").

53. Benjamin Franklin, letter to Sarah Bache, January 26, 1784, in *The Founders' Constitution,* vol. 3, ed. Philip B. Kurland and Ralph Lerner (Chicago: University of Chicago Press, 1987), 381.

54. Ibid.

55. The Marquis de Lafayette, letter to George Washington, March 9, 1784, in *The Papers of George Washington,* ed. Abbot and Twohig, 190.

56. Ibid.

57. Myers, *Liberty without Anarchy* 157.

58. Thomas Jefferson, letter to George Washington, April 16, 1784, in *The Papers of Thomas Jefferson* vol. 7, ed. Julian P. Boyd (Princeton, N.J.: Princeton University Press, 1953), 106.

59. Ibid., 107.

60. Nathanael Greene, letter to Joseph Reed, May 14, 1784, in *The Papers of General Nathanael Greene,* vol. 13, ed. Roger N. Parks (Chapel Hill: University of North Carolina Press, 2005), 311, 312.

61. Thomas Jefferson, letter to George Washington, April 16, 1784, in *The Papers of Thomas Jefferson,* vol. 7, ed. Julian P. Boyd, 107.

62. Ibid., 108.

63. *The Papers of Thomas Jefferson,* vol. 10, ed. Julian P. Boyd (Princeton, N.J.: Princeton University Press, 1954), 6.

64. *Connecticut Courant,* January 13, 1784, 2.

65. Ibid.

66. Ibid. The lack of connection to state institutions was undoubtedly the strongest argument against the applicability of the Articles' Nobility Clause. Did opponents of the Cincinnati truly believe that any private organization with a hereditary component was prohibited? It is possible that some did, but more likely the Cincinnati represented a unique category. As retired military officers, they clearly had a greater connection to the state than would, say, an organization of tailors. Membership in the Cincinnati was conditional upon the member having been selected previously and employed by the United States for high military office. A hereditary organization of former delegates to the Confederation Congress likely would have raised similar concerns. The history of nobility in Europe also would have suggested reasons to be concerned, particularly about hereditary orders of military heroes.

67. [Stephen Moylan], *Observations on a Late Pamphlet Entitled Considerations on the Society or Order of the Cincinnati* (Philadelphia: Robert Bell, 1783), 18, 21.

68. Ibid., 20.

69. "To Cassius," *Connecticut Courant,* January 20, 1784, 1.

70. Member of the Society of Cincinnati, *A Reply to a Pamphlet, Entitled Considerations on the Society or Order of the Cincinnati* (Annapolis: Frederick Green, 1783), p. 7, 8, 18, 19.

71. Myers, *Liberty without Anarchy,* 58.

72. Winthrop Sargent's Journal, May 5, 1784, in *The Papers of George Washington,* ed. Abbot and Twohig, 333.

73. George Washington, "Observations on the Institution of the Society," May 4, 1784, in *The Papers of George Washington,* ed. Abbot and Twohig, 330.

74. Winthrop Sargent's Journal, 334–35; see also George Washington, letter to James Madison, December 16, 1786, in *The Papers of George Washington,* ed. Abbot and Twohig, 457 (describing Washington's role in the reform of the Society).

75. See, for example, *Newport Mercury,* May 29, 1784, 2.

76. Society of the Cincinnati, *A Circular Letter, Addressed to the State Societies of the Cincinnati* (Philadelphia: E. Oswald and D. Humphreys, 1784), 2.

77. Ibid., 2–3.

78. Ibid., 3.

79. "From the Independent Gazetteer," *New-Haven Gazette,* July 29, 1784, 1.

80. George Washington, letter to Arthur St. Clair, August 31, 1785, in *The Papers of George Washington: Confederation Series,* vol. 3, ed. W. W. Abbot and Dorothy Twohig (Charlottesville: University Press of Virginia, 1994), 212–13.

81. Nathanael Greene, letter to George Washington, August 29, 1784, in *The Papers of General Nathanael Greene,* vol. 13, ed. Roger N. Parks, 383.

82. Ibid.

83. Hume, "Early Opposition to the Cincinnati," 618–22. The Society continues in existence today and has a large headquarters on Massachusetts Avenue in Washington, D.C.

84. "Report of a Committee of the New York State Society of the Cincinnati," July 6, 1786, in *The Papers of Alexander Hamilton,* vol. 3, ed. Harold C. Syrett (New York, London: Columbia University Press, 1962), 675, 676.

85. Edmund Randolph, *Germanicus* (Philadelphia, 1794), 53.

86. John M'Culloch, *A Concise History of the United States,* 2d ed. (Philadelphia: John M'Culloch, 1797), 168.

87. Myers, *Liberty without Anarchy,* 63.

88. John Adams, *A Defence of the Constitutions of Government of the United States of America* (London, 1788; New York: Da Capo Press, 1971), 207–09.

89. Jefferson's Observations on Demeunier's Manuscript, in *The Papers of Thomas Jefferson,* vol. 10, ed. Julian P. Boyd, 51. In 1786, Jefferson would report to Washington from Paris that he had "never heard a person in Europe, learned or unlearned, express his thoughts on this institution, who did not consider it dishonourable and destructive to our governments," and he concluded that the Society should be eradicated completely. Thomas Jefferson, letter to George Washington, November 14, 1786, in ibid., 531, 532–33.

90. It is perhaps worth noting that "[o]f the ninety-nine men who signed the Declaration of Independence or were members of the Constitutional Convention, only eight are known to have had fathers who attended college." Carl J. Richard, *The Founders and the Classics* (Cambridge, Mass.: Harvard University Press, 1994), 51.

91. Noah Webster, "Sketches of American Policy," *St. Gazette of South Carolina,* January 26, 1786, 2.

92. Ibid.

93. Noah Webster, *Sketches of American Policy* (Hartford: Hudson and Goodwin, 1785), 26.

94. James Madison, "The Federalist No. 44," in *The Federalist Papers,* ed. Garry Wills (Toronto, New York: Bantam Books, 1982), 227.

95. Alexander Hamilton, "The Federalist No. 84," in ibid., 436.

96. Ibid., 435.

97. "On the Safety of the People, from the Restraints Imposed upon the Senate," *Pennsylvania Gazette,* October 24, 1787, 3.

98. William Bentley, *Extracts from Professor Robison's "Proofs of a Conspiracy"* (Boston: Manning and Loring, 1799), 11; see also Thomas Jefferson, "A Bill for the More General Diffusion of Knowledge, 1779," in *The Papers of Thomas Jefferson,* vol. 2, ed. Julian P. Boyd (Princeton, N.J.: Princeton University Press, 1950), 526, 527 (stating that liberal education should be available "without regard to wealth, birth or other accidental condition or circumstance").

99. "To the Honorable the Members of the Convention of Virginia," *Pennsylvania Gazette,* May 28, 1788, reprinted in *The Documentary History*

of the Ratification of the Constitution, vol. 9, ed. John P. Kaminski and Gaspare J. Saladino (Madison: State Historical Society of Wisconsin, 1990), 889, 893.

100. Ibid.

101. "Isaac Backus on Religion and the State, Slavery, and Nobility, Feb. 4, 1788," in *The Debate on the Constitution,* ed. Bernard Bailyn (New York: Library of America, 1993), 931, 933.

102. "To the People of Pennsylvania," *Pennsylvania Gazette,* November 7, 1787, 2.

103. *The New-Jersey, Pennsylvania, Delaware, Maryland, and Virginia Almanac* (Baltimore: Samuel and John Adams, 1790).

104. David Ramsay, *A Dissertation on the Manner of Acquiring the Character and Privileges of a Citizen of the United States* (Charleston, 1789), 3, quoted in Wood, *The Radicalism of the American Revolution,* 169.

105. Pennsylvania Constitution of 1790, art. 9, sec. 24. Such state constitutional provisions may provide additional bases for legal challenges to legacy preferences.

106. South Carolina Constitution of 1790, art. 9, sec. 5.

107. Kentucky Constitution of 1792, art. 7, cl. 26.

108. *Boston Gazette,* May 30, 1791, 1.

109. Ibid.

110. *Pennsylvania Gazette,* September 7, 1791, 2–3.

111. William Morrison, *A Sermon Delivered at Dover* (Exeter, N.H.: Henry Ranlet, 1792), 38.

112. "The American—No. 4," *Connecticut Courant,* January 28, 1793, 1.

113. For example, *City Gazette and Daily Advertiser,* June 29, 1791, 2.

114. Thomas Paine, "The Rights of Man," in *The Complete Writings of Thomas Paine,* vol. 1, ed. Philip S. Foner (New York: Citadel Press, 1945), 241, 269, 367, 368; see also "The American—No. 3," *Connecticut Courant,* January 21, 1793, 1 ("Stupidity or insanity are the portion of half the crowned heads in Europe").

115. Thomas Paine, *Letters, by the Author of Common Sense* (Albany: Charles R. and George Webster 1792), 21.

116. Ibid., 3.

117. *New York Daily Gazette,* January 27, 1794, 2.

118. Ibid.

119. Quoted in Wood, *The Radicalism of the American Revolution* 180.

120. *Federal Galaxy,* August 18, 1798, 3.

121. The great exception, of course, was the contemporary law of chattel slavery, under which slave status descended to the children of slaves. Slavery, however, was an exception to every vital constitutional principle. Slaves lacked freedom of speech, rights to habeas corpus and trial by jury, and rights to form legally recognized families. That slaves were also excluded from the general prohibition on hereditary privilege is thus not particularly surprising. With the passage of the Thirteenth Amendment, however, slavery was permanently banished from America, and with it any notion of hereditary slave status. The Thirteenth Amendment is thus a further anti-hereditary privilege gloss on the original Nobility Clauses. That revolutionary Americans failed to live up to their professed principles in the area of slavery is no reason for modern Americans to water down those principles, particularly when the primary revolutionary failure has been erased by civil war and constitutional amendment.

122. This does not mean, however, that government may never employ certain hereditary distinctions. For the narrow category of permissible uses of hereditary distinctions, see Carlton F.W. Larson, "Titles of Nobility, Hereditary Privilege, and the Unconstitutionality of Legacy Preferences in Public School Admissions," *Washington Law Review* 84 (2006): 1413–18. For an analysis and distinction of *Kotch* v. *Board of River Port Pilot Commissioners,* 330 U.S. 552 (1947), a case upholding certain hereditary privileges with respect to river boat piloting licenses, see ibid., pp. 1410–12.

123. Akhil Reed Amar and Neal Kumar Katyal, "Bakke's Fate," *UCLA Law Review* 43 (1996): 1745.

124. 238 U.S. 347 (1915).

125. Ibid., 357.

126. *Atwater* v. *Hassett,* 111 P. 802, 812 (Okla. 1910).

127. *Guinn,* 238 U.S. at 363–64. For an extensive analysis of *Guinn* and its companion cases, see Benno C. Schmidt, Jr., "Principle and Prejudice: The Supreme Court and Race in the Progressive Era," *Columbia Law Review* 82 (1982) 835.

128. *Grutter* v. *Bollinger,* 539 U.S. 306, 332 (2003); compare *Brown* v. *Board of Education of Topeka*, 347 U.S. 483, 493 (1954) ("[E]ducation is

perhaps the most important function of state and local governments. . . . It is doubtful that any child may reasonably be expected to succeed in life if he is denied the opportunity of an education.").

129. Abraham Bell and Gideon Parchomovsky, "Givings," *Yale Law Journal* 111 (2001): 549.

130. Harold S. Wechsler, *The Qualified Student: A History of Selective College Admission in America* (New York: Wiley, 1977), 4.

131. Jerome Karabel, *The Chosen: The Hidden History of Admission and Exclusion at Harvard, Yale, and Princeton* (Boston: Houghton Mifflin, 2005), 1, 22–23, 76, 128–29.

132. Ibid., 77–136.

133. Quoted in ibid., 107; see also Robert K. Fullinwider and Judith Lichtenberg, *Leveling the Playing Field: Justice, Politics, and College Admissions* (Lanham, Md.: Rowman and Littlefield, 2004), 83–84 (discussing introduction of legacy preferences at Dartmouth in 1922); Wechsler, *The Qualified Student*, 162–68 (discussing limitations on class size as a means of reducing Jewish enrollment at Columbia in the 1920s).

134. Karabel, *The Chosen*, 116.

135. Ibid., 135.

136. For example, Lani Guinier, "Admissions Rituals as Political Acts: Guardians at the Gates of Our Democratic Ideals," *Harvard Law Review* 117 (2003): 130 (noting growth in selectivity at the University of Texas from the 1960s to 2001).

137. Daniel Golden, *The Price of Admission: How America's Ruling Class Buys Into Elite Colleges—And Who Gets Left Outside the Gates* (New York: Crown Publishers, 2006), 261–64.

138. Ibid., 125.

139. Stephen Holmes and Cass R. Sunstein, *The Cost of Rights* (New York: W.W. Norton, 1999) (arguing that all rights entail corresponding costs to the government).

140. Mark Kishlanksy, *A Monarchy Transformed* (London: Allen Lane, Penguin Press, 1996), 24, 57.

141. For an argument applying the 1866 Civil Rights Act to prohibit legacy preferences in private universities, see Chapter 8 by Steve Shadowen and Sozi Tulante in this volume.

142. For example, Karabel, *The Chosen*, 262 (discussing growing importance of federal research money at Harvard in the 1950s).

143. Compare Golden, *The Price of Admission,* 246 (quoting Senator John Edwards as stating legacy preferences were "a birthright out of eighteenth-century British aristocracy, not twenty-first century American democracy").

Chapter 8

1. The preferences, in both private and public universities, also may violate state public accommodation laws that prohibit ancestry discrimination, and international conventions that prohibit discrimination based on birth or descent. See Steve Shadowen, "Personal Dignity, Equal Opportunity, and the Elimination of Legacy Preferences," *George Mason University Civil Rights Law Journal* (forthcoming October 2010).

2. See, for example, *Grutter* v. *Bollinger,* 539 U.S. 306, 368 (2003) (Thomas, J., concurring in part and dissenting in part) (stating, without analysis, that "the Equal Protection Clause does not . . . prohibit the use of unseemly legacy preferences or many other kinds of arbitrary admissions procedures"); *Hopwood* v. *Texas,* 783 F.3d 932, 946 (5th Cir. 1996) (stating in dicta that "an admissions process may also consider an applicant's . . . relationship to school alumni"); *Rosenstock* v. *Board of Governors of the University of North Carolina,* 423 F. Supp. 1321 (M.D.N.C. 1976) (upholding legacy preferences where plaintiff did not contend that they used a suspect classification); Charles W. Collier, "Affirmative Action and the Decline of Intellectual Culture," *Journal of Legal Education* 55 (2005): 3, 5. But see *Gratz* v. *Bollinger,* 135 F. Supp. 2d 790, 802 (E.D. Mich. 2001) (referring in dicta to legacy status as a "suspect criter[ion]"); Ernest Gellhorn & D. Brock Hornby, "Constitutional Limitations On Admissions Procedures and Standards—Beyond Affirmative Action," *Virginia Law Review* 60 (1974): 1006 (legacy preferences cannot survive even rational-basis scrutiny under the Equal Protection Clause).

3. *Fullilove* v. *Klutznick,* 448 U.S. 448, 531 n.13 (1980) (Stewart, J., dissenting).

4. Ibid., 531.

5. Jerome Karabel, *The Chosen: The Hidden History of Admission and Exclusion at Harvard, Yale, and Princeton* (New York: Houghton Mifflin Harcourt, 2005), 549.

6. See *Hack* v. *President & Fellows of Yale College,* 237 F.3d 81 (2d Cir. 2000); see generally *Lebron* v. *National Railroad Passenger Corporation,* 513 U.S. 374 (1995).

7. Civil Rights Act of 1866, ch. 31, sec. 1, 14 stat. 27 (re-enacted in the Enforcement Act of 1870, ch. 114, secs. 16, 18, 16 stat. 140). Section 1 of the act originally provided, in relevant part, "that all persons born in the United States and not subject to any foreign power, excluding Indians not taxed, are hereby declared to be citizens of the United States; and such citizens, of every race and color, . . . shall have the same right, in every State and Territory in the United States, to make and enforce contracts, to sue, be parties, and give evidence, to inherit, purchase, lease, sell, hold, and convey real and personal property, and to full and equal benefit of all laws and proceedings for the security of person and property, as is enjoyed by white citizens." The portion of this act that we are concerned with—the prohibition on discrimination in the right "to make and enforce contracts"—is currently codified at 42 U.S.C. sec. 1981 (1991).

8. For example, Title VII of the 1964 act, 42 U.S.C. sec. 2000e(f), protects only "employees"—not independent contractors or others—in the workplace. The more capacious language of the 1866 act protects all "persons." See, for example, *Brown* v. *J. Kaz, Inc.,* 581 F.3d 175 (3d Cir. 2009).

9. See, for example, *Grutter* v. *Bollinger,* 539 U.S. 306 (2003) (public school admissions); *Runyon* v. *McCrary,* 427 U.S. 160 (1976) (private school admissions); *Doe* v. *Kamehameha Schools,* 470 F.3d 827 (9th Cir. 2006) (en banc) (private school admissions); *Jett* v. *Dallas Independent School District,* 491 U.S. 701 (1989) (public school employment); *St. Francis College* v. *Al-Khazraji,* 481 U.S. 604 (1987) (private school employment); *Amini* v. *Oberlin College,* 440 F.3d 350 (6th Cir. 2006) (private school employment)._

10. Gordon S. Wood, *The Radicalism of the American Revolution* (New York: Knopf, 1992); see also Mark E. Brandon, "Family at the Birth of the American Constitutional Order," *Texas Law Review* 77 (1999): 1206–17, 1223–25; Richard Delgado, "An Equality 'From The Top': Applying An Ancient Prohibition To An Emerging Problem Of Distributive Justice," *UCLA Law Review* 32 (1984): 109–13; Roderick M. Hills, Jr., "You Say You Want a Revolution? The Case against the Transformation of Culture through Antidiscrimination Laws," *Michigan Law Review* 95 (1997): 1600–02; James W. Torke, "Nepotism and the Constitution: The

Kotch Case—A Specimen in Amber," *Loyola Law Review* 47 (2001): 611–18.

11. Wood, *The Radicalism of the American Revolution,* 175.

12. Ibid., 180 (quoting Stephen Burroughs, *Memoirs of Stephen Burroughs of New Hampshire,* vol. 3 [Boston: Northeastern University Press, 1988]).

13. *The Radicalism of the American Revolution,* 180; see also Bernard Bailyn, *The Ideological Origins of the American Revolution,* enlarged ed. (Cambridge, Mass.: Harvard University Press, 1992), 319 (Revolution ensured that "the status of men flowed from their achievements and from their personal qualities, not from distinctions ascribed to them at birth"); Harry V. Jaffa, *A New Birth of Freedom: Abraham Lincoln and the Coming of the Civil War* (Lanham, Md.: Rowman and Littlefield, 2000), 408 ("if the American Revolution meant anything at all, it meant that no man ought to be limited by the condition into which he is born").

14. Thomas Jefferson, *Autobiography,* in *Thomas Jefferson: Writings,* ed. Merrill D. Peterson (New York: Library of America, 1984), 32. Jefferson believed that inherited privileges were a principal cause of European poverty. See Joseph J. Ellis, *American Sphinx: The Character of Thomas Jefferson* (New York: Alfred A. Knopf, 2005), 112; see also Yehoshua Arieli, *Individualism and Nationalism in American Ideology* (Cambridge, Mass.: Harvard University Press, 1964), 78.

15. Thomas Jefferson, Letter to George Washington (April 16, 1784), in *Thomas Jefferson: Writings,* 791. Jefferson wrote this letter to urge Washington to oppose the hereditary privileges granted by the Society of the Cincinnati. Those privileges were also opposed by John Adams and Benjamin Franklin, who participated in drafting the Declaration. See Carlton F.W. Larson, "Titles of Nobility, Hereditary Privilege, and the Unconstitutionality of Legacy Preferences in Public School Admission," *Washington University Law Review* 84 (2007): 1393–95. Larson illuminates the dispute over the Cincinnati and its importance in understanding the Founders' rejection of hereditary privileges. See ibid., 1387–99; see also Wood, *The Radicalism of the American Revolution,* 241.

16. Thomas Jefferson, letter to Roger C. Weightman (June 24, 1826), in *Thomas Jefferson: Writings,* 1517; see also Thomas Jefferson, "First Inaugural Address" (March 4, 1801), in *Thomas Jefferson: Writings,* 494

(the foundation of American society is "our equal right to the use of our own faculties, to the acquisitions of our industry, to honor and confidence from our fellow-citizens, resulting not from birth but from our actions and their sense of them").

17. One Paine biographer asserts that "there are so many common elements between Paine's first American writings and the Declaration that some historians have claimed that Paine himself secretly wrote it, or that Jefferson copied him so thoroughly that it amounted to the same thing." Craig Nelson, *Thomas Paine: Enlightenment, Revolution, and the Birth of Modern Nations* (New York: Viking, 2006), 98.

18. Thomas Paine, *Common Sense,* in *Thomas Paine, Collected Writings,* ed. Eric Foner (New York: Library of America, 1995), 16 (emphasis in original); see generally Arieli, *Individualism and Nationalism in American Ideology,* 71 (noting "the great influence of Common Sense on the independence movement and on the rise of American democracy"); Sean Wilentz, *The Rise of American Democracy: Jefferson to Lincoln* (New York: W. W. Norton, 2005), 23 ("Paine considered aristocratic government, established by a parasitic caste of the pedigreed and privileged, as the chief author of human misery").

19. Paine, *Common Sense,* 36.

20. Pauline Maier, *American Scripture: Making The Declaration of Independence* (New York: Knopf, 1997), 165; Joseph J. Ellis, "The Enduring Influence of the Declaration," in *What Did The Declaration Declare?* ed. Joseph J. Ellis (New York: St. Martin's, 1999), 19.

21. Helen Hill, *George Mason: Constitutionalist* (Gloucester, Mass.: Peter Smith, 1966), 136–37 (quoting Virginia Declaration of Rights in 1776, as originally drafted by Mason).

22. Thomas Jefferson, Letter to Henry Lee (May 8, 1825), in *Thomas Jefferson: Writings,* 1501.

23. Carl Becker, *The Declaration of Independence: A Study in the History of Political Ideas* (New York: Alfred A. Knopf, 1972), 27; see also Allen Jayne, *Jefferson's Declaration of Independence: Origins, Philosophy and Theology* (Lexington: University Press of Kentucky, 1998), 56.

24. John Locke, *Two Treatises of Civil Government* (1689) (New York: E. P. Dutton, 1953), 6–7, 64–67. Jefferson likely read Filmer as well as Locke's rejection of him. See Becker, *The Declaration of Independence,* 27.

25. Locke, *Two Treatises,* 118, 179, 189, 164.

26. John Adams, *Papers of John Adams,* vol. 1, ed. Robert J. Taylor et al. (Cambridge, Mass.: Belknap Press of Harvard University Press, 1977), 167–68.

27. Benjamin Franklin, To William Franklin: Journal of the Negotiations in London (March 22, 1775), in *The Papers of Benjamin Franklin,* vol. 21, ed. William B. Wilcox (New Haven, Conn.: Yale University Press, 1978), 540, available at http://www.franklinpapers.org/franklin/.

28. Benjamin Franklin, letter to Sarah Bache (January 26, 1784), in *Writings of Benjamin Franklin,* vol. 9, ed. Albert H. Smyth (New York: Macmillan Company, 1906), 162. This letter, like Jefferson's of April 1784 to George Washington (see note 14), was prompted by the controversy over the Society of the Cincinnati. Franklin described the Society as "an Attempt to establish something like an hereditary Rank or Nobility," which he rejected because "all *descending* Honours are wrong and absurd; [and] the Honour of virtuous Actions appertains only to him that performs them, and is in its nature incommunicable." Letter to George Whatley (May 23, 1785), in *Writings of Benjamin Franklin,* vol. 9, 336 (emphasis in original).

29. Larson, "Titles of Nobility," 1406 (quoting *New York Daily Gazette,* January 27, 1794, 2); see also Mark Puls, *Samuel Adams: Father of the American Revolution* (New York: Palgrave Macmillan, 2006), 214 (quoting letter to Elbridge Gerry [April 19, 1784], in *The Writings of Samuel Adams,* ed. Harry Alonzo Cushing [New York: G. P. Putnam's Sons, 1904], 299) (people may not properly "exalt themselves & their family upon the ruins of the common liberty").

30. On the continuities of the egalitarian nature of the Declaration and the 1787 Constitution, see Eric Foner, *Tom Paine and Revolutionary America* (New York: Oxford University Press, 2005), 205–09.

31. U.S. Constitution, art. 4, sec. 4.

32. Akhil Reed Amar, *America's Constitution: A Biography* (New York: Random House, 2005), 276–78; see generally *The Federalist* No. 39 (James Madison), in *The Debate on the Constitution: Federalist and Antifederalist Speeches, Articles and Letters During the Struggle Over Ratification,* vol. 2 (New York: Library of America, 1993), 27 (consent must be "derived from the great body of the society, not from any inconsiderable proportion, or of a favored class of it"); *The Federalist* No. 22 (Alexander Hamilton), in *Debate on the Constitution,* vol. 1 (consent of the people is the "pure original fountain of all legitimate authority"); *The Federalist* No. 77 (Alexander Hamilton), in *Debate on the Constitution,* vol. 1 (concentrating powers of

appointment in "a few families" would lead "to an aristocracy or an oligarchy").

33. U.S. Constitution, art. 1, sec. 9, cl. 8, sec. 10, cl. 1.

34. See Larson, "Titles of Nobility," 1375. Torke notes that the ban on granting titles of nobility is closely related to the guarantee of a republican form of government because prohibiting positions from being passed lineally keeps them available to all. Torke, "Nepotism," 615 and nn.358–60 (citing *The Federalist* No. 85 [Alexander Hamilton], No. 39 [James Madison], No. 36 [Alexander Hamilton]).

35. U.S. Constitution, art. 3, sec. 3, cl. 2.

36. Amar, *America's Constitution,* 243.

37. U.S. Constitution, art. 1, secs. 9, 10.

38. See Akhil Reed Amar, "Attainder and Amendment 2: Romer's Rightness," *Michigan Law Review* 95 (1996): 215; see also J.M. Balkin, "The Constitution of Status," *Yale Law Journal* 106 (1997): 2350. Numerous other provisions similarly reflect an insistent effort to stamp out hereditary distinction, although sometimes in more subtle ways. See, for example, Torke, "Nepotism," 615–16 (requirement of presidential appointments with the advice and consent of the Senate guards against "family attachment") (quoting *The Federalist* No. 76 [Alexander Hamilton]); Delgado, "Equality," 112 (title of "President" was chosen to avoid exalted, noble title); ibid., 112 n.90 (noting preamble's reference to "We the People" and Fifth Amendment's guarantee of due process to all "persons"). Madison emphasized the egalitarian nature of voting qualifications for the House of Representatives: "Who are to be the electors of the Federal Representatives? Not the rich more than the poor; not the learned more than the ignorant; not the haughty heirs of distinguished names, more than the humble sons of obscure and unpropitious fortune. . . . No qualification of wealth, of birth, of religious faith, or of civil profession, is permitted to fetter the judgment or disappoint the inclination of the people." *The Federalist* No. 57 (James Madison), in *Debate on the Constitution,* vol. 2, 213–14. Contemporaries noted that even the Senate, which some saw as having an aristocratic flavor, was composed "without one distinction in favor of the birth, rank, wealth or power of the senators or their fathers." Wilentz, *The Rise of American Democracy,* 33 (quoting *Independent Gazeteer* [Philadelphia], November 6, 1787). Following independence, the constitutions drafted by both former colonies and new states reflected the revolutionary rejection of hereditary privilege. See, for example, Robert J. Harris, *The Quest*

for Equality: The Constitution, Congress, and the Supreme Court (Baton Rouge: Louisiana State University Press, 1960), 18–19; Franklin B. Hough, *American Constitutions* (Albany, N.Y.: Weed Parsons and Co., 1872). The new states similarly rejected hereditary punishment, as shown by provisions that enjoined the use of bills of attainder or corruption of blood penalties. See generally Max Stier, Note, "Corruption of Blood and Equal Protection: Why the Sins of the Parents Should Not Matter," *Stanford Law Review* 44 (1992): 730–31. After the Revolution, the states also abolished the remnants of feudal land law, including primogeniture and fee tail. See Wood, *The Radicalism of the American Revolution,* 183. Repealing these hereditary land laws "laid the axe to the root of Pseudo-aristocracy." Thomas Jefferson, Letter to John Adams (October 28, 1813), in *Thomas Jefferson: Writings,* 1308.

39. Amar, *America's Constitution,* 125.

40. See William E. Nelson, *The Fourteenth Amendment: From Political Principle to Judicial Doctrine* (1988): 16–17.

41. Jacobus TenBroek, *Equal Under Law,* enlarged ed. (New York: Collier Books, 1965), 75 (quoting William Goodell, *Views of American Constitutional Law in Its Bearing upon American Slavery* [1844]); see also Theodore Parker, The Relation of Slavery to a Republican Form of Government: A Speech Delivered at the New England Anti-Slavery Convention (May 26, 1858), http://memor0y.loc.gov/cbi-bin/query.

42. Balkin, "Constitution of Status," 2350 n.113 (quoting Frederick Douglass, "The Constitution of the United States: Is It Pro or Anti-Slavery?" in *The Life and Writings of Frederick Douglass: Pre-Civil War Decade 1850–1860,* vol. 2, ed. Philip S. Foner [New York: International Publishers, 1950], 478); see generally Michael Lind, *The Next American Nation: The New Nationalism and the Fourth American Revolution* (New York: Free Press, 1995), 379–83 (discussing Douglass's contribution to idea of equal rights).

43. See, for example, Daniel A. Farber and John E. Muench, "The Ideological Origins of the Fourteenth Amendment," *Constitutional Commentary* 1 (1994): 249 ("Perhaps the most important source of anti-slavery Republicanism was the Declaration of Independence"); TenBroek, *Equal under Law,* 85 n.20, 118.

44. Abraham Lincoln, Eulogy on Henry Clay at Springfield, Missouri, (July 6, 1852), in *Abraham Lincoln, Speeches and Writings, 1832–1858,* ed. Don E. Fehrenbacher (New York: Library of America, 1989), 269. As Jaffa

shows, "One might epitomize everything Lincoln said between 1854 and 1861 as a demand for recognition of the Negro's human rights, as set forth in the Declaration of Independence." Jaffa, *New Birth*, at 290.

45. Abraham Lincoln, Speech on the *Dred Scott* Decision at Springfield, Illinois (June 26, 1857), in *Abraham Lincoln, Speeches and Writings, 1832–1858*, 400.

46. Seventh Lincoln-Douglas Debate, at Alton, Illinois (October 15, 1858), in *Abraham Lincoln, Speeches and Writings, 1832–1858*, 811. Benjamin Wade had made the same point in the Senate in 1854, arguing that the Declaration was incompatible with slavery because the assertion of a right of one person to control another was equivalent to "the divine right of every king, and every emperor, and every monarch, to reign over his subjects, and the right of privileged orders everywhere." *Congressional Globe,* 33rd Cong., 1st sess., app. 311 (1854). To assert such a right was to contradict the "principle [that] was established by the American Revolution." Ibid., app. 310.

47. Abraham Lincoln, Letter to Henry L. Pierce and Others (April 6, 1859), in *Abraham Lincoln, Speeches and Writings 1859–1865,* ed. Don E. Fehrenbacher (New York: Library of America, 1989), 18–19. In asserting that the "irrepressible conflict" was between a "republic or democracy" in the North and a "ruling aristocracy" in the South, Senator Seward was voicing a prevailing northern view. See William Seward, "On the Irrepressible Conflict," in *The World's Famous Orations,* vol. 9, ed. William J. Bryan (New York: Funk and Wagnalls, 1906), 177–85; see also Eric Foner, *Free Soil, Free Labor, Free Men: The Ideology of the Republican Party before the Civil War* (New York: Oxford University Press, 1995), 50, 65, 70; Eugene D. Genovese, *The Political Economy of Slavery: Studies in the Economy and Society of the Slave South,* 2d ed. (Middletown, Conn.: Wesleyan University Press, 1989), 297. Southerners agreed that the war was a clash between a society founded on the proposition "that all men are equal and that equality is right," thus forming a "horizontal plane of a democracy," and another society contending that "all men are not equal, that equality is not right," and thus forming "a social aristocracy." Wilentz, *The Rise of American Democracy,* 745 (quoting L.W. Spratt, "Report on the Slave Trade," *DeBow's Review* 24 [1858]: 473–74); see also ibid., 773, 775; Arieli, *Individualism,* 206, 299; Elizabeth Fox-Genovese and Eugene D. Genovese, *The Mind of the Master Class: History and Faith in the Southern Slaveholders' Worldview* (Cambridge: Cambridge University Press, 2005),

114–15. With the coming of war, therefore, the clarion call in the North was to end southern aristocracy. See, for example, Arieli, *Individualism,* 309; Wilentz, *American Democracy,* 673.

48. Message to Congress in Special Session (July 4, 1861), in *Abraham Lincoln, Speeches and Writings, 1859–1865,* 259. Lincoln's opposition to slavery was also an extension of the Republicans' Free Labor ideology: "I want every man to have the chance—and I believe a black man is entitled to it—in which he can better his condition." Abraham Lincoln, Speech at New Haven, Connecticut (March 6, 1860), in *Abraham Lincoln, Speeches and Writings, 1859–1865,* 144. For a more complete discussion of the influence of Free Labor ideology on the 1866 act and the Equal Protection Clause, see Steve Shadowen, Sozi Tulante, and Shara Alpern, "No Distinctions Except Those Which Merit Originates: The Unlawfulness of Legacy Preferences In Public and Private Universities," *Santa Clara Law Review* 49 (2009): 88–91.

49. Lincoln's critics immediately recognized the significance of the Gettysburg Address in confirming the centrality of the Declaration's principle of equality and its extension to encompass African Americans. See David Herbert Donald, *Lincoln* (New York: Simon and Schuster, 1995), 465–66.

50. See *Scott* v. *Sandford,* 60 U.S. 3939 (1856) (discussed more fully below). Today, as well as in 1866, Congress has by statute extended citizenship to the foreign-born children of U.S. citizens, as well as all persons born in the United States. See Shadowen et al., "No Distinctions," 95 n. 218. This limited use of citizenship-by-lineage does not, however, discriminate based on lineage in any meaningful sense. The only persons discriminated against are the foreign-born children of non-U.S. citizens. Denying automatic U.S. citizenship to those children is integral to the existence of a nation-state.

51. *Congressional Globe,* 39th Cong., 1st sess. 434 (1866) (Sen. Trumbull). As summarized by Professor Epps, "the 'lords of the lash' had been refuted by the egalitarian armies of the North, made up of laborers—the men southerners had scorned as 'mud-sills of society' and former slaves. They had humbled aristocrats like Jefferson Davis and Robert E. Lee. The equality genie was out of the bottle." Garrett Epps, *Democracy Reborn: The Fourteenth Amendment and the Fight for Equal Rights in Post-Civil War America* (New York: Henry Holt and Co., 2006), 108–09.

52. *Congressional Globe,* 39th Cong., 1st sess. 434 (1866) (Sen. Trumbull) (1866 act was intended to protect the civil rights that had been "intended to be secured by the Declaration of Independence and the Constitution of the United States originally").

53. Ibid., 531; see also Robert J. Reinstein, "Completing the Constitution: The Declaration of Independence, the Bill of Rights and Fourteenth Amendment," *Temple Law Review* 66 (1993): 403 ("According to the Republicans [of the 39th Congress], the principle of equal treatment that they then constitutionalized had originated in the founding. The Founders had rejected the doctrine that the right to rule could be vested in families and dynasties; and, to the Republicans, it was a short step to prohibit caste distinctions and class legislation based on the inheritance of race."); John Harrison, "Reconstructing the Privileges or Immunities Clause," *Yale Law Journal* 101 (1992): 1412 ("Trumbull derived his ban on race discrimination [in the 1866 act] from the more general principle of the equality of citizens."); Shadowen et al., "No Distinctions," 79–80 nn. 134–40 (detailing congressional statements to this effect).

54. See generally *Congressional Globe,* 39th Cong., 1st sess. 574, 601 (1866) (Sen. Hendricks) (1866 act responds to Sumner's call for equality under law); David Herbert Donald, *Charles Sumner and the Rights of Man* (New York: Random House, 1970), 152–61(discussing Sumner's leadership on issues of equality); John P. Frank and Robert F. Munro, "The Original Understanding of 'Equal Protection of the Laws,'" *Columbia Law Review* 50 (1950): 141 ("the fundamental working legal theory of equality before the law, or equal rights, or equal protection was formulated for American law by Sumner, and popularized under his leadership").

55. Charles Sumner, *The Works of Charles Sumner,* vol. 13 (1873–1883) (Charleston, S.C.: BiblioBazaar, 2008), 175–78 .

56. Charles Sumner, "The Slave Oligarchy and Its Usurpations," Speech, November 2, 1855, http://www.archive.org/details/slaveoligarchyan00sum nrich); see generally Donald, *Charles Sumner and the Rights of Man,* 208 (when Lincoln "said he never had an idea, politically, that did not spring from the Declaration, he used words which Sumner could have echoed").

57. *Congressional Globe,* 39th Cong., 1st sess. 673–87 (1866) (Sen. Sumner). This was days after the Senate had passed the 1866 act, but before the House had acted; after House modifications, the Senate passed the revised bill on March 15, 1866, and subsequently overrode President Johnson's veto on April 6, 1866.

58. Ibid., 674 (1866). Sumner believed that the Revolution had been a war of democracy against aristocracy, and that the same contest had been continued in the Civil War. David Donald, *Charles Sumner and the Coming of the Civil War* (New York: Knopf, 1961), 229–30.

59. *Congressional Globe,* 39th Cong., 1st sess. 680, 681, 683, 684 (1866) (Sen. Sumner). All italics were supplied by Sumner.

60. See Reinstein, "Completing the Constitution," 388–89 ("the consistency of the references to and reliance upon the Declaration in relation to the Civil Rights Act and Section 1 [of the Fourteenth Amendment] is remarkable").

61. *Congressional Globe,* 39th Cong., 1st sess. 344 (1866) (Senator Wilson); see also Shadowen et al., "No Distinctions," 78–80 nn. 129–40 (detailing additional congressional statements to the same effect).

62. *Congressional Globe,* 41st Cong., 2d sess. app. 547 (Rep. Prosser) (debate on Enforcement Act of 1870).

63. Advocates believed that the Equal Protection Clause was "almost entirely declaratory of the great natural rights of men already embodied in the Declaration of Independence, lying at the foundations of all Republican governments, and expressed in the Constitution itself." TenBroek, *Equal Under Law,* 232; see also Shadowen et al., "No Distinctions," 79 n. 136 (detailing additional congressional statements to the same effect); ibid., 80 n. 140 (showing that the public likewise understood the Equal Protection Clause to codify and extend to African Americans the Declaration's prohibition on hereditary privilege).

64. *Congressional Globe,* 39th Cong., 1st sess. 2961 (1866) (Sen. Poland).

65. *Congressional Globe,* 37th Cong., 2d sess. 1639 (1862) (Rep. Bingham) (referring, in debate on slavery in District of Columbia, to Acts of the Apostles 17:26 and 10:34).

66. *Congressional Globe,* 34th Cong., 3d sess. app. 140 (1857) (Rep. Bingham) (debate on Lecompton constitution). Bingham revered the Massachusetts law that granted the franchise to all men "in no wise dependent upon complexion or the accident of birth," *Congressional Globe*, 37th Cong., 2d Sess. 1639 (1862) (Rep. Bingham), and the Northwest Ordinance that protected "all the inhabitants without respect to complexion or birth," *Congressional Globe,* 37th Cong., 3d sess. 265 (1863) (Rep. Bingham).

67. *Congressional Globe,* 34th Cong., 3d sess. app. 140 (1857) (Rep. Bingham).

68. Ibid. (emphasis in original).

69. *Congressional Globe,* 39th Cong., 1st sess. 1291 (1866) (Rep. Bingham); see also ibid., 1094 (Rep. Bingham) (Equal Protection Clause protects every person "no matter what his color, no matter beneath what

sky he may have been born, . . . no matter how poor, no matter how friendless, no matter how ignorant"); ibid., 158 (Rep. Bingham) (Equal Protection Clause requires states to "respect the rights of the humblest citizen"); see generally Garrett Epps, "Second Founding: The Story of the Fourteenth Amendment," *Oregon Law Review* 85 (2006) 905 (Bingham was driven by the "idea of a republic, which is not governed by an elite, but is radically egalitarian").

70. *Congressional Globe,* 39th Cong., 1st Sess. 158 (1866) (Rep. Bingham).

71. Ibid., 432 (Rep. Bingham); *accord* ibid., 429, 431 (Rep. Bingham). When later explaining the meaning of the Equal Protection Clause, Bingham again invoked the Declaration. *Congressional Globe,* 42d Cong., 1st Sess. app. 86 (1871) (Rep. Bingham). Most Republicans believed that Congress had constitutional authority to pass the 1866 act before ratification of the Fourteenth Amendment because "equality of civil rights is the fundamental rule that pervades the Constitution." *Congressional Globe,* 39th Cong., 1st sess. 1836 (1866) (Rep. Lawrence). Bingham agreed that equality was the foundation of the Constitution, but asserted that Congress lacked authority to pass the act until the amendment was ratified. ibid., 1291–92 (Rep. Bingham).

72. Wood, *The Radicalism of the American Revolution*, 169; see also *United States* v. *Wong Kim Ark,* 169 U.S. 649, 665 (1898) ("the term 'citizen' seems to be appropriate to republican freemen."); *Congressional Globe,* 39th Cong., 1st Sess. 1116 (1866) (Rep. Wilson) (birth in the jurisdiction "makes a man a subject in England, and a citizen here").

73. *Congressional Globe,* 39th Cong., 1st sess. 1159 (1866) (Rep. Windom); see also ibid., 1757 (Sen. Trumbull) ("The equality of rights is the basis of a commonwealth.") (quoting Chancellor Kent).

74. *Congressional Globe,* 39th Cong., 1st sess. 1837 (1866) (Rep. Lawrence); see also *Congressional Globe,* 39th Cong., 2d sess. 40 (1866) (Sen. Morrill) ("the genius of republicanism is equality, impartiality of rights and remedies among all the citizens," and "Congress at its last session enacted that every person born in the United States is a citizen thereof, and entitled to protection in his civil rights").

75. In the 1850s the Know-Nothings sought to reserve public offices to native-born Protestants, restrict immigration from Ireland and Germany, and prevent recent immigrants from voting by implementing a twenty-one-year naturalization period. See, for example, Michael F. Holt, "The Antimasonic

and Know Nothing Parties," in *History of U.S. Political Parties,* vol. 1, ed. Arthur M. Schlesinger, Jr. (New York: Chelsea House, 1973), 593.

76. Sumner, "The Slave Oligarchy," 12.

77. Ibid., 13.

78. Abraham Lincoln, Speech at Chicago, Illinois (July 10, 1858), in *Abraham Lincoln, Speeches and Writings, 1832–1858,* 456.

79. Epps points to the speech as "a startling clear exposition of the belief of an entire generation of Republicans that inspired a constitutional revolution after the Civil War." Epps, *Democracy Reborn,* 35.

80. Carl Schurz, True Americanism: A Speech Delivered in Faneuil Hall, Boston (April 18, 1859), in Carl Schurz, *Speeches, Correspondence and Political Papers of Carl Schurz,* vol. 1, ed. Frederic Bancroft (New York: G.P. Putnam's Sons, 1913), 54, 57, 58, 67–68. Emphasis in original. The rejection of privilege was announced in the Declaration, and the Founders intended the nation's institutions "to be the living incarnation of this idea." Ibid., 58.

81. See *Annals of Congress,* 16th Cong., 2d sess. 555, 557 (1820) (Rep. Smyth); ibid., 615–16 (Rep. McLane); see generally James H. Kettner, *The Development of American Citizenship, 1608–1870* (Durham: University of North Carolina Press, 1978), 312–14. The great compromiser, Henry Clay, negotiated the admission of Missouri on condition that its constitution would never be construed to impair the rights of any U.S. citizen, intentionally leaving ambiguous and unresolved the issue of whether free blacks were U.S. citizens.

82. *Dred Scott* v. *Sandford* 60 U.S. 393, 404–05, 407, 417 (1856).

83. See Kettner, *The Development of American Citizenship,* 322 (the decision "called into question, by the majority's challenge to birthright citizenship, the status of natives born of unnaturalized alien parents").

84. *Congressional Globe,* 39th Cong., 1st sess. 529 (1866) (Sen. Johnson); see also ibid., 525 (Sen. Davis); *accord* ibid., 499 (Sen. Cowan).

85. See *Congressional Globe,* 39th Cong., 1st sess. 505, 529 (1866) (Sen. Johnson); ibid., 1120 (Rep. Rogers); see also ibid., 1295 (Rep. Latham).

86. *Dred Scott,* 60 U.S. at 581–82 (Curtis, J., dissenting).

87. *Congressional Globe,* 39th Cong., 1st sess. 1776–77 (1866) (Sen. Johnson).

88. See Ira Berlin, *Slaves Without Masters: The Free Negro in the Antebellum South* (New York: Random House, 1974), 161–62 n.39.

89. *Congressional Globe,* 39th Cong., 1st sess. 1776 (1866) (Sen. Johnson).

90. See, for example, *Congressional Globe,* 39th Cong., 1st sess. 1117 (1866) (Rep. Wilson); ibid., 1124 (Rep. Cook); ibid., 1152 (Rep. Thayer); ibid., 1266 (Rep. Raymond); ibid., 1291 (Rep. Bingham); ibid., 1756 (Sen. Trumbull); ibid., 1832 (Rep. Lawrence); ibid., 1160 (Rep. Shellabarger); ibid., 1263 (Rep. Broomall). The Republicans had begun a legal assault on the *Dred Scott* citizenship-by-lineage analysis even before the conclusion of the war. Lincoln's attorney general, for example, published an exhaustive analysis concluding, based on the principle of birthright citizenship, that free Negroes were U.S. citizens. See 10 Op. Att'y. Gen. 382, 399 (1862) ("It is an error to suppose that citizenship is ever hereditary. It never 'passes by descent.' It is as original in the child as it was in his parents"). The opinion gave the narrowest possible reading to *Dred Scott,* asserting that almost all of it was "of no authority as a judicial decision." Ibid., 412.

91. See, for example, *Congressional Globe,* 39th Cong., 1st sess. at 2226–27 (1866) (Rep. Wilson); ibid., 1124 (Rep. Cook).

92. Ibid., 1757 (Sen. Trumbull); see generally Gerald L. Newman, "Back to Dred Scott?" *San Diego Law Review* 24 (1987): 491–92 (Republicans "refused the invitation to create a hereditary caste of voteless denizens, vulnerable to expulsion and exploitation").

93. *Congressional Globe,* 39th Cong., 1st sess. 1757 (1866) (Sen. Trumbull); ibid., 1832 (Rep. Lawrence) ("Children born here are citizens without any regard to the political condition or allegiance of their parents.") (quoting Standford's Ch. R. 583). Citizenship by lineage was then the prevailing rule in continental Europe. See *United States* v. *Wong Kim Ark,* 169 U.S. 649, 667 (1898). The 1866 act and, later, the Fourteenth Amendment, rejected that principle "in the most explicit and comprehensive terms," in favor of "the fundamental principle of citizenship by birth within the jurisdiction." Ibid., 675. The act determines citizenship "by the place of nativity, irrespective of parentage." Ibid., 690. See generally Epps, "Second Founding," 910 (Republicans required that membership in society "is not based on race or blood or country of origin, but on simple shared humanity").

94. *Congressional Globe,* 39th Cong., 1st sess. 1262 (1866) (Rep. Broomall).

95. *Congressional Globe,* 39th Cong., 1st sess. 2891 (1866) (Sen. Conness). The Republicans understood that "race," as well as what today is sometimes called "ethnicity," ultimately collapses into family lineage, and they rejected discrimination and any citizenship test based on it. Many

contemporary Americans keenly experience the collapsing of race/ethnicity into family lineage. Fourteen-year-old Alma Singer realized that, given her forebears' lineage, her own race/ethnicity could be classified in any of sixteen different ways. Alma then recounted this dialogue with her mother: "Then again, you could always just stick with half English and half Israeli, since—" "I'M AMERICAN!" I shouted. My mother blinked. "Suit yourself," she said and went to put the kettle on to boil. Nicole Krauss, *The History of Love* (New York: W. W. Norton, 2005), 97.

96. See, for example, Kenneth L. Karst, "The Supreme Court 1976 Term Foreward: Equal Citizenship Under the Fourteenth Amendment," *Harvard Law Review* 91 (1977) 14 (under the act "citizenship and equality were melded into a single policy"); Farber and Muench, Ideological Origins, 264, 277 (Republicans closely tied the act's substantive rights to the concept of national citizenship); Shadowen et al., "No Distinctions," 97 n. 220 (detailing Congressional statements that link the guarantee of equality to national citizenship). Reviewing the legislative history of the Citizenship Clause, the Department of Justice recently concluded that Congress should not attempt to restrict birthright citizenship because, "in America, a country that rejected monarchy, each person is born equal, with no curse of infirmity, and no exalted status, arising from the circumstances of his or her parentage." *Citizen Reform Act of 1995; Hearing on H.R. 1363 Before the H. Comm. On the Judiciary,* 104th Cong. 4 (1995) (statement of Assistant Attorney General Walter Dellinger), http://www.usdoj.gov/olc/deny.tes.31.htm.

97. *Congressional Globe,* 39th Cong., 1st sess. 1836 (1866) (Rep. Lawrence). Congress created an express exception from the act's substantive protections for some distinctions, such as those based on gender, age, and mental competence, that are not a basis for the denial of citizenship. See Shadowen et al., "No Distinctions," 97 n. 221. The need for this express exception confirms the general rule that a distinction that cannot deny citizenship—and certainly a distinction that Congress expressly rejected as a basis for citizenship—cannot be the basis for discrimination in the act's substantive provisions.

98. Congress included birthright citizenship in the Fourteenth Amendment in order to remove any doubt as to the constitutionality of the grant of that citizenship in the 1866 act. See Shadowen et al., "No Distinctions," 98 n. 228.

99. *Congressional Globe,* 39th Cong., 1st sess. 1292 (1866) (Rep. Bingham).

100. Ibid.; see also ibid., 1090 (Rep. Bingham) (Equal Protection Clause meant to protect "all persons, whether citizens or strangers"). Bingham had routinely contrasted the Magna Carta, which applied to "freemen," and therefore "secured no privileges to vassals or slaves," to the Fifth Amendment, which protected "all persons" and was therefore "a new gospel to mankind." *Congressional Globe,* 37th Cong., 2d sess. 1638 (1862) (Rep. Bingham) (Constitution protects all persons "[n]o matter upon what spot on the earth's surface they were born; no matter whether an Asiatic or African, a European or an American sun first burned upon them; no matter whether citizens or strangers; no matter whether rich or poor"); see also *Congressional Globe,* 36th Cong., 2d sess. 83 (1861) (Rep. Bingham) ("The Constitution has the same care for the rights of the stranger within your gates as for the rights of the citizen."); *Congressional Globe,* 37th Cong., 3d sess. 266 (1863) (Rep. Bingham) (Constitution "is no respecter of persons [and] declares that the poor and the rich, the citizen and the stranger within your gates, are alike sacred before the sublime majesty of its laws"). Bingham heaped scorn on the Lecompton constitution's idea that all freemen are equal when they form a social compact; instead, the Declaration provides that all persons are equal, and there is "no inferior class of human beings" outside the social compact. *Congressional Globe,* 35th Cong., 1st sess. 402 (1858) (Rep. Bingham). Natural rights are "as imperishable as the human soul, and as universal as the human race." *Congressional Globe,* 34th Cong., 3d sess. app. 136 (1857) (Rep. Bingham).

101. For a description of this legislative history, see Shadowen et al., "No Distinctions," 100 nn. 231–32.

102. *Congressional Globe,* 39th Cong., 2d sess. 40 (1866) (Sen. Morrill) (debate on African-American suffrage in the District of Columbia).

103. Ibid., 41.

104. See, for example, *Romer* v. *Evans,* 517 U.S. 620, 629 (1996) (invalidating state law that discriminated against persons based on their sexual preferences); *Massachusetts Board of Retirement* v. *Murgia,* 427 U.S. 307, 312 n.4 (1976) (upholding state statute imposing mandatory retirement age for police); *Lindsey* v. *Normet,* 405 U.S. 56, 73 & n.22 (1972) (invalidating state bond requirements for poor persons who appealed adverse property-law decisions).

105. See, for example, *Georgia* v. *McCollum,* 505 U.S. 42, 59 (1992) (invalidating racially motivated use of peremptory challenges in jury selection); *Ristaino* v. *Ross,* 424 U.S. 589, 596 n.8 (1976) (denying right of minority criminal defendant to specifically examine potential jurors regarding racial

prejudice); *Frontiero* v. *Richardson,* 411 U.S. 677, 686 (1973) (subjecting gender distinctions to heightened scrutiny).

106. *Hirabayashi* v. *United States,* 320 U.S. 81 (1943), at 100.

107. *Oyama* v. *California,* 332 U.S. 633 (1948).

108. Ibid., 641–42.

109. Ibid., 640, 641, 644, 646; ibid. (discrimination based on whether "parents can[ ] be naturalized"); ibid., 642 (discrimination based on "the father's nationality" and on whether "the father is ineligible for citizenship"); ibid., 647 (discrimination "because of his father's country of origin"); ibid., 641 ("the California law points in one direction for citizens . . . whose parents cannot be naturalized, and in another for all other children"). The dissent confirmed that the discrimination found unlawful by the majority was that "against sons of persons ineligible for citizenship." Ibid., 685 (Reed, J., dissenting); see also ibid., 686.

110. *Cockrill* v. *California,* 268 U.S. 258 (1925) at 262.

111. *Oyama* v. *California,* 332 U.S. at 645, 660 n.27; see also ibid., 686 (Reed, J., dissenting) ("the Court's decision is that the presumption denies Fred Oyama [that is, the child] the equal protection of the laws because grantees are treated differently if they are sons of ineligible aliens than if they are the sons of others"). The dissenters in *Korematsu* v. *United States,* 323 U.S. 214 (1945), had earlier made clear that the proscription on discrimination based on "ancestry" is not confined to racial or ethnic groups. Justice Jackson concluded that Korematsu was entitled to be judged on his own merits rather than on who his parents were or what they might have done: "Even if all of one's antecedents had been convicted of treason, the Constitution forbids its penalties to be visited upon him, for it provides that 'no Attainder of Treason shall work Corruption of Blood, or Forfeiture except during the Life of the Person attainted.' Article 3, s 3, cl. 2. But here is an attempt to make an otherwise innocent act a crime merely because this prisoner is the son of parents as to whom he had no choice, and belongs to a race from which there is no way to resign." Ibid., 243 (Jackson, J., dissenting); see also ibid., 242 (Murphy, J., dissenting) ("All residents of this nation are kin in some way by blood or culture to a foreign land . . . [But] [t]hey must . . . be treated at all times as the heirs of the American experiment and as entitled to all the rights and freedoms guaranteed by the Constitution.").

112. See note 103.

113. *Plyler* v. *Doe,* 457 U.S. 202 (1982).

114. Ibid., 216 n.14.

115. Ibid., 219–20. Justice Powell's concurring opinion reached the same conclusion, for the same reasons. See ibid., 238.

116. Ibid., 220 (majority opinion) (quoting *Trimble* v. *Gordon,* 430 U.S. 762, 770 (1977)); see also ibid., 223 (legislation affected "a discrete class of children not accountable for their disabling status").

117. Ibid. (quoting *Weber* v. *Aetna Casualty & Surety Co.*, 406 U.S. 164, 175 [1972]).

118. Ibid., 221–22; see also *Zobel* v. *Williams,* 457 U.S. 55, 70 (1982) (Brennan, J., concurring) (Constitution "requires attention to individual merit, to individual need"); *Miller* v. *Albright,* 523 U.S. 420, 476 (1998) (Breyer, J., dissenting) ("this Court, I assume, would use heightened scrutiny to review discriminatory laws based upon ancestry, say, laws that denied voting rights or educational opportunity based upon the religion, or the racial makeup, of a parent or grandparent"); *Nordlinger* v. *Hahn,* 505 U.S. 1, 30 (1992) (Stevens, J., dissenting) (state tax exemption for children of homeowner parents denies equal protection because it "establishes a privilege of a medieval character" by "treat[ing] [children] differently solely because of their different heritage").

119. In his famous dissent in *Plessy* v. *Ferguson,* 163 U.S. 537, 559 (1896) (Harlan, J., dissenting), Justice Harlan wrote that race discrimination is unlawful because, "The humblest is the peer of the most powerful. The law regards man as man, and takes no account of his surroundings or of his color when his civil rights as guaranteed by the supreme law of the land are involved." See also *Regents of University of California* v. *Bakke,* 438 U.S. 265, 320 (1978) (plurality opinion) ("a State's distribution of benefits or imposition of burden [cannot] hinge[] on ancestry or the color of a person's skin"); ibid., 355 (Brennan, J., concurring in part and dissenting in part) ("human equality is closely associated with the proposition that differences in color or creed, birth or status, are neither significant nor relevant to the way in which persons should be treated").

120. *Rice* v. *Cayetano,* 528 U.S. 495 (2000).

121. Ibid., 517 (emphasis added); see also *Parents Involved in Community Schools* v. *Seattle School District No. 1*, 127 S. Ct. 2738, 2767 (2007) (quoting this passage from *Rice*); *Fullilove* v. *Klutznick,* 448 U.S. 448, 531, 541 n.13 (1980) (Stewart, J., dissenting) (discussed in text accompanying notes 2–3). Similarly, Justice Scalia's opinion in *Adarand Constructors, Inc.* v. *Pena,* 515 U.S. 200, 239 (1995) (Scalia, J., concurring in part and concurring in the judgment),

noted that a classification based on race "is alien to the Constitution's focus upon the individual, . . . and its rejection of dispositions . . . based on blood, see U.S. Const. art. III § 3 ['(N)o Attainder of Treason shall work Corruption of Blood']; U.S. Const. art. I, § 9, cl. 8 ('No Title of Nobility shall be granted by the United States')."

122. *Weber* v. *Aetna Casualty & Surety Co.,* 406 U.S. 164 (1972) at 175, 176.

123. *Mathews* v. *Lucas,* 427 U.S. 495 (1976) at 505; see also ibid., 520 n.3 (Stevens, J., dissenting) (government must be "especially sensitive to discrimination on grounds of birth"); *Trimble* v. *Gordon,* 430 U.S. 762, 770 (1977) (out-of-wedlock children "can affect neither their parents' conduct nor their own status").

124. *Kotch* v. *Board of Riverport Pilot Commissioners for Port of New Orleans,* 330 U.S. 552 (1947), at 565 (Rutledge, J., dissenting).

125. Ibid., 564 (majority decision).

126. Ibid., 561.

127. See Torke, *Nepotism,* 563.

128. Ibid.; see also ibid., 588–92; Larson, "Titles of Nobility," 1412. The *Kotch* majority opinion is in significant tension with the judicial opinions that were faithful to Congress's intent in the immediate aftermath of the Civil War. See, for example, *Slaughterhouse Cases,* 83 U.S. 36, 113 (1872) (Bradley, J., dissenting) (Fourteenth Amendment prohibits states from "pass[ing] a law of caste, making all trades and professions, or certain enumerated trades and professions, hereditary"); ibid., 105, 109 (Field, J., dissenting) (Equal Protection Clause was "intended to give practical effect to the Declaration of 1776," and therefore "all grants of exclusive privileges, in contravention of this equality, are against common right, and void"); In re *Ah Fong,* 1 Fed. Cas. 213, 218 (C.D. Cal. 1874) (Field, J.) (Equal Protection Clause prohibits "[d]iscriminating and partial legislation, favoring particular persons").

129. *Grutter* v. *Bollinger,* 539 U.S. 306, 332 (2003).

130. 448 U.S. at 531.

131. *Runyon* v. *McCrary,* 427 U.S. 160 (1976).

132. *St. Francis College* v. *Al-Khazraji,* 481 U.S. 604 (1987).

133. Ibid., 613.

134. Ibid., 610–11 (citations omitted).

135. Ibid., 611–12 (citations omitted).

136. Ibid., 613 (emphasis added).

137. Ibid., 611–613 (emphasis added).

138. See, for example, Dictionary.com, http://dictionary.reference.com/ (last visited August 26, 2008) ("ancestry" defined as "1. family or ancestral descent, lineage"); *Rice* v. *Cayetano,* 528 U.S. 495, 517 (2000) (inquiry into "ancestral lines" demeans dignity of individuals); *Miller* v. *Albright,* 523 U.S. 420, 471 (1998) (Breyer, J., dissenting) ("ancestry" discrimination includes that based on identity of parent or grandparent). The Court in *Cayetano* noted that a statute granting a benefit based on having only one sixty-fourth of a particular type of ancestry, or having ancestors who resided in a particular location—regardless of their racial group—may well be "racial" legislation. *Rice,* 528 U.S. at 514 ("it is far from clear" that this "would not be a race-based qualification").

139. *Al-Khazraji,* 481 U.S. at 613 n. 5.

140. Ibid., 613.

141. See *McDonald* v. *Santa Fe Trail Transportation Co.*, 427 U.S. 273, 295-96 (1976).

142. See *Al-Khazraji,* 481 U.S. at 609–10 (Court is "quite sure" that the act prohibits "discrimination by one Caucasian against another").

143. The act provides that all citizens shall have the same right to make and enforce contracts "as is enjoyed by white citizens." For a discussion of that phrase, see Shadowen et al., "No Distinctions," 114–18.

144. *Grutter* v. *Bollinger,* 539 U.S. 306 (2003). In *Grutter,* the Court upheld the University of Michigan Law School's race-conscious admissions policy. The Court held that the policy was subject to strict scrutiny under the Equal Protection Clause, that the school had a compelling interest in obtaining a diverse student body, and that the means of achieving that goal were appropriately narrow because race was only one factor in a holistic evaluation of each application.

145. Ibid., 316, 325.

146. See Shadowen et al., "No Distinctions," 122–25.

147. Michael J. Sandel, *Justice: What's the Right Thing to Do?* (New York: Farrar, Strauss, and Giroux, 2009), 183.

148. Ibid.

149. *Brown* v. *Board of Education,* 347 U.S. 483 (1954).

150. *Plyler* v. *Doe* 457 U.S. (1982) at 227; see also ibid., 249 (Burger, C.J., dissenting) ("fiscal concerns alone could not justify discrimination against a suspect class or an arbitrary and irrational denial of benefits to a particular group of persons"); *Saenz* v. *Doe,* 526 U.S. 489, 506-07 (1999) (same).

151. See Chapter 5, 111–18.

152. Ibid.

153. Ibid. Students from families with annual incomes of $200,000 or more are more than five times as likely as other students to be admitted to an elite university. Jamillah Moore, *Race and College Admissions: A Case For Affirmative Action* (Jefferson, N.C.: McFarland and Co., 2005), 166.

154. See Shadowen et al., "No Distinctions," 59–60.

155. See text at note 59.

156. See Chapter 5, 116.

157. See Shadowen et al., "No Distinctions," at 128.

158. That is, 30 percent of 3.5 percent to 5.1 percent.

159. See Shadowen et al., "No Distinctions," 130–31.

Chapter 9

1. *Grutter* v. *Bollinger,* 288 F.3d 732 (6th Cir. 2002), aff'd, 539 U.S. 306 (2003).

2. While we heard argument on *Grutter*'s companion case evaluating the quota-based admissions policy of the University of Michigan's undergraduate admissions, we did not issue a decision before the case was appealed to and decided by the Supreme Court. The Supreme Court held in *Gratz* v. *Bollinger*, as I believe that we would have, that the undergraduate admission standard's use of race violated the Fourteenth Amendment because the methodology used was not narrowly tailored to the purpose of creating a diverse student body since it did not provide individualized consideration of a minority applicant. 539 U.S. 244, 271 (2003).

3. Anya Perret, "Dartmouth Twice as Likely to Admit Legacy Applicants," *The Dartmouth*, April 18, 2008.

4. Ashley Jefferson and Laura Welch, "At Villanova U., It's All in the Family," *The Villanovan,* October 4, 2007.

5. Max Hall, "A Legacy's Leg Up," *Cavalier Daily,* January 16, 2008 (noting that legacy applicants also receive special access to the admissions program).

6. Tina Mao, "Duke Study: Legacy Admits Often Underperform," *The Chronicle,* September 9, 2008.

7. Thomas J. Espenshade and Chang Y. Chung, "The Opportunity Cost of Admission Preferences at Elite Universities," *Social Science Quarterly* 86, no. 2 (June 2005): 293.

8. Chapter 8 of this book argues that legacy preferences at private universities are legally suspect, an issue we do not take up in this chapter.

9. For example, the Duke study of the academic profiles of Duke legacy students compared to students whose parents were college-educated at another university, "A Social Portrait of Legacies at an Elite University," noted that campus diversity suffered as a result of legacy admissions because "legacies were more likely to be white, Protestant, U.S. citizens and private school-educated." Mao, "Duke Study." Indeed, this was likely part of the goal. As Malcolm Gladwell and Jerome Karabel have noted, when Harvard, Yale, and Princeton's admission systems were merit-based, by 1922, one-fifth of the class was Jewish. Malcolm Gladwell, "Getting In," *The New Yorker,* October 10, 2005 (citing Jerome Karabel, *The Chosen: The Hidden History of Admission and Exclusion at Harvard, Princeton, and Yale* [New York: Houghton Mifflin Harcourt, 2005]). Believing this to be bad for fundraising and that it would undermine the reputation of the universities, the schools put the "character" questions on the applications as a way to determine less numeric qualities of their applicants like their family histories and religions in order to keep the number of Jews in the school below a certain threshold.

10. Akhil Reed Amar and Neal Kumar Katyal, "*Bakke's* Fate," *UCLA Law Review* 43 (August 1996): 1749.

11. Perret, "Dartmouth Twice as Likely to Admit Legacy Applicants" (noting that "one of the interesting things I've seen [as director of admissions] is the growing diversity of the legacy applicants themselves, mirroring the increased diversity of our student body in terms of gender, race and ethnicity, citizenship," [Dartmouth Dean Maria Laskaris] said).

12. At least one school is, however, using a unique version of legacy preferences to improve its campus diversity. Georgetown College, a college with a historically white student body, has begun applying legacy preferences to applicants with family members who graduated from Bishop College, a historically black college that closed its doors in 1998. William H. Crouch, "Broader Diversity Enriches the College Experience," *Courier Journal,* November 15, 2009, H1.

13. See Daniel Golden, "Aiding Mainly Whites, Legacy Policy Gets Embroiled in Debate over Affirmative Action," *Wall Street Journal,* January 15, 2003.

14. Interestingly, some opponents of affirmative action based for minority students actually benefited from affirmative action for students of privilege and education. It is possible, if not likely, that George W. Bush would not have been admitted to Yale had he not been the son and grandson of Yale graduates on his father's side, as well as the nephew of Yale graduates on his mother's (Walker) side of the family. See Michael Kinsley, "How Affirmative Action Helped George W.," CNN.com, January 20, 2003, http://www.cnn.com/2003/ALLPOLITICS/01/20/timep.affirm.action.tm/ (noting that, while then-president Bush spoke out against affirmative action,"If our President had the slightest sense of irony, he might have paused to ask himself, 'Wait a minute. How did I get into Yale?' It wasn't because of any academic achievement: his high school record was ordinary. It wasn't because of his life experience—prosperous family, fancy prep school—which was all too familiar at Yale. It wasn't his SAT scores: 566 verbal and 640 math.").

15. College Quality, Affordability, and Diversity Improvement Act of 2003, S. 1793, 108th Cong. (2003).

16. Golden, "Aiding Mainly Whites, Legacy Policy Gets Embroiled in Debate over Affirmative Action."

17. Adam Liptak, "A Hereditary Perk that Founding Fathers Failed to Anticipate," *New York Times,* January 15, 2008.

18. U.S. Constitution, amend. 14.

19. *Buckley* v. *Valeo*, 424 U.S. 1, 93 (1976).

20. "Based on the 'national policy to discourage racial discrimination in education,' the IRS ruled that 'private school not having a racially nondiscriminatory policy as to students is not 'charitable' within the common law concepts reflected in sections 170 and 501(c)(3) of the Code." *Bob Jones University* v. *United States*, 461 U.S. 574, 579 (1983) (citing Revenue Ruling 71–447, 1971–2 Cum.Bull. 230, 231).

21. *Grutter*, 539 U.S. at 368. He added a footnote stating that "Were this court to have the courage to forbid the use of racial discrimination in admissions, legacy preferences (and similar practices) might quickly become less popular—a possibility not lost, I am certain, on the elites (both individual and institutional) supporting the law school in this case." Ibid. at 368 n.10.

22. *Rosenstock* v. *Board of Governors of University of North Carolina,* 423 F. Supp. 1321, 1327 (D.C.N.C. 1976).

23. *Palmore* v. *Sidoti*, 466 U.S. 429 (1984).

24. *Korematsu* v. *United States*, 323 U.S. 214 (1944).

25. *Reynolds* v. *Sims*, 377 U.S. 533, 555 (1964).

26. *Crandall* v. *Nevada*, 73 U.S. (6 Wall.) 35 (1867).

27. *Adarand Constructors, Inc.* v. *Peña*, 515 U.S. 200, 227 (1995).

28. *San Antonio Independent School District* v. *Rodriguez*, 411 U.S. 1 (1973).

29. See Chapter 8.

30. Ibid.

31. *Craig* v. *Boren*, 429 U.S. 190, 197 (1976).

32. *Clark* v. *Jeter*, 486 U.S. 456, 461 (1988).

33. *Weber* v. *Aetna Casualty and Surety Co.*, 406 U.S. 164, 175 (1972).

34. Ibid.

35. *Romer* v. *Evans,* 517 U.S. 620 (1996).

36. *Kimel* v. *Florida Board of Regents*, 528 U.S. 62, 83 (2000) (applying the rational basis test to age discrimination because there is not a 'history of purposeful discrimination" based on age and " discrimination does not define a discrete and insular minority" because all persons experience all ages if they live out their normal lifespans).

37. *University of Alabama* v. *Garrett*, 531 U.S. 356 (2001).

38. *McGowan* v. *Maryland,* 366 U.S. 420, 425–56 (1961).

39. See *U.S. Railroad Retirement Board* v. *Fritz*, 449 U.S. 166 (1980).

40. See, for example, *Romer* v. *Evans*, 517 U.S. 620 (1996); *City of Cleburne* v. *Cleburne Living Center, Inc.*, 473 U.S. 432 (1985).

41. In *Rosenstock*, Judge Ward applied the rational basis test because the Supreme Court had found that the right to a university education was not a fundamental interest and he found that children of alumni are not a suspect criteria. *Rosenstock,* 423 F. Supp. at 1327. However, as I previously noted, this decision is not binding on future cases involving this issue.

42. *Grutter*, 539 U.S. at 329.

43. Ibid.

44. *Grutter*, 539 U.S. at 329.

45. Ibid. at 330–32.

46. Ibid. at 333.

47. See, for example, Brianna Barzola, "Princeton to Review Legacies' Academic Performance," *Brown Daily Herald,* April 12, 2007 (reporting that Brown dean of admissions James Miller commented that "alumni support is an important component of sustaining the University. 'We and all other private universities rely heavily on the efforts of our alumni to sustain ourselves. We rely on

our graduates to staff committees, donate money, recruit students and do a whole variety of things that [alumni of] public institutions don't do. In turn, I think it's important for us to continue to have continuity with families,' he said.").

48. Mao, "Duke Study."

49. Jacques Steinberg, "Of Sheepskins and Greenbacks," *New York Times,* February 13, 2003, A24.

50. Ibid.

51. Jacques Steinberg, "Before College, Costly Advice Just on Getting In," *New York Times,* July 19, 2009, A1.

52. Jonathan Meer and Harvey S. Rosen, "Altruism and the Child-Cycle of Alumni Giving," Working Paper No. 13152, National Bureau of Economic Research, June 2007.

53. Ibid.

54. See Chapter 5.

55. Ibid.

56. Mao, "Duke Study."

57. In the past, universities might have also argued that using legacy preferences is important to boosting their position in the *U.S. News and World Report* rankings (given that legacies are more likely to accept offers to attend), but this contention is weakened by the magazine's decision to drop admissions "yield" from its ranking methodology.

Chapter 10

1. Daniel Halperin, "Does Tax Exemption for Charitable Endowments Subsidize Excessive Accumulation?" Social Science Research Network, June 10, 2008, 19, http://ssrn.com/abstract=1143458.

2. *Giving in America: Toward a Stronger Voluntary Sector* (Washington, D.C.: Commission on Private Philanthropy and Public Needs, 1975), 18, https://archives.iupui.edu/handle/2450/889.

3. Daniel Golden, "Admissions Preferences Given to Alumni Children Draws Fire," *Wall Street Journal,* January 15, 2003, 1.

4. Debra Thomas and Terry Shepard, "Legacy Admissions Are Defensible, Because the Process Can't Be 'Fair,'" *Chronicle of Higher Education,* March 14, 2003, http://chronicle.com/weekly/v49/i27/27b01501.htm.

5. Thomas D. Snyder, Salley A. Dillow, and Charlene M. Hoffman, *Digest of Education Statistics: 2007* (Washington, D.C.: National Center

for Education Statistics, March 2008), Table 349, http://nces.ed.gov/programs/digest/d07/tables/dt07_349.asp?referrer=list.

6. Golden, "Admissions Preferences Given to Alumni Children Draws Fire," 1.

7. William F. Buckley Jr., "Civil Rights for Old Boys," *New York Times,* January 24, 2003, A23, http://www.nytimes.com/2003/01/24/opinion/civil-rights-for-old-boys.html.

8. *University of California Regents* v. *Bakke,* 438 U.S. 265 (1978).

9. Ibid.

10. *Grutter* v. *Bollinger* (02-241) 539 U.S. 306 (2003).

11. *Runyun* v. *McCrary* 427 U.S. 160 (1976); *Gratz* v. *Bollinger* 539 U.S. 244 (2003); *Regents of the University of California* v. *Bakke*, 438 U.S. 265 (1978).

12. *Annual Report: Fiscal Year 2008,* Harvard University Office of Sponsored Programs, 2008, 11, 16, http://vpf-web.harvard.edu/osp/pdfs/OSP_FY08_Annual_Report.pdf.

13. *Harvard University Financial Report: Fiscal Year 2008,* Harvard University, 2008, 17, http://vpf-web.harvard.edu/annualfinancial/.

14. Snyder et al., *Digest of Education Statistics 2007,* Table 345, http://nces.ed.gov/programs/digest/d07/tables/dt07_345.asp.

15. Ibid., Table 341, http://nces.ed.gov/programs/digest/d07/tables/dt07_341.asp.

16. Joint Committee on Taxation, *Estimates of Federal Tax Expenditures for Fiscal Years 2007–2011* (Washington, D.C.: Government Printing Office, September 24, 2007), 31, http://www.house.gov/jct/s-3-07.pdf.

17. Ibid.

18. Charles E. Grassley, "Wealthy Colleges Must Make Themselves More Affordable," *Chronicle of Higher Education,* May 30, 2008.

19. Jane G. Gravelle, "Tax Issues and University Endowments," Memorandum to Honorable Max Baucus, Chairman, Senate Committee on Finance, Honorable Chuck Grassley, Ranking Member, Senate Committee on Finance, Congressional Research Service, August 20, 2007.

20. *Giving in America,* 104.

21. Ibid, 19.

22. Internal Revenue Service, "Charitable Contributions for Use in Preparing 2008 Returns," Publication 526, Cat. No. 15050A, 3.

23. "Charitable Contributions; Private Schools Operated by Charitable Oragnization," July 25, 1983, http://counsel.cua.edu/Tax/publications//RR83-104.cfm.

24. Daniel Golden, *The Price of Admission: How America's Ruling Class Buys Its Way into Elite Colleges—and Who Gets Left Outside the Gates* (New York: Random House, 2006).

25. Anthony Carnevale and Stephen J. Rose, "Socioeconomic Status, Race/Ethnicity and Selective College Admissions," in *America's Untapped Resource: Low-Income Students in Higher Education*, ed. Richard D. Kahlenberg (New York: Century Foundation Press, 2004), 107–15.

26. Ibid. Some estimates run even higher. See Chapter 1, 4.

27. Jennifer Cheeseman Day and Eric C. Newburger, "The Big Payoff: Educational Attainment and Synthetic Estimates of Work-Life Earnings," U.S. Census Bureau, Current Population Reports, July 2002.

28. See, for example, William G. Bowen, Martin A. Kurzweil, and Eugene M. Tobin, *Equity and Excellence in American Higher Education* (Charlottesville, Va.: University Press of Virginia, 2005).

29. Daniel Golden, Testimony to the U.S. Senate Committee on Finance, December 5, 2006, http://finance.senate.gov/imo/media/doc/120506dgtest.pdf.

30. Princeton University Office of Development, 2007–2008 AG Campaign Reports, http://giving.princeton.edu/ag/progress/08reports.xml.

31. Jonathan Meer and Harvey S. Rosen, "Altruism and the Child-Cycle of Alumni Donations," Princeton University, CEPS Working Paper No. 150, May 2007, 1, http://www.princeton.edu/~ceps/workingpapers/150rosen.pdf.

32. Ibid., 48.

33. Ibid., 29.

34. Charles E. Grassley, "Report Card on Tax Exemptions and Incentives for Higher Education: Pass, Fail, or Need Improvement?" Opening Statement, Senate Finance Committee Hearing, December 5, 2006, http://finance.senate.gov/imo/media/doc/120506cg.pdf.

35. "Tax-Exempt Status for Your Organization," Publication 557, Internal Revenue Service, revised June 2008, 50. Gravelle, "Tax Issues and University Endowments," 4.

Index

Note: page numbers followed by *f* and *t* refer to figures and tables, respectively.

About the Contributors

Eric L. Bloom is an attorney at Hangley Aronchick Segal & Pudlin. He is a 2002 graduate of the Dickinson School of Law, where he was a comments editor for the *Dickinson Law Review* and a member of the Appellate Moot Court Board. While attending Dickinson, he concurrently earned a master's degree in business administration from the Smeal College of Business Administration of the Pennsylvania State University.

John Brittain is a professor of law at the University of the District of Columbia, David A. Clarke School of Law, and a public interest civil rights lawyer with a career spanning over forty years. He is formerly chief counsel and senior deputy director, Lawyers Committee for Civil Rights Under Law; law school dean at the Thurgood Marshall School of Law at Texas Southern University in Houston; and veteran law professor at the University of Connecticut School of Law. He has served as the president of the National Lawyers' Guild, a member of the Executive Committee and the Board of the ACLU, and legal counsel to NAACP at the local level and national office of the General Counsel. In 1993, the NAACP awarded him the coveted William Robert Ming Advocacy Award for legal service to the NAACP without a fee. He is a school desegregation specialist and one of the original counsel in *Sheff* v. *O'Neill*, a landmark case decided by the Connecticut Supreme Court in 1996. He earned a bachelor's degree and law degree from Howard University.

Chad Coffman is the president of Winnemac Consulting, LLC. Prior to joining Winnemac, he was a principal at Chicago Partners, LLC. He has extensive experience directing and managing large and complex litigation consulting matters across a wide variety of disciplines as well as managing analysis related to securities class actions, antitrust examinations, and labor discrimination cases. He has testified as an expert witness and also has acted as an independent expert in several mediations. He has a bachelor's degree in economics from Knox College and a master's degree in public policy from the University of Chicago.

Daniel Golden is an editor at large for Bloomberg News, specializing in education coverage. In 2004, as a reporter at the *Wall Street Journal,* he won a Pulitzer Prize for a series of articles about college-admissions preferences for children of alumni and donors. He has received many other journalistic honors, including two George Polk awards, and has also worked for the *Boston Globe* (1981–99) and Conde Nast Portfolio (2007–09). He is the author of *The Price of Admission: How America's Ruling Class Buys Its Way Into Elite Colleges and Who Gets Left Outside the Gates* (Crown, 2006). He received a bachelor's degree from Harvard College.

Richard D. Kahlenberg is a senior fellow at The Century Foundation and writes about education, equal opportunity, and civil rights. Previously, he was a fellow at the Center for National Policy, a visiting associate professor of constitutional law at George Washington University, and a legislative assistant to Senator Charles S. Robb (D-VA). He is the author of four books: *Tough Liberal: Albert Shanker and the Battles Over Schools, Unions, Race, and Democracy* (Columbia University Press, 2007); *All Together Now: Creating Middle-Class Schools through Public School Choice* (Brookings Institution Press, 2001); *The Remedy: Class, Race, and Affirmative Action* (Basic Books, 1996); and *Broken Contract: A Memoir of Harvard Law School* (Hill & Wang/Farrar, Straus & Giroux, 1992). In addition, he is the editor of six Century Foundation books: *Rewarding Strivers: Helping Low-Income Students Succeed in College* (2010); *Improving on No Child Left Behind: Getting Education Reform Back on Track* (2008); *America's Untapped Resource: Low-Income Students in Higher Education* (2004); *Public School Choice vs. Private School Vouchers* (2003); *Divided We Fail: Coming Together Through*

Public School Choice: The Report of The Century Foundation Task Force on the Common School (2002); and *A Notion at Risk: Preserving Public Education as an Engine for Social Mobility* (2000). He graduated *magna cum laude* from Harvard College and *cum laude* from Harvard Law School.

Donya Khalili is an attorney at Susman Godfrey, LLP. She served as a law clerk to the Honorable Boyce F. Martin, Jr., on the United States Court of Appeals for the Sixth Circuit from 2009 to 2010 and to the Honorable Thomas N. O'Neill, Jr., on the United States District Court for the Eastern District of Pennsylvania from 2008 to 2009. Among her many civic engagements, she has served on the American Constitution Society National Board of Directors and the Bronfman Fellowship Alumni Advisory Board. She received her undergraduate degree from Yale University and is a graduate of the University of Pennsylvania School of Law, where she was on the board of the *Journal of Constitution Law* and was a senior editor for the *Journal of Law and Social Change.*

Carlton F. W. Larson is a professor of law at the University of California, Davis, School of Law, where he teaches constitutional law and legal history. He previously served as a litigation associate at the Washington, D.C., law firm of Covington & Burling and as a law clerk to Judge Michael Daly Hawkins of the United States Court of Appeals for the Ninth Circuit. He has been published in *University of Pennsylvania Law Review, Washington University Law Review, Law and History Review*, and *The Yale Law Journal*, among others. He received his undergraduate degree *summa cum laude* in history from Harvard University and his law degree from Yale Law School, where he served as an articles editor of *The Yale Law Journal.*

Michael Lind is co-founder of the New America Foundation and policy director of its Economic Growth Program. He has taught at Harvard University and The Johns Hopkins University and writes frequently for the *Financial Times*, the *New York Times, Democracy Journal,* and other publications. He has appeared on C-SPAN, National Public Radio, CNN, the Business News Network, *PBS NewsHour* and other programs, and has a weekly column in *Salon* magazine. He is the author of *Made in Texas: George W. Bush and the Southern Takeover of American Politics* (New America/Basic Books, 2003), *The American Way of Strategy* (Oxford University Press, 2006), *What Lincoln Believed* (Doubleday, 2005), and *The Next American Nation: The New Nationalism and the Fourth American Revolution* (Free Press, 1995), and he is coauthor (with Ted Halstead) of *The Radical Center: The Future of American Politics* (Doubleday, 2001). He graduated from the University of Texas at Austin, received a master's degree in international relations from Yale University, and a law degree from the University of Texas Law School.

Boyce F. Martin, Jr., was nominated to the United States Court of Appeals for the Sixth Circuit in the spring of 1979 and was confirmed that fall. He served as chief judge from October 1, 1996, until September 30, 2003. Before his nomination to the Sixth Circuit, he was a member of the Kentucky Court of Appeals from its creation in 1976 and served as its first chief judge. Prior to that, he was a Judge of the Jefferson Circuit Court. Before joining the judiciary in 1974, he practiced law in Louisville after serving as the United States attorney for the Western District of Kentucky. He also served as a law clerk to the Honorable Shackelford Miller, Jr., on the United States Court of Appeals for the Sixth Circuit. He has served as chairman of the board of trustees of the I. W. Bernheim Foundation, operator of the Bernheim Arboretum. He has also served as a trustee at Davidson College and as a trustee and chairman of the board of trustees at Hanover College. He received a bachelor's degree from Davidson College and a law degree from the University of Virginia School of Law.

Tara O'Neil has extensively researched legacy preferences for the past three years. She received a bachelor's degree in criminal justice and sociology from the University of Scranton. Currently, she is working at the law firm of Hangley Aronchick Segal & Pudlin and is pursuing a graduate degree at Drexel University.

Peter Sacks is an author, journalist, and social critic. His essays on education and American culture have appeared in the *Nation*, the *Chronicle of Higher Education*, the *Boston Review*, the *Los Angeles Times*, the *New York Times*, *Change* magazine, *Education Week*, and many other publications. A former economist and staff writer at metro dailies on both coasts, he covered business and economics and completed several awarding-winning journalism projects and received a Pulitzer Prize nomination. His recent book, *Tearing Down the Gates: Confronting the Class Divide in American Education*, won the 2009 Frederic W. Ness Book of the Year Award from Association of American Colleges and Universities. He also is the author of *Standardized Minds: The High Price of America's Testing Culture and What We Can Do to Change It* (Perseus Publishing, 2000). His undergraduate degree is from the University of Washington.

Peter Schmidt is a senior writer at the *Chronicle of Higher Education*, covering affirmative action, state and federal higher-education policy, education research, and issues related to academic freedom. He has covered school desegregation, urban education, immigrant education, and education research for *Education Week*, and has reported for the Associated Press, the *Detroit Free Press*, the *Northern Virginia Daily*, and the *Ann Arbor News*, and he has written for the *Boston Globe*, the *Wall Street Journal*, *USA Today*, and the *Weekly Standard*. His work has won awards from the Society of Professional Journalists, the Education Writers Association, the Virginia Press Association, and the National Council on Crime and Delinquency. He is the author of *Color and Money: How Rich White Kids Are Winning the War over College Affirmative Action (Palgrave Macmillan, 2007) and* writes about race, class, and college access on his blog, colorarandmoney.com.

Steve Shadowen is an attorney at Hangley Aronchick Segal & Pudlin. A leading national attorney in commercial litigation, he is an adjunct professor of law at the Pennsylvania State University Dickinson School of Law and a member of the advisory board of the Institute for Consumer Antitrust Studies at the Loyola University Chicago School of Law. He has previously written on the subject of legacy preferences for the *Santa Clara Law Review* and the George Mason University *Civil Rights Law*

Journal. He graduated *summa cum laude* from St. Edward's University in Austin, Texas, and *cum laude* from the Georgetown University Law Center.

Brian Starr is a research analyst for Winnemac Consulting, LLC. He graduated *cum laude* with a bachelor's degree in economics from Knox College and is pursuing a master's degree in public policy at the Harris School of Public Policy at the University of Chicago.

Sozi P. Tulante is an attorney at Hangley Aronchick Segal & Pudlin. He has written on legacy preferences and is active in commercial and human-rights litigation. He was a law clerk to the Honorable Reginald C. Lindsay of the United States District Court for the District of Massachusetts from 2004 to 2005. He graduated *cum laude* in 2001 from Harvard Law School, where he was a member of the *Harvard Human Rights Journal*, and *cum laude* in 1997 from Harvard College.